D0910054

THE POLITICS OF DE-INDUSTRIALISATION
THE CONTRACTION OF THE WEST EUROPEAN
SHIPBUILDING INDUSTRY

THE POLITICS OF DE-INDUSTRIALISATION

THE CONTRACTION OF THE WEST EUROPEAN SHIPBUILDING INDUSTRY

Bo Stråth

CROOM HELM
London ● New York ● Sydney

© 1987 Bo Stråth
Croom Helm Ltd, Provident House,
Burrell Row, Beckenham, Kent BR3 1AT

Croom Helm Australia, 44–50 Waterloo Road,
North Ryde, 2113, New South Wales

Published in the USA by
Croom Helm
in association with Methuen, Inc.
29 West 35th Street
New York, NT 10001

British Library Cataloguing in Publication Data

Stråth, Bo
    The politics of de-industrialisation :
    the contraction of the West European
    shipbuilding industry.
    1. Shipbuilding industry — Europe
    I. Title
    338.4′762382′0094   VM299.7.E85
    ISBN 0–7099–5401–8

Library of Congress Cataloging-in-Publication Data
Stråth, Bo, 1943-
    The politics of de-industrialisation.

    Bibliography: p.
    Includes index.
    1. Shipbuilding industry — Europe — History — 20th
century. I. Title.
VM299.7.E85S77   1987   338.4′76238′094   87-6780
ISBN 0-7099-5401-8

Filmset by Mayhew Typesetting, Bristol, England
Printed and bound in Great Britain by Mackays of Chatham Ltd, Kent

Contents

Preface

I started this study in 1979. In the autumn of that year I interviewed a prominent representative of the Danish shipbuilding industry about the 'crisis'. By then unemployment in Denmark had passed the 200,000 mark. 'The politicians must do something', he argued. 'If not we'll have a revolution well before we have 300,000 unemployed'. I knew what he meant, since just a few months earlier I had been in Britain to discuss the same 'crisis' with people in both the shipbuilding industry and the unions. I had witnessed there the almost hysterical public reaction when British unemployment passed 2 million. There too there were warnings of social and political upheaval and massive protests if this trend continued. Some even prophesised the collapse of the political and economic system.

However, whilst the period since the end of the 1960s has been revolutionary in terms of technological and economic restructuring, with a dramatic increase in unemployment (the peak of which may not yet have been reached), the predictions of massive social unrest have been confounded. Indeed, throughout Europe the 1980s have been a period of social and political calm with a marked tendency to stable, and rather conservative, government. In Denmark unemployment went above 300,000 without any signs of revolution and there was less attention paid in Britain when unemployment exceeded 3 million than when it passed 2 million.

Why then did the revolution predicted by the Danish director not happen? What factors stabilised the political process in the wake of economic and technological restructuring? What factors defused the tensions produced by the restructuring?

The historical study reported here poses these questions by focusing on how mass redundancy with minimal social upheaval was achieved in 10 shipbuilding regions in Western Europe. But can the study of a single industry serve any more general purpose?

A British yard manager wanted to know whether it served any purpose at all when he asked me over lunch what good my study could do for his failing industry. After some hesitation I told him that I had no immediate recipe, but that he could regard me as a social pathologist. 'So then you mean that I am a corpse', he angrily replied.

I should of course have foreseen his reaction. Nevertheless, I maintain that my metaphor was a good one. I was studying the impact of a radically changed environment on an industry in an attempt to understand the social and political processes involved. This can be compared with the study of pathology by doctors in order to promote health. The wider questions of how unemployment could have been avoided and how it can be cured are beyond the immediate scope of my study, but hopefully this industry study provides a foundation for discussing these wider questions.

I am indebted to many people for their assistance in different ways during the completion of this study. Above all I must thank Professor Jörgen Weibull, University of Gothenburg, who persuaded me to undertake this work. I am very much indebted to him. He engaged me in a shipbulding history project which he initiated in 1978 as a new professor of history in Gothenburg. Since then it has been a privilege to have him as a friend and mentor and to enjoy his encouragement and competent criticism. I dedicate this book to him. Dr Thommy Svensson, my colleague within the research project on the contraction of the West European shipbuilding industry at the University of Gothenburg, Frank Wilkinson, of the Labour Studies Group, Department of Applied Economics at the University of Cambridge, and Professor Edward Lorenz, South Bend, Indiana, have all saved me from many shortcomings. Their positive criticism and relevant suggestions have inspired and encouraged me. Their support during difficult phases of the work was invaluable. I thank Frank Wilkinson, not only for his brilliant suggestions and capability to catch in a few words the core of a complicated context, but also for his assistance with the editing.

Professor Tony Slaven, University of Glasgow, helped me with many valuable comments and with research facilities during a stay in Glasgow.

Anne-Marie Mureau, Geneva, inspired me during a time when the working title of this book was still 'At the fall of Icarus' with long discussions about the difficulties involved in the concept of international co-operation.

For very valuable comments on special points and for stimulating discussions about different parts of the study I want to thank Dr Mark Almond, Oxford; Dr Reynald Bourque, Montreal; Finn Breitenstein, Copenhagen; Professor Jürgen Brockstedt, Berlin; Dr Peter Flieshardt, Bremen; Jakob Fuchs, Copenhagen; Raymond Glasgow, Geneva; Professor Yannick Guin, Nantes; Dr Heiner Heseler, Bremen; Professor Hartmut Kaelble, Berlin; Jane Kenrick, Cambridge; Bengt Jakobsson, Stockholm; Professor Jürgen Kocka, Bielefeld; Dr Jean-Pierre Le Crome, Nantes; Heinz Meinking,

Bremen; Dr Joseph Melling, Liverpool; Professor Magnus Mörner, Gothenburg; Professor Martin Osterland, Bremen; Dr Alastair Reid, Cambridge; Professor Christopher Smout, St Andrews; Dr Martin Stopford, Newcastle; Professor Rolf Torstendahl, Uppsala; Professor Heinrich Volkmann, Berlin; Henk Vos, Amsterdam; and First Secretary Dr Anders Åslund, Moscow.

I also want to thank all those people who have given me time for interviews, in some cases a considerable amount of time, and who have also helped me with source materials and other things. In all they are some 150 people, listed at the end of the book.

In Kiel, Professor Hain Rebas supported me with research facilities, and Mr Reinhold Wulff and Mrs Jennegien Grundtner helped me with problems of translation and typing. In Glasgow, Mrs Isabel Burnside, Miss Eileen Maher and Mrs Aileen Philidis gave me the same help. For the editing of the final manuscript I am very grateful to Jane Kenrick, Ann Newton and Frank Wilkinson, Cambridge, and for typing the final version to Shani Douglas, Anne Mason, Sharon Metcalfe, Sue Moore and, above all, Betty Clifton, Cambridge.

Lectures at the University of Cambridge, the University of Glasgow, the University of Liverpool, the University of St Andrews, the Free University of Berlin and the University of Bremen, and papers for conferences at the Centre de Documentation du Mouvement Ouvrier et du Travail, Nantes, and, for the IIIrd and the IVth Shipbuilding Conferences in London and Helsinki, respectively, and for the VIIth International Conference on Labour Market Segmentation in Santiago de Compostela, gave me the opportunity to discuss my results.

Although my indebtedness is great to all the people mentioned it goes without saying that I bear full responsibility for the final version, with all the shortcomings that there may still be.

An international comparative study like this is expensive. Support by the Swedish Council for Research in the Humanities and Social Sciences (HSFR) and by the German Alexander von Humboldt Foundation has been indispensable. HSRF was the main sponsor of the project for three years and contributed to the costs of publishing. The AvH Foundation generously made it possible for me to carry out research in Germany and Britain for almost two years. I also want to thank the Institute for Advanced Studies in the Humanities at the University of Edinburgh where I was an honorary research fellow for three months. For additional financial support I also want to thank Adlerbertska Forskningsfonden Letterstedtska Föreningen and Knut och Alice Wallenbergs Stiftelse.

Last but not least my thanks go to Maud for her quiet support and wonderful patience during the writing of this book, which is dedicated, besides to Jörgen Weibull, to Peter, Niklas and Johan.

Bo Stråth
Gothenburg

To my friend and mentor *Jörgen Weibull*

and to *Peter, Niklas and Johan*

1

The State: A Force for Change and Insurance Against Failure

INTRODUCTION

The spectacular collapse of the West European shipbuilding industry happened during a short period after 1975. The same processes of contraction took place in the steel and coal industries and before that in the textile industry. In this context, therefore, shipbuilding could be regarded as an example of a more general process of de-industrialisation of important basic industries in Western Europe.

It would be an exaggeration to say that nobody took any notice of the collapse of West European shipbuilding. On the contrary, there were massive government attempts to prevent its decline, by means of subsidies in various forms. But, despite unemployment figures in many shipbuilding regions as high as in the 1930s, and well above the average national figures of around 10 per cent, there has been much less political turbelence and social protest over this issue than during the inter-war period,[1] no general crisis of legitimacy in the wake of economic stagnation, and hardly any radicalisation of workers' political attitudes. The shipyard workers directly concerned have fought against these developments, but their fights have certainly not developed into massive social protest or upheaval. My aim here is to distinguish those factors in the slimming-down process in shipbuilding which have served to prevent the rise of co-ordinated protest and social unrest of a more general nature. Therefore, the main question of this book will be: *Which factors have contributed to the relatively trouble-free contraction process in West European shipbuilding?*

It must be emphasised, however, that the focus on the undramatic character of the process does not imply the assumption of a syn-chronised or linear process of social and political evolution. It is not

1

a matter of building a static funtionalist model capable *a priori* of containing all kinds of tensions and conflicting or competing interests. Rather, the subject of the book is that process of adjustment which has permitted conflicts and tensions, initiatives and their repercussions to have stability as their end result. The final outcomes of integration and compromise as perceived here are rather the expression of shifting realignments in the balance of power and of functions of conflict and coercion.[2] This study therefore deals with the interaction between different political actors and social and economic processes, and with the undramatic performance as a consequence of a process which does not exclude challenges to the social fabric from within and from without.[3] When looking for an explanation of how this has been maintained there will, for the reasons discussed below, be a focus on the role of the state and the international market — i.e. on the nation state in its international economic context.

STRUCTURAL CHANGES AND COLLAPSE

An anonymous author writing 75 years before Adam Smith published the *Wealth of nations* pointed out that:

> Ships are built in the Plantations of cheaper Materials, and might be also by cheaper Labour. Materials there for Building, are cheaper. 'Tis true indeed, that Iron, Sails and Rigging, are bought in *Europe* and therefore must be dearer in the Plantations; however, these things are carried either in Ships that otherwise must carry empty Holds and Ballast, so that they are not dearer for the Carriage: Besides, the Customs upon these things to *England*, are drawn back upon their Exportation; so that they are cheaper than in *Holland*. But, if these things are something dearer, Timber, Rozin, Pitch and Tar, are so much cheaper; that at a medium, Materials are nothing near so dear in our Plantations.[4]'

It was to be more than 250 years, however, before developments took the course this author suggested. The geographical restructuring of modern shipbuilding has been a lengthy process and represents the less spectacular subplot to the story of the collapse of the industry. That collapse was shown most clearly in the rapid downturn after 1975, but to understand both the subplot and the main story it is necessary to return to the immediate post-war years.

The driving force behind the growth of the shipbuilding industry after World War II was the development of seaborne trade. Ever increasing amounts of oil transported over longer and longer distances were especially important. This impressive growth was in turn, of course, a consequence of the general economic growth after World War II. The 25–30 years after 1945 were, despite minor recessions, a long period of expansion.

Expansion in the industrial centres of Western Europe, the US and Japan required the importing of raw materials. By the middle of the 1970s, around 75 per cent of the world trade tonnage was seaborne and, if measured in tonmiles, seaborne trade is even more important, reaching 95 per cent, as commodities are transported over longer distances by ship.

The average growth rate for seaborne trade in the period between 1950–73 was 8.2 per cent per year, a figure considerably above the rates of economic growth in Western industrial societies. However, the demand for seaborne transport has increased even more than this 8.2 per cent p.a. would indicate, since transport *distances* have increased all the time. The growth rate, measured in tonmiles from 1962–73, was 12.2 per cent per year.[5]

Transport distances increased more for oil than for dry cargoes, but for other reasons too, the transportation of oil increased dramatically. Cheap oil was an important stimulus to post-war economic expansion in the industrial centres. Japan has no oil of its own, Europe shifted its source of energy from its own coal reserves to imported oil, and oil production in the US could not keep up with the demand for oil there. The importance of oil in seaborne trade was especially clear during the Korean boom of 1951–53, and during the Suez boom of 1956–7 (see Table 1.1).

The 1960s brought the first signs of structural problems in the economy of growth. By the end of the decade it was obvious that the Bretton Woods agreement was a very weak basis for the international economy, and problems were accentuated in 1971 when the United States lost its currency hegemony. Moreover, the 1960s and the beginning of the 1970s brought the opening of new oilfields in the North Sea, in Indonesia (offshore) and in Algeria, all of which were close to the industrial centres of Europe and Japan, and therefore decreased the need for sea transport. The opening of the Suez Canal in 1974 had the same consequence.

Thus the beginnings of a downturn in the demand for shipping were already clear when in 1973 the October war between Israel and

Table 1.1: Growth rates for seaborne oil and dry cargoes 1962–1973 and distribution of seaborne trade between oil and dry cargoes in 1962 and 1973 respectively (annual averages)

	1962–1973	1962	1973
Growth rate:			
oil cargoes (tonnes)	10.7 pc		
dry cargoes (tonnes)	6.9		
all trades	8.7		
oil cargoes (tonmiles)	14.5		
dry cargoes (tonmiles)	8.8		
all trade (tonmiles)	12.2		
Oil cargoes. Share of seaborne trade		42.9 pc	52.3 pc
Dry cargoes. Share of seaborne trade		57.1	47.7

Source: OECD, *Maritime Transport*, 1971, p. 27, and 1978, p. 29.

Egypt and the Arab reaction to it produced a dramatic drop in the international oil trade and, consequently, in international trade in general.

The impact of the oil crisis on world trade is shown in Table 1.2. 1976 was the exception to the rule — a year when there was a general need to build up stocks following the price shock and the uncertainty it produced. But between 1973 and 1979 the share of oil in total seaborne trade decreased from 52.3 per cent to 48.7 per cent.

Of the West European countries concentrating on tanker production, Sweden made the most thoroughgoing adjustments to the changed conditions, a fact that must be related to the high wage costs found there. As a by-product of this development, the Swedish industry became a model for the International Metalworkers' Federation, which at its conferences in 1964 and 1967 was therefore able to argue that high wage costs were acceptable so long as productivity was high enough.[6]

These developments in Sweden involved conversion to the production of comparatively unsophisticated types of ships, and brought with them unforeseen difficulties. Old professional skills and technological knowhow were lost in the new streamlined tanker yards. The new Arendalsvarvet outside Gothenburg, completed in 1963 and built on the model of the conveyor belt system in car factories, though in the vanguard of Western European technology,[7] was economically backward from the very start. Its designers had not foreseen the trend towards very large crude carriers (VLCCs) and ultra-large crude carriers (ULCCs), and the yard was too small to build either. The Arendalsvarvet example demonstrates the

Table 1.2: World seaborne trade, 1974–1981 (thousand million metric tonmiles)

	1974	1975	1976	1977	1978	1979	1980	1981
A. Oil & Products[1]	10867	10016	11546	11552	11223	11180	10000	8950
- % change	5.1	−7.8	15.3	0.1	−2.8	−0.4	−10.6	−10.5
B. Dry Cargo[2]	5765	5635	5875	6050	6390	7015	7370	7460
- % change	11.2	−2.3	4.3	3.0	5.6	9.8	5.1	1.2
C. Total Trade	16632	15651	17421	17602	17613	18195	17370	16410
- % change	7.2	−5.9	11.3	1.0	0.1	3.3	−4.5	−5.5

Sources: 1. OECD & LBS estimates. 2. Fearnley & Egers Review

problems involved in judging trends correctly.

The general development in world trade is clearly reflected in the development of the composition of the world market for shipping. The Cape of Good Hope route, after the closure of the Suez Canal, both permitted and demanded huge ships, and their pattern influenced other cargoes and dock design. VLCCs and ULCCs were increasingly built as owners started to take advantages of the reductions in the direct cost of transporting oil that were associated with increased tanker size. Similar reductions in unit transport cost were found to apply to bulk carriers.[8]

At the beginning of the 1950s, the share of tankers in the total world merchant fleet was one fifth and by the middle of the 1970s almost a half. Of all the ships built in 1970, 47.8 per cent were tankers. In 1975 the proportion had risen to 66.5 per cent (see Figure 1.1).[9] At the same time, the need for extensive transport of other raw materials such as iron ore, coal, phosphate, cereals and so on increased, apparently justifying the breakthrough into bulk-carriers.

The need for new types of ship, rapid economic development, and political factors such as the temporary closure of the Suez Canal created a fertile breeding ground for technical innovations in shipbuilding. Tankers and bulk carriers were built in ever-increasing sizes, and the technology of construction meant large-scale operations not only for the transport industry but for the shipbuilding industry itself. New techniques changed the working practices of the yards and what had hitherto been a predominantly craft-oriented production process became more industrialised. Japan invested in new and larger shipbuilding berths from the 1950s onwards, concentrating on greenfield sites with integrated steelmaking facilities. At the same time the Japanese developed highly successful design and

Figure 1.1: Tankers under construction or on order 1950–1980 as a percentage of total world tonnage under construction (grt)

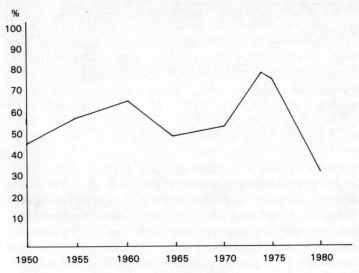

Source: Kappel and Rother, pp. 780–81 (revised).

construction methods for the new ships which, when implemented, reduced construction time considerably. Japan was also at the forefront in the devleopment of high-tensile steel plate, which made possible a reduction in bulk and weight. The amount of steel per gross register tonne (grt) was reduced by as much as 36 per cent between 1958 and 1964. In the 1960s, covered berths were introduced in Sweden to reduce the impact of the weather on production. Numerical control was also developed for cutting the steel plates which are welded together to form the hull. The 1970s saw the development of computerised systems which integrated the whole production process from design to material and workload flow, and these came into more general use in the 1980s (CADCAM). As these changes were introduced, craft work was broken down into smaller and more specialised operations, although this did not necessarily mean an end to skilled labour but rather a restructuring of professional skills.[10]

Shipbuilding output, measured in grt, increased tenfold between 1950 and 1975. However, shipbuilding has always been characterised by severe cyclical fluctuations where the speculative element has been obvious. This has been an industry of 'feast and famine', and the reasons for this are many. On the one hand, the fact that the supply capacity cannot increase much in the short run and the fact that shipbuilding outputs only represents a small percentage of the world merchant fleet results in large price fluctuations for even small fluctuations in demand. On the other hand, prices of raw materials vary more than prices of manufactured goods, and, as raw materials constitute the major share of seaborne goods, this produces large variations in freight prices, which in turn result in a rapidly changing demand for ships.[11]

Shipowners, and consequently the shipbuilders themselves, have tended to over-react in an almost manic-depressive way to general economic cycles, which has magnified the cyclical fluctuations to a greater extent than in most other industries. The rapid development from 1950 to 1975 was interrupted by a depression between 1958 and 1964 (in Japan 1962). The many pessimistic evaluations then prevailing gave way to a period of extreme optimisim from 1964 until 1975, and the years before the collapse are generally referred to as either 'the bonanza years' or 'the crazy years'. Both expressions are good descriptions of the period.

The contraction after 1975 is obvious from Table 1.3, as is the temporary recession after 1958 and the powerful expansion thereafter. However, from the point of view of employment, the expansion was fictitious. The table shows the change to large-scale tanker and bulk carrier production. Building the new types of ships with new, less labour-intensive techniques, meant that the amount of plate manufactured by each employee increased dramatically. As Table 1.4 shows, there was no expansion in employment corresponding to the expansion in tonnage figures, but contraction after 1975 affected employment dramatically.

Developments from the late 1950s until 1975 affected different countries differently, as Table 1.3 and 1.4 show. In Western Europe, Sweden, and to a lesser extent West Germany, followed Japan. The Swedish yards concentrated on series production of standard ships, especially tankers, with striking effects on employment when the tanker market collapsed (Table 1.4). In the group of 'others', the NICs, above all South Korea, followed Japan, with a 10-year time-lag, and conquered new market shares from Western Europe. In the UK there was an almost constant contraction after World War II, while in the other West European countries the structural shift to the Pacific was concealed only by the growth of the market as a whole. The spectacular downturn after 1975 made these developments clearly visible for the first time, although many

Table 1.3: Tonnage launched 1958–1983, million grt

Country	1958	1960	1970	1975	1977	1980	1984	% change 1975–1983
UK	1.4	1.5	1.2	1.3	1.1	0.2	0.2	−84.6
West Germany	1.4	1.1	1.7	2.5	1.4	0.5	0.5	−80.0
Sweden	0.8	0.7	1.7	2.5	2.1	0.3	0.2	−92.0
France	0.5	0.6	1.0	1.3	0.9	0.3	0.2	−84.6
Netherlands	0.6	0.6	0.5	1.0	0.4	0.1	0.1	−80.0
Belguim	0.1	0.1	0.2	0.2	0.2	0.1	0.1	−50.0
Denmark	0.3	0.2	0.5	1.0	0.6	0.2	0.4	−60.0
Japan	2.1	1.7	10.5	18.0	9.9	7.2	9.4	−47.8
Others	2.1	2.0	4.2	8.1	7.6	5.0	6.5	−19.7
World	9.3	8.5	22.0	35.9	24.2	13.9	17.7	−50.7

Source: Lloyds Annual Summaries, 1958–84.

Table 1.4: Employment in shipbuilding 1957–1982 (1000s)

	1957	1965	1971	1975	1978	1982	1975–1982	(1957–1975)
UK	294.0	221.4	189.4	78.4	72.1	60.0[c]	−26	(−80)
West Germany	92.8	73.2	67.4	46.8	31.3	27.6	−41	(−70)
Sweden	30.8	28.7	29.0	23.7	14.8	8.0	−66	(−69)
France[a]	38.9	29.1	32.2	32.9	25.4	23.9	−27	(−39)
Netherlands	55.8	46.8[b]	47.6	49.7	39.3	34.4	−31	(−44)
Belgium	16.3	9.4	12.4	6.1	5.2	4.0	−33	(−75)
Denmark	23.9	24.0	25.3	16.6	12.0	11.2	−33	(−53)
Japan	108.2	169.3	246.5	183.0	137.0	116.0	−37	(+7)

Sources 1957–71: background material to the Shipbuilding Conferences of the International Metal Workers' Federation (IMF Archives, Geneva); 1975–82: OECD Statistics (OECD Directorate for Science, Technology and Industry).
Notes: a. Excluding naval construction; b. 1966; c. After 1978 the British statistics are exclusive of naval construction. The official figure for 1982, 28,500, should therefore be 60,000 (employment statistics British Shipbuilders) to make the British development commensurable.

The figures are based on official statistics. The principles used in the reports differ from country to country so that, for instance, only the large yards are included in Germany and Sweden, and military production is excluded from the French figures. Military production there could be estimated to be about the same as for merchant production. Consequently, the figures cannot be used for comparisons *between* the countries but only *inside* them and then only as a rough measure. In, for instance, Sweden, so-called 'grey labour' was often hired at peak periods, implying that employment in reality was higher than reported. In France, too, a system of subcontracting has often been used.

Table 1.5: Share of world shipbuilding production in 1956 and 1982 (per cent)

	1956	1982
France	4.0	<2
Italy	4.3	<2
Netherlands	6.3	<2
Sweden	7.7	<2
West Germany	17.3	3.7
UK	23.1	2.6
Japan	24.4	48.5
South Korea	—	8.3
Spain	—	3.3
Brazil	—	3.0
Taiwan	—	2.7
Others	12.9	21.9

Source: Verband de Deutschen Schiffbauindustrie, Hamburg.

decision-makers continued to interpret the collapse as a cyclical phenomenon to be bridged in a Keynesian way.

In the debate about the causes of the crisis (as the contraction process was generally referred to), not only in shipbuilding but in the economy as a whole one, numerous references have been made to Kondratieff's theory of long waves.[12] According to this theory, 20–25 years of growth are followed by 20–25 years of stagnation. Each stage of development is characterised *inter alia* by different leading sectors, by distinctive technologies, by shifting entrepreneurial styles. Kondratieff's theory of long waves has also been considered by other economists and economic historians, among them Schumpeter, who has seen periods of stagnation as favourable to the development of a new spirit of entrepreneurship and a re-orientation which has prepared the ground for the development of a new era of growth. For Schumpeter this was a necessary process, not in a Marxian-Hegelian sense of immanent laws of historical development but as a 'scientific statement about the tendencies present in an observable pattern'.[13]

The perspective implicit in such theories is a more or less deterministic one. Although a number of factors which result in growth or stagnation have been considered, much less attention has been focused on the question of why they should emerge and disappear. An iron economic law has been laid down, which leaves little room for — and less interest in — the free play of human action. History is explained by history itself in a Hegelian manner. With the historian's hindsight everything can be made deterministic. However, such determinism has little to say about decision-making situation as the decision-makers themselves experienced it. Therefore, such theories are not so much explanatory as a way of systematising economic development. Furthermore, such models only consider the endogenous forces of change. External factors such as the development of world markets and the change in relative costs between countries are not considered. These factors have been decisive for development within the European shipbuilding industry. It therefore goes without saying that long-wave theories have little part to play in this book. The many references to them in the debate over the causes of the development in shipbuilding and other basic industries have only served to confuse that debate.

It has already been stated that the focus of this study is not economic development itself but rather the interaction between developments in economic and social structures and political action. The restructuring process has been a response to the demands of the market, but if in pure market terms it would have been possible to buy more cheaply in other parts of the world and thus enable individual national shipbuilding industries to survive, the priorities of the managed economy have dictated other considerations. One common denominator of the whole West European shipbuilding industry has been the massive input of government subsidies in various forms. That development and the rationale behind it will be discussed in a later section.

THE RESPONSE OF THE UNIONS

Modern shipbuilding developed on a craft basis, giving much control of the working process to the labour force and conversely limiting the direct on-the-job control exercised by management. This feature of the industry has traditionally given great power to shipbuilding unions and has promoted management to attempt to reduce craft control by industrialising the production process. In Sweden this attempt began as early as the 1910s, but it was not until the 1950s and 1960s that increasing specialisation and mechanisation in building giant tankers effectively introduced a more factory-like production process in Swedish yards. Management in Germany and France also favoured capital-intensive production, but in Britain management retained a labour-intensive strategy — limiting capital investment and reducing the burden of overheads in the form of capital assets in periods of depression. Thus management response to craft control clearly varied from country to country but no ship-building country entirely succeeded in introducing full factory production to supplant craft skills.[14]

The craft basis of the industry in Britain has also contributed to the distinctive features of union organisation. Sectional interests have predominated, with workers identifying themselves as 'boiler-makers' or 'platers' rather than as shipyard workers, while the latter identification has been more typical of Continental yards. Conse-quently, in Britain unions are organised on a trade or craft basis, while in Europe industry-wide unions have been more typical. But irrespective of the form of organisation and the degree of craft basis and labour intensity, worker control of the job process has con-tributed to a reputation for militancy and radicalism among shipyards workers, who have frequently played a leading role in general labour movement struggles, and in the general promotion of working-class interests.

Yet there is no simple or direct link between the radicalism of shipyard workers and the nature of their work process. In Britain, union militancy in the industry frequently took the form of disputes between craft rather than a generalised opposition of labour to management. In Sweden there were distinct regional variations in militancy between the Communist-dominated yards in Gothenburg and the Social-Democratic stronghold in Malmö. The different pace and setting of industrialisation and different worker-employer rela-tionships led to the rise of different political traditions.[15] Similar differences can be seen in radical Bremen and reformist Kiel in Gemany,[16] and regional variations in militancy such as those between Clydeside and Tyneside were also notable in Britain. Thus shipyard worker militancy has been influenced by many factors in local and national environments.[17]

Given the severity of the decline of the industry and the radical tradition of shipbuilding unionism some observers believed that, as in the inter-war years, the growing level of unemployment in ship-building would induce a new working-class militancy, bringing an end to union co-operation with government, and challenging the legitimacy of the welfare state and the political framework of social democratic capitalism.[18] It is the purpose of this study to examine to what extent these prognostications have proved true.

THE BREMEN STUDIES

In 1980 and 1981, at the University of Bremen, two extensive studies were published on the reaction of shipbuilding workers to the crisis, one of which also covered workers in other contracting industries.[19] The conclusions of the two studies are consistent and convincing: that the crisis has not been a spur to collective action at a grassroots level directed against the employer. Instead, it was found that most workers looked towards the state for some solution to the crisis. In the first study mentioned, four-fifths of the workers interviewed looked to government measures to solve the crisis, and in the second, 84 per cent of the shipyard workers regarded the state as the body which could intervene in the crisis and at least bring about improvements.

This is not to say, however, that the state was seen as capable of acting outside the market economy. The vast majority of shipyard workers considered the re-establishment of shipbuilding capital as the best and indeed the only solution to the problem of creating secure employment. Thus, rather than regarding the employer as a class adversary, they tended to identify the interests of the enterprise with their own interests and with their experience of the growth of the welfare state and the managed economy, they provide very few examples of a perspective critical of shipbuilding capital. Overwhelmingly, theirs is a perspective of co-operation with employers in which the state is seen as having a co-ordinating role.

Such feelings of solidarity with the enterprise have created tensions between employees of different companies when, during the contraction process, companies have been merged or workers transferred from one enterprise to another. For example, such feelings were responsible for much of the resistance to a merger between the large yards in Bremen.

When the unions took the field, therefore, it was not to fight the bosses but rather to pressurise governments into taking responsibility for the crisis and its handling. They wanted the state, by legal means and temporary subsidies, to make it possible for the employer to avoid the crisis which was manifesting itself in the form of reduced employment. In this context the state was seen as a body above group interests in society, to be used more or less by employers or employees depending on their actual degree of influence.

There is obviously a qualitative difference between this kind of crisis awareness and the much more straightforward opposition between labour and capital found earlier in the history of industrial relations, a perspective which had as its point of departure a trust and a confidence by the workers in their own strength and in the potential of the union's to protect their interests. This shift in perspective finds its most palpable expression in the increasing involvement of the unions in national tripartite bodies for social bargaining. It did not, however, mean that the unions necessarily came to be seen as out of touch with their members. The German studies indicate great confidence in the unions despite their changed roles, and in one of the studies almost half of the shipyard workers saw no opportunity for the unions to intervene. They referred instead to the impracticability of forcing employers to employ workers who were 'objectively' regarded as superfluous. Lastly, the crisis situation in particular yards was not interpreted as a breakdown of the whole economy but as as a regional or as a trade problem. Each group of workers seemed to believe that the crisic could be individually overcome even at the cost to themselves of reduced income and transfer to other trades, which in turn would imply individual mobility.

THE 'OBSCURE JUNGLE' OF SUBSIDIES

The wealth of subsidies that has supported shipbuilding is almost impossible to survey, at least if one is to try to calculate their size in real terms rather than simply detail the forms they take. The inventive power and ingenuity of politicians has been great when introducing new kinds of support for the failing industry, but the fact that it has been in the interest of every government to minimise the figures published has not made the survey easier.

The OECD has used the following typology for forms of public subsidy in shipbuilding:

A. *Protection of the national market*
   1. Custom duties on ships
   2. Import restrictions
   3. Government purchasing
B. *Direct subsidies*
C. *Fiscal assistance*
   1. Customs duty exemption or rebates for imported materials and parts
   2. Tax exemption or rebates

D. *Finance for investment and research*
  1. Facilities for the equipment of yards
  2. Loans or grants for the reorganisation and conversion of yards
  3. Contributions to research
  4. Assistance for the development of shipbuilding capacity abroad
E. *General facilities for financing the activities of yards*
  1. Provision of guarantees of finance on favourable terms (see item F.1)
  2. Public ownership or participation
F. *Export credit facilities*
  1. Provision of credits on favourable terms
  2. Export credit insurance
G. *Assistance to customers*
  1. Home market credit schemes
  2. Demolition and/or modernisation subsidies
  3. Operating subsidies

For some items the size of the support has been estimated by the OECD; for others an estimate is impossible. This is especially true of the different forms of guarantee, where it is not known to what extent they have been redeemed. The real value of favourable low interest loans is also difficult to evaluate.

Such problems are compounded by the noticeable tendency to develop a new political language to disguise subsidies, for example, by calling grants, 'loans'. Officially, a loan may be made, but both sides are well aware that it will never be repaid. Grants have also been classified as 'interest' and 'instalment-free loans', while formal loans have been transformed into direct capital contributions.

Other measures have been used besides types of subsidy. Military orders, more for employment than for defence reasons, have brought indirect government support through the defence budget. In Germany, so-called short-time working (*Kurzarbeit*) has often been introduced, meaning that the unemployment insurance has provided considerable sums to keep the yards running. In all these cases, however, OECD data is based on information given by the governments of member states, and a critical evaluation of the sources is therefore difficult. Yet another problem in assessing the scope of subsidies is that most subsidy surveys (others have been made, for example, by the EEC and different national and international federations of the shipbuilding industry) give a static view so that it is impossible to follow developments over time.

But even if a precise estimation is difficult it was commonly held in the industry at the beginning of the 1980s that 40 per cent of the price of a new ship in Western Europe was paid by government subsidies in one form or another. However, the size of subsidies is of no immediate interest for the question at the centre of this study, and will be indicated only by some examples. The aim here is not to calculate the total size of subsidies but to elucidate how the subsidy system has been developed and how it has influenced the relationships between the governments, the employers and the unions.

Subsidies in shipbuilding were the subject of heated debate as early as 1960. Structural problems in a rapidly changing industry had produced government interventions by the 1950s, but the cash flow from governments began in a more consistent way in the 1960s as a West European response to the Japanese challenge.

In the earlier period in Western Europe, the shipowner usually paid a part of the price during the construction period and the rest on delivery of the ship. But the rapidly increasing demands of shipowners in the 1950s and 1960s created financing difficulties. Norwegian shipowners in particular looked for credit abroad, since the Norwegian credit market was too small to serve their needs, and gradually the granting of credit by shipbuilders became a weapon of competition. The usual credit terms in Europe were 50 per cent of the order sum over five years, but Japanese shipbuilders escalated credits to improve their competitiveness and by 1961 credits covering 70 per cent of the order sum over a period of seven years had become fairly general, very often with no instalments during the first two years after delivery.

As shipbuilders became more and more concerned with being able to offer better credit terms than their competitors, governments became increasingly involved in the problem of securing funds. Credits were generally supplied by government-backed financial institutions, and the outcome was a period of prosperity for shipowners and shipbuilders alike, coupled with a sharp increase in the size of the world fleet and shipbuilding capacity above the level of shipping requirements. The high profits returned by shipowners attracted so many newcomers to the industry that the freight market collapsed in 1958; between 1958 and 1964 shipbuilders struggled to sell their products. In this context, credit schemes which had been devised by governments to cope with a situation of high demand came to be seen by the same governments as a solution to the problem of low demand.[20] Credit competition intensified, and in

15

the period of expansion after 1964 and, above all, from 1970 to 1975, credit schemes became an institution. During the contraction phase from the second half of the 1970s onwards they generally covered 80 per cent of the contract value at 7.5 per cent over 8.5 years.

In 1971, at the height of the boom in shipbuilding, the Danish Ship Credit Fund published a study where the principal question put forward was:

> Why has this internationally regarded industry been enclosed by a jungle of support measures and countermeasures and why have governmental funds in a number of countries over the years given billions in direct contributions to the yards, besides a long string of favourable treatments in other respects?[21]

The study finds one answer in the feelings of crisis provoked by the growth of the Japanese industry beginning in the 1960s. With the beginning of this geographical and structural shift in the market and the introduction of new production methods, employment stagnated and even decreased in West European shipbuilding. The credit option was now no longer enough to win orders and export credit systems were also developed. As this second form of government intervention grew in importance, a number of countries were able to offer foreign shipowners credit on better terms than the yards themselves could arrange on the free capital markets. In Sweden the semi-state-owned AB Svensk Exportkredit was founded in 1962. It guaranteed credit of up to 50 per cent of construction costs with an instalment period of ten years and 20 per cent paid on delivery. The outstanding 30 per cent was founded by the yards themselves who could organise finance on the international capital market within the framework of the government credit guarantee.

However, in late 1967, faced with temporary currency problems and a relatively high level of state-guaranteed interest (7 per cent), the industry asked for yet further assistance. At this point the Swedish government attempted to intervene directly to shape the industry, making it a condition of more favourable treatment that the industry agree to a voluntary and far-reaching series of mergers. Ironically, the inquiry set up to investigate the industry saw the need for mergers less in the international context than as a means of avoiding a labour shortage, mainly in Gothenburg.[22] With hindsight it is easy to smile, but it should be remembered that at this time Swedish shipbuilding was booming and Sweden was Japan's most successful

West European competitor. Any difficulties in the industry were regarded as temporary, and confidence bred by the ever-increasing production figures still made it difficult to identify the underlying theme of radical structural change. The yards successfully defended themselves against government proposals for mergers and, when the government tried to put pressure on them by threatening to withdraw credit aid, argued that a 50 per cent reduction in production would be the outcome. As a result, the government surrendered and gave new guarantees.[23]

In some ways the credit schemes themselves increased the problems of the industry. The running down of the Gothenburg yards was accelerated by currency speculation (signing contracts in dollars and refinancing them in Swiss francs and other currencies), and up to the end of 1967 some Swedish yards had higher income from interest than from sales. But this was a period when the dollar was rising. The American loss of financial hegemony at the beginning of the 1970s meant that exchange rates began to move in the opposite direction, and the Swedish yards suffered a currency squeeze.

Similar credit schemes were found in other countries. In Great Britain export promotion measures were undertaken in 1965, when 80 per cent of orders were offered on a ten-year credit at 5.5 per cent interest. In Germany, the first financing programme for shipbuilding was introduced by the government in 1962, guaranteeing refinancing of 50 per cent of the order sum at 5.5 per cent.[24] At the same time, the Conservative government initiated a programme of mergers resulting in the creation of a state-owned concern with yards in Kiel and Hamburg.[25]

Credit competition in Western Europe in the 1960s developed a system with interest rates of about 5–6 per cent, and instalment periods of eight to ten years or even more. Attempts within the OECD to harmonise credit terms resulted in protracted and tough talks. A special working party for shipbuilding had been appointed within the OECD in 1963 and produced its first report on subsidies in 1965. So many different forms of subsidy already existed at this point that those countries which had concentrated on credit schemes demanded concessions from those using other forms of subsidy as compensation for reducing credits. France, for example, had introduced direct production subsidies of some 17 per cent and would not accept any obligation to reduce them unless all forms of subsidy, including credit, were abolished. The outcome was an agreement in May 1969 on 6 per cent interest for up to 80 per cent of the order sum over eight years, i.e. an agreement to keep the existing levels.[26]

In December 1970, the minimum interest was increased to 7.5 per cent but, as in 1969, a number of countries introduced escape clauses.[27] By then credit subsidies to bridge temporary problems had become a permanent and necessary phenomenon within West European shipbuilding.

It is interesting to speculate what role increasing government intervention played in the development of production. Were subsidies a factor in the development of new types of ships with new technology, or were they only a consequence of changed market conditions? In Sweden, restructuring had its roots in the inter-war period when a fruitful symbiosis developed between Swedish tanker builders and Norwegian shipowners, who increasingly specialised in oil freight,[28] Swedish shipbuilders had always tended to follow the Japanese lead and this trend was sustained (though not initiated) in the 1950s by government subsidies. The Arendalsvarvet yard, for example, was planned before credit facilites were introduced. On the other hand, direct government backing for restructuring was demonstrated in 1973 (two years before the collapse of the market),[29] when the state-owned Uddevallavarvet some 50 miles north of Gothenbeerg became a tanker yard.

In Germany the government provided investment support between 1967 and 1970 with the explicit aim of modernising the shipbuilding industry.[30] As a result the new building dock for 750,000 ton tankers at Howaldtwerke-Deutsche Werft (HDW) in Kiel was ready for production in 1976, one year after the collapse of the market.[31] The streamlining of Chantiers d'Atlantique in St Nazaire, France may also be viewed in such a context. It would seem, therefore, that government intervention began as a response to the threat posed by Japan and the market, but went on to encourage the transformation of production, either indirectly or as a result of conscious political choice.

As early as 1963 yet another solution was proposed in the form of incentives to scrap surplus tonnage.[32] This suggestion was to remain in abeyance for more than 15 years until it was revived in talks within the OECD and the EEC about a worldwide scrap-and-build scheme. Also in the 1960s, the West European governments tried to cope with the crisis by a contraction of capacity,[33] but while the number of yards was reduced by rationalisations and mergers, productive capacity was thereby increased.[34]

The 1970s brought a qualitative change in government intervention in West European shipbuilding. The old credit subsidies to the industry as a whole remained but there was a new trend towards company-specific subsidies, as money was increasingly given to bail out individual yards in response to pressure from workers in the industry. By the end of the 1970s, this kind of more spectacular government assistance would dominate the political debate on shipbuilding, and the trend accelerated after the collapse of the market in 1975, culminating in the nationalisation of the large yards in Great Britain and Sweden in 1977.

Even before 1975, this development was discernible. In Great Britain the first suggestion of government-led restructuring occurred with the programme of mergers put forward by the Geddes report of 1966,[35] and continued at the beginning of the 1970s with the reconstruction of the Upper Clyde. In Germany, for the same reasons, the government initiated a merger programme at the end of the 1960s, which was however only partly successful in the face of significant resistance within the industry. In Sweden, the government intervened to save Götaverken in Gothenburg in co-operation with a private shipping company. In France this form of direct intervention had a longer tradition, having begun as early as 1951 with the first Act. Since that date there had existed a national strategy of co-operation between the government and the largely non-profitable industry in which direct intervention was an important part.

The credit war was in the long run, however, a hopeless strategy which could not prevent the shift of production to regions with lower costs and where subsidies were also used. But the character of this rear-guard action was not as obvious at the time as it is now. Few drew the appropriate conclusions from the rise of the Japanese industry, perhaps partly because the violent fluctuations in the price of the product peculiar to shipbuilding helped hide from decision-makers the shift in long-term competitiveness.[36] Instead there was a general process of adaptation, with the aim of maintaining market shares or, in the most optimisitic case, of regaining lost shares. The process of adaptation was eased by general economic growth which meant that other trades could absorb redundancies.

The oil crisis in the mid-1970s occasioned and legitimised political action of a more immediate and spectacular interventionist kind. On the one hand, general economic stagnation meant that other industries also succumbed, and the need for rescue operation grew. Actions were now governed by hopes for a change for the better in a few years, and the earlier sense of a need for structural modernisation gave way to a cyclical perspective. This was especially clear in Sweden, where first the Social Democratic government and after 1976 the centre right government tried to solve the crisis in a

19

Keynesian way. If, however, the trend was especially obvious in Sweden, it nevertheless held throughout Western Europe. Numerous studies carried out by governments, unions and shipbuilders in these years prophesised, or rather hoped for, a turn of the market in two or three years. Their strategies all aimed at riding out the storm, and the promise of better times was pushed steadily further into the future.

After 1982 the structural perspective gradually reasserted itself but now it was much more realistic.[37] The ambition of governments became to cope with an unavoidable retreat as flexibly as possible. In several countries the objective became to maintain two or three trimmed down yards for building sophisticated, high technology merchant ships. In Great Britain, plans to separate and privatise the 'profitable' military sector merely underlined this tendency.

WHY SUBSIDISE SHIPBUILDING?

It is not clear exactly why shipbuilding has been given such massive support, by comparison with other industries, when in most countries its contribution to GNP and to industrial employment has never been more than a few per cent.[38] It has been argued that the share of subcontractors is especially high in shipbuilding and that therefore many more people are involved than those directly employed by the yards. Economically, however, this argument is hardly relevant,[39] although it may serve to increase the political impact of changes in the sector. There is more sense in the argument that shipbuilding derives its national importance from its role in particular regions. The industry totally dominates many shipbuilding regions of Western Europe, and this in turn gives employers and employees, in co-operation with local and regional authorities and politicians, considerable strength as a pressure group. Moreover, unlike in another hard hit industry, textiles,[40] the vast majority of employees are men and (except in France) organised in unions, and this, too, may serve to explain the power of the shipbuilding lobby.[41]

It has also often been argued that shipbuilding owes its preferential treatment to considerations of national security. However, it may still be asked why ships should be produced in each individual country when it is considered quite natural to import other war materials such as aircraft, tanks and guns. The fragility of the argument is perhaps best demonstrated by the fact that the US in peace-time has always had a relatively negligible shipbuilding industry.[42]

Overall, the pressure group argument seems more powerful, while the argument about national security makes better sense if modified to include the need for national symbols, itself related to national security. Ships are, as far as it is known, the only industrial products besides aeroplanes which are the objects of christening. The industry is associated with pride and *machismo*: it is difficult to imagine textiles in such a role.

It was Keynes who supplied the politicians with a model justifying increasing government intervention. In the wake of the inter-war depression Keynes provided the real middle way between Fascism, Communism and National Socialism by postulating the possibility of national economic management to promote continuous growth, full employment, and rising social benefits. The ultimate failure of such a strategy lies in Keynes's overestimation of the potential for rational management by experts under democratic political conditions and his disregard of the fact that politics are a constant *flow* or *process* (rather than a steady state), in which inputs provoke outputs which in turn require inputs at a new level. The capacity of the market to adjust to leverage at the microeconomic or firm level gave rise to more and more government intervention, and the declining role of market allocation over time has inevitably drawn governments into microeconomic control. This has been an especially distinctive feature in shipbuilding where not only the individual enterprises but also every new order (i.e. the individual end products themselves) have become the subject of government decisions.

Keynesian economic management was based on the assumption of rational manipulation of aggregate market forces from above but, in so far as the model ignored the destabilising forces of political pressure within the bargaining and power triangle formed by governments, employers and unions, it found a way of keeping capitalist democracy working in the short term while weakening further its long-term conditions of existence.[43] Thus the political context of the Keynesian paradigm provides a framework in which it is possible to interpret both the rapidly increasing propensity for government intervention in shipbuilding from the 1960s or earlier, and the long-term impossibility of such a strategy as demonstrated after 1982.

Developments in West European shipbuilding since the 1960s have followed two lines, subsidies and capacity reduction, based on two different assumptions about the future. Subsidies imply the hope

21

for a later upturn in the market, while reductions in capacity are carried out on the assumption that there will be no such upturn. Logically the two principles are mutually incompatible, but in spite of this they have been pursued simultaneously. It is the emphasis which has changed over time, from the first to the second. The beginning of the 1980s seems crucial for this change in emphasis. Before then political pressure from the electorate took the form mainly of demands for subsidies to save industries in trouble. From the beginning of the 1980s onwards, in the wake of increasing rivalry between different groups in the stagnating economies of Western Europe, there have been increased resistance to 'gambling with taxpayers' money'.

In this context, the concept of the 'political market' of the West European democracies can be deployed to explain the link between the two basically incompatible strategies. In the political market votes are bought and in that market changes in public opinion made it sensible for politicians to shift from subsidies to capacity reduction. I am deliberately not going to use the concept in this reductionist sense of the rational calculation of how to maximise votes, but in the sense of politicians' sensibility to pressures and to changing opinions in a process of social bargaining. It is *not* a matter of a functionalist concept presuming an analogy between politicians and profit-seeking entrepreneurs.

The development of the subsidy programme had meant that governments came to possess both the administrative apparatus and the experience to support the industry — a fact which lent weight to workers' expectations that politicians would be prepared to intervene, expectations that were further reinforced by the experience of the 'friendly' state committed to welfare. This in turn meshed with workers' perceptions that the problems of the industry lay outside the scope of conventional class politics or industrial relations bargaining. But unlike the subsidy programmes and the dramatic rescue that followed in their wake, subsequent developments did not, and indeed could not, produce a solution favourable to the unions or to the industry. From the early 1980s onwards, as governments came to face the real impact of the international market, the industry suffered a continuous decline, and the granting of one concession after another by the unions at best served to carve out temporary resting places on the slide into oblivion. To explain why this period did not see a renaissance of large-scale union protest there is a need to look more deeply at the hints from the Bremen study about the distinction between collective and individual experiences of the crisis. For, as the critics grew, so the structure and size of the groups that experienced collective threats to their livelihood changed, and with them perceptions of the risks faced by marginalised individuals. On the other hand, if we are to ask why governments now felt able to cut the life support system to an industry they had earlier succoured, we must remember that, as the industry and its workforce shrank and as other sectors began to decline, the number and weight of the votes that shipbuilding had at its disposal to use in the political market also declined. As a result, the state was able to legitimise a progressive retreat from its previous commitments.

QUESTIONS AND PROBLEMS

The section about subsidies has revealed the considerable extent of state involvement in a non-profitable industry. A great deal of money has been spent on the contraction process over more than two decades. The credit policies of the 1960s, during a period of general economic growth when redundancy could be more easily absorbed, were conditioned by a desire to maintain the industry in the interests of the national economy and maybe, too, for 'symbolic' security reasons. Despite a degree of recognition of the structural changes underway, some retained their faith in the possibility of constructing a industry capable of competing in the world market. In the 1970s, the desire to protect employment came to the fore far more clearly. At the beginning of the acute phase the market downturn was still seen as a cyclical fluctuation to be bridged by Keynesian policies of government support. The 1980s have been characterised by attempts to withdraw from the giant subsidies of the earlier period, by strategies based on a much more pessimistic and realistic view of the industry's future. Such a change could in its turn be related to an increased propensity for other groups to hold their own in the zero-sum play of the stagnating economy, which certainly has meant growth in certain sectors and continued general growth, though at a slower pace, but also a declining share of wages in the GNP of Western industrial societies. (This development is discussed in Chapter 9.)

The study looks at all three levels of the industry — workers/ unions, management and government — and asks the following questions:

1. How have industrial policies in shipbuilding been formed? What content have these industrial policies had? How, when and why have there been changes? What have been the roles of governments and interest organisations?

2. What views about the future existed when policies were formed? When did the picture of the crisis as a deeply structural and persisting one, rather than transient and cyclical, become clear and how did patterns of action then change?

3. How have the unions acted in their relations with employers and government, and in what respects has the shift from growth to stagnation implied changed patterns of action?

4. What has been the union attitude to contraction? In what forms have reductions been approved? To what extent has such a disposition meant a strain on the workers' solidarity?

5. What effects has the struggle for government money had on the workers' unity?

6. What forms of action have there been and to what extent have their members been mobilised?

7. To what extent have union demands on governments been sustained by employers and their trade organisations?

8. What have been the union positions on the advance of the NICs? What reactions has the Japanese advance provoked?

9. To what extent have the national unions in their international federations represented national rather than group interests?

Each of these questions has been examined in a dynamic context which makes it possible to ask if and when institutional, ideological, and programmatic changes have occurred and power relationships changed. The historical perspective makes it possible to study the development of tensions between enforced decisions of a short-term kind and their more long-term, often unintended effects. It is the combination of a chronological and geographical comparison which makes it possible to throw more light upon political and union activities.

The questions are posed on three different levels: the local, the national, and the international. Questions 1, 3, 6 and 7 about industrial policies and union strategies above all refer to the local and national planes; questions 2, 4 and 5 about attitudes and views on the future prospects, and their effects on workers' unity, to all three levels; and questions 8 and 9 about the international implications to the national and international planes.

The case studies on which the analysis is based are as follows:

At the local level:
- in West Germany, AG Weser and Bremer Vulkan in Bremen;
- in Sweden, Götaverken and Eriksberg in Gothenburg, Kockums in Malmö and Öresundsvarvet in Landskrona;
- in Great Britain, John Browns (UIE), and Govan, on the Clyde;
- in France, Chantiers Dubigeon-Normandie in Nantes and Chantiers d'Atlantique in St Nazaire;
- in Denmark, Burmeister and Wain in Copenhagen;
- in the Netherlands, NDSM in Amsterdam.

At the national level:
- the governments, the federations of shipbuilding industry and the metal workers' national unions in West Germany, France, the UK, Sweden, Denmark and the Netherlands.

At the international level:
- The International Metal Workers' Federation (IMF) in Geneva and the European Metal Workers' Federation (EMF) and the EEC in Brussels.

The local level is the basis of the investigation, where the study focuses on the experiences, actions and reactions of the men in the building docks and berths of some of the large West European yards. It is there that the intensive analysis was carried out, creating a map of what they have had in common and in what respects they have differed.

The national and international levels present a unifying framework in each case, but it is a framework which has always changed in interaction with the local level. The industry's and the unions' national policies are to a large extent — but not only — a reflection of what happens locally. But national union policies affect, in their turn, the actions of the local unions. The national unions have been particularly important in talks about mergers, where much local rivalry has existed. Government policies, too, have changed over time, with or without a change of the party in power and to a greater or lesser extent in response to local pressure.

Co-operation between national industries and their unions is mirrored in the international organisations, where national factors are important and can be more easily studied. In fora where national interests are set against each other they are more easily accessible than in their national environments where they are often implicit and therefore more difficult to identify.

2

West Germany: Political Division and Local Action

In West Germany shipbuilding is regionally constructed. In 1980, whereas shipyard employment was less than 1 per cent of the total labour force in manufacturing industry, in Bremen and Emden 25 per cent of industrial workers were in shipbuilding, and in Kiel this proportion was 33 per cent. Moreover, these latter figures exclude workers employed by firms subcontracting to shipbuilders. Between 1972 and 1977 the five largest shipyards together had a 70 per cent share of the turnover in German shipbuilding. These were AG Weser (owned by the Krupp concern) and Bremer Vulkan (the German-Dutch concern Thyssen-Bornemisza) in Bremen; Nordseewerk (the German Thyssen concern) in Emden; Blohm & Voss (the German Thyssen concern) in Hamburg; and Howaldtwerke Deutsche Werft (HDW) (state-owned *via* the Salzgitter concern) with plants in Kiel and Hamburg. AG Weser also controlled the Seebeck yard in Bremerhaven some 40 miles down the Weser.

All the large yards belong to steel concerns. This is mainly the result of a deliberate strategy within the German steel industry in the 1920s, aimed at vertical integration.[1] One consequence of belonging to a vertically integrated organisation is that it makes possible a relatively rapid shift to production areas other than new construction. By 1979 only 52.4 per cent of turnover came from new construction.[2]

Being a part of large conglomerates and the federal political structure of Germany together have combined to make the yards pawns in a game between the industrial giants, the federal government (*Bundesregierung*), and the *Länderregierungen* in the four coastal states (*Länder*) of Schleswig-Holstein, Hamburg, Bremen, and Lower Saxony. This first became clear at the beginning of the 1960s with the introduction of the first structural rationalisation and federal government aid programme. More than 10,000 employees were then made redundant but in a generally expanding economy it was relatively easy for them to find new jobs.

In 1965, faced with the Japanese challenge, the Conservative federal government initiated a new concentration scheme in a general climate of optimism concerning the prospects for ship-building. This stage of modernisation implied staking all on big ships in series production: Howaldtwerke in Kiel, for example, was streamlined into a tanker yard with a 750,000 ton dock. Originally the government intended to carry through the concentration programme in co-operation with private industry. However, private industry withdrew, doubtful about the scale of investment required, and the government continued on its own. The state-owned Howaldtwerke, with yards in Hamburg and Kiel, was merged with the Deutsche Werft in Hamburg, creating the state-owned HDW in which the federal government held three-quarters of the shares and the remaining quarter was held by the *Land* Schleswig-Holstein.[3]

The unions agreed to the rationalisation programme despite the loss of another 10,000 jobs, but this was at a time when the economy was growing. The cuts were achieved largely by early retirement and voluntary redundancies. The belief in the future of shipbuilding remained unshakeable but since then the reduction in employment has been considerable (see Table 2.1)[4].

Table 2.1: Employment in German shipbuilding, 1975–1984

	1975	1980	1984
AG Weser	5,000	2,800	—
Bremer Vulcan	5,700	4,200	4,000
HDW Kiel	8,900	7,500	4,800
HDW Hamburg	6,600	5,100	2,000
Nordseewerk	4,800	3,600	2,900

UNIONS AND WORKS COUNCILS

In Germany unionisation is by broad industry grouping, not by trade. In the shipbuilding industry all blue collar workers and a significant number of white collar workers belong to IG Metall.[5] There is also a separate white collar union, DAG. In this study the focus will be on IG Metall, the union to which the vast majority of employees in German shipbuilding belong.

There is in the structure of the representation of German workers' interests a tension between centralising and decentralising tenden-cies.[6] This results from the parallel system of representation, the

the one introduced by law (the works councils (*Betriebsräte*) at the enterprise level), the other by voluntary association in the union movement.

Formally, the two systems are independent of one another. Unionised or not, all employees of the enterprise elect their members to the works council which has rights of co-determination with management on personnel and social affairs. The works councils have their origin in the Works Councils Law of 1920. Amendments at the beginning of the 1950s and in the 1970s have not altered their general character. The works council's responsibilities are for the wage structure, the regulation of working hours, overtime and short-time working, job classification, and the hiring, transfer and lay-off of employees. However, they have no right to call strikes and disagreements with management have to be settled by conciliation or by arbitration in the Labour Court, and in strictly economic matters the councils only have the right to be kept informed.

Wage negotiations and strike decisions are the prerogative of the unions, even if the differential between union-negotiated wages and earnings is especially high in Germany, as a result of the influence of works councils on the wage *incentive* system.[7] Although in many respects a highly centralised organisation, IG Metall's negotiations are mainly conducted at the regional (*Bezirksleitung*) rather than the national (*Vorstand*) level. Consequently, for shipbuilding the centre for collective bargaining is the Hamburg *Bezirksleitung* rather than the *Vorstand* in Frankfurt. This decentralisation of bargaining creates the basis for regional differences in bargaining within the union.[7]

Although formally independent of the unions the great majority of the members of work councils are loyal union members. The unions are also important for the works councils as a source of expert knowledge and training. Moreover, lists of candidates for the elections to the works councils are compiled by the unions, although there are other lists, since there are council members who are not union members. For instance, at HDW in Kiel a non-union list got some 600 votes out of 3,000 in the elections in 1978 and 1981, and at HDW in Hamburg the chairman of the council was expelled from IG Metall after having successfully campaigned on a list of his own not approved by the union.[8] However, the main importance of works councils has not been the establishment of a system competing with the unions, but rather their enormous influence at local level, which has in turn considerably influenced the higher echelons of the union hierarchy.[9]

28

Finally, it should be underlined that the relationship between the unions and the Social Democratic Party, SDP, is less close than it is, for instance, in Scandinavia. In the Weimar Republic the unions were tied to different political parties. After World War II such alignments were abandoned. However, the personal ties, if not the organisational ones, are strong between the members of IG Metall and the SDP, and the degree of overlapping membership is high among officials.

THE 'STRANGE COALITION'

Up until April, 1983 there was a strange coalition between the *Länder* governments, the shipbuilding industry and IG Metall concerning shipbuilding policy in Germany. The coalition broke down when we [IG Metall] couldn't agree on further employment cuts (Gerd Lilienfeld, IG Metall, *Bezirk* Hamburg. Interview, May 1983).

In 1973 the union position on the future prospects of the shipbuilding industry was the same optimistic one as that of the Federation of the German Shipbuilding Industry (VDS). They shared the view that a major investment programme was needed, that this had to be guaranteed by the government, that, in principle, all subsidies should be abolished but that, as long as they existed in other countries, Germany too had to keep them, and that German shipbuilding had a future. IG Metall argued for the necessary restructuring, for investment aid to be dependent on job-creation and for the unions and the government to be guaranteed real control in that respect.[10]

Though all three parties in the 'strange coalition' after 1975 were in agreement as to principles, the unions laid most stress on employment. This did not mean maintaining capacity at any price. Necessary reductions were accepted, but they argued that such reductions must be made in a socially responsible way, under government and union supervision, and linked to plans for investments in new production areas. Subsidies should not be given 'blindly', but made conditional on restructuring. Reorganisation in turn was to be governed by private interests and market economic principles, and there should be a development plan which took employment into consideration. The inevitable disappearance of jobs in shipbuilding should be offset by diversification in production.[11]

At the beginning of the crisis in 1977 union officials in IG Metall went so far as to argue that, in the framework of such a national

29

plan, the yards with the best chances of survival should be publicly named and distinguished from those where capacity reduction would have to be introduced.[12] This was a much more radical proposal than the 'cheese-cutter principle' by which cuts of equal size are made at every yard, and which, when the crisis deepened, became the only possible way to balance competing local interests. The proposal was rapidly withdrawn from the union scheme for handling the crisis. Probably the proposal was also too radical for the VDS; although its professed commitment to a market solution pointed in that direction, in practice they would have had difficulties in listing the condemned member enterprises.[13] Therefore both the union and the industry not only agreed in theory on a market economic solution, but also found each other, in practice, ready to diverge from that principle.[14]

IG Metall's idea of creating new jobs in new production areas is much easier to implement in a growing economy than in a stagnating one. The idea has been constantly repeated but has remained an empty phrase. Shipbuilding has been treated as a sectoral problem. However, the solution is not a sectoral one (see Chapter 4, pp. 102–4 on active labour market policy).

IG METALL: A CHANGE OF STRATEGY

At the seventh national shipbuilding conference of IG Metall in March 1978, the need for restructuring and reducing capacity receded into the background. Instead, it was argued that capacity should not in the short term be adapted to low demand, which was seen as a cyclical phenomenon. The proper strategy would be to increase the demand for ships by government measures within the framework of the EEC. The federal government was asked to prepare an 'intermediate plan' guaranteeing full employment at the yards and in the regions in which they were situated. The more radical restructuring in 1977 was put aside for the time being.[15]

This new emphasis must be related to the worsening situation in shipbuilding. More immediate measures were demanded than a long-term restructuring plan. The new emphasis meant, of course, demands for more temporary government subsidies in the hope of weathering the crisis. This was not incompatible with the views of the VDS, which nevertheless had clearer understanding than did IG Metall of the structural features of the crisis.[16] The unions and employers were therefore united in demanding government money, although for the former the money was intended to tide them over the crisis, and for the latter to adjust the structure of the industry to a new situation.[17]

Even if IG Metall resisted 'every unilateral adjustment of capacity to the sinking demand for ships' as 'having no perspective', they generally regarded the position of VDS positively.[18] IG Metall proposed a transformation of most of the subsidies into direct building aid, which assumed that it would be possible to get orders at unprofitable rates. Although this was certainly not the strategy favoured by VDS, they did not resist it. Thus the ever deepening crisis in shipbuilding did not result in the traditional conflict between capital and labour but in a common campaign for more money. The campaign was directed at the federal government, and this common objective united IG Metall and VDS, supported by the *Länder* governments, in the 'strange coalition'.

In March 1980, IG Metall received with approval a VDS report on shipbuilding situation.[19] The report was said to be a 'further step towards a closer structural linkage of yard planning and political influence by government bodies'. The state was still the common denominator for both IG Metall and VDS: its role was to guarantee that 'the policy without perspective' of the EEC Commission (i.e. a definite reduction in capacity) would not be pursued. Reduction yes, but only to the same extent as the creation of new jobs.[20]

The demands of the union and of the shipbuilding industry were met with appreciation by the federal government. The federal Minister of Finance at the time, Hans Matthöffer, stated: 'By and large we made the industry's proposal our own'.[21] In January 1979 new subsidies were introduced. They totalled some DM 660 m for the three-year period 1979–81. They were calculated to cover 10 per cent of the order sum on average, but the yards could in individual cases go up to 20 per cent, the original amount demanded by the industry.[22] Not only the size but also the form of the new support was close to the wishes of the industry. In addition to the new package there were also older subsides (a hangover from previous attempts to restructure the industry) and, in all, more than DM 1 bn was allocated for the three years. In addition, the Federal Ministry of Defence ordered seven frigates to be built in the next few years.

However, two conditions went with the new aid. First, structural rationalisation, implying job cuts and diversification of production, had to be carried out. At the same time, the federal and the *Länder* governments were made responsible for a programme for the development of new jobs in new industries in the coastal region. The

31

second condition was that the *Länder* governments participate in the undertaking, and the federal government demanded one third of the DM 660 m from them.

The first of the conditions was soon lost sight of in the generally stagnating economy, where the creation of new jobs in new labour-intensive industries was easier said than done. As to the second condition, it was the cause of much conflict between the different political levels as to who was to pay the bill.[23]

STRAINS IN THE 'STRANGE COALITION'

The first real strains in the 'strange coalition' became apparent in the spring of 1981. Wide difference opened between IG Metall and VDS on the one side and the *Länder* governments on the other. The latter were not prepared to continue the subsidies on the same scale as previously: an attitude which had immediate consequences. The *Länder* governments and the other interested parties in the coastal region had to agree in order to get federal money. The disagreement in 1981 caused by the *Länder* goverments' refusal to contribute as much as previously meant that the federal government refused a subsidy of DM 180 m for 1982.

The continuing crisis and the pronounced reluctance of the new federal Conservative-Liberal government (which succeeded the Social Democratic-Liberal administration in October 1982) to proceed with subsidies to industries with poor future prospects brought new tensions into the strange coalition.

The federal government demanded a plan for the creation of a competitive industry in return for considering any more subsidies. The demand was not new: it had been made by the Social Democratic Liberal government in 1979. What was new was that the demand was now made more vigorously. In order to consider new subsidies at all, the federal Conservative-Liberal government demanded a common forward-looking concentration scheme for the whole shipbuilding industry. The four coastal *Länder* governments were put under pressure in the spring of 1983, when they met with the shipbuilding industry and the unions to try to agree on such a scheme.

The conference was held in April 1983 in Hamburg, after the federal parliamentary elections and those for the *Landes* parliament in Schleswig-Holstein in March. (The question was too hot to be handled before the elections.) A reduction in employment of 9,000 men at the large yards was decided upon. The *Länder* governments, two Social Democrat (Bremen and Hamburg) and two Conservative (Schleswig-Holstein and Lower Saxony), agreed with the ship-building industry on that figure. The unions disagreed and protested[24] and in Bremen and Hamburg tensions developed within the Social Democratic party.

According to the plan, the labour force was to be cut by 4,000 at HDW yards in Kiel and Hamburg, by 3,000 in Bremen and Bremerhaven and by 500 at Blohm & Voss in Hamburg. The Federation of the Shipbuilding Industry (VDS) would have preferred to close whole yards immediately. However, this was politically impracticable.[25] In return for the cuts the federal government was expected to pay some DM 250 m annually. However, the federal government refused. Employment was reduced according to plan in Hamburg and Kiel. In Bremen, AG Weser collapsed in August/September 1983 but made it clear that no federal money could be expected.[26]

This lack of support from the federal government should not be mistaken for a total withdrawal from the subsidy policy. Total subsidies from the 1960s until 1982 have been estimated at some DM 12 bn.[27] In May 1982 the federal government granted another DM 650 m in direct yard aid for the period 1984–86. The aid to shipowners was DM 230 m for 1983 and DM 250 m for 1984. The federal resistance was to *further* increase in the subsidy scheme, called for by the Bremen Senate and the Social Democratic opposition.[28]

At the 1983 conference in Hamburg the president of the VDS, M. Budczies, argued that 9,000 people had to go and that the closure of whole yards had to be considered. The 'social plans' for a 'soft landing' when the labour force was reduced had so far cost DM 20,000–25,000 per redundant worker. That figure had to be reduced. Furthermore, M. Budczies said that foreign workers on average tended to be ill much more often than their German counterparts, and should therefore be the first to go.[29] IG Metall could not agree to this, and the strange coalition broke down.

IG Metall's counter strategy was formulated in August 1983. It can be summed up as follows: no more redundancy or closure of yards, no changed rules for the social plans and no special treatment of foreign workers.[30] No further reduction in the productive capacity of the German shipbuilding industry could be accepted. Demand should be stimulated by a gigantic Keynesian overall growth and employment programme costing at least DM 20 bn a year, coupled with an investment programme in alternative production. Subsidies to shipowners should be increased from 12.5 to 17.5 per cent but these were to be regarded as a step towards the nationalisation of the industry, a long-term union goal. A tripartite body should immediately elaborate a national plan for the industry.

Against the IG Metall strategy stood that of VDS, largely supported by the *Länder* governments, aimed at a continued gradual contraction. They considered that subsidies were necessary, but not for any expansionist purpose. Their goal was to maintain minimal employment in shipbuilding. The absolute level of such a contracted industry was a political question. In May 1983, one month after the Hamburg conference, Budczies set out some of the conditions which would affect decisions for the maintenance of the size decided upon at the conference: tax-free aid of 12.5 per cent of the order sum to German shipowners and direct building aid of 10 per cent, on average, of all export orders. If these conditions were not met, another 6,000 jobs would have to disappear, in addition to the 9,000 decided upon in Hamburg.[31]

The important question is that of why the union found it impossible to agree about the redundancy of 9,000 men and left the strange coalition. Since 1978 the policy of the union had not been to resist all redundancies but to insist that every reduction had to be compensated for by new jobs in other production areas and to insist that there could be no more talk of a new 'unilateral' adjustment, 'without perspectives', to market demand. But in practice that strategy had long since been undermined by local developments allowing a gradual contraction within the framework of 'social plans', as a rule without compulsory redundancy. By halting recruitment, early retirement and voluntary redundancy, the employment contraction was brought about quite smoothly, so that IG Metall's strategy had not up to that date been severely tested. But there was an increasing credibility gap between the public union statements about no job losses and local developments. How did that gap influence IG Metall?

At the beginning of the 1980s it was obvious that without further government contributions the large yards were threatened by immediate bankruptcy. It was also obvious that the political will to assist the yards had decreased considerably since the 1970s when the problems of the industry were regarded as cyclical and optimism still existed about the future.[32] The growing political resistance to calls for help was probably assisted by an increasing resistance in public opinion to loss-covering financial contributions to an industry the future of which was in doubt, and the increasing need to control the huge budget deficits involved. Moreover, the continuous contraction process had considerably decreased the labour force in the yards so that the potential for protest was much smaller. Closing an enterprise with 2,000–3,000 employees is less sensational and therefore politically less risky than it is with one with 7,000–8,000 employees. In short, the Social Democratic federal government was no longer prepared to increase its support for shipbuilding without a plan for the structure of the industry which gave reasonable prospects for long-term survival.[33] Thus when there was disagreement within the 'strange coalition' in March 1981 the writing was on the wall.

Federal pressure in the spring of 1981 patched up the coalition again, temporarily. The Social Democratic Bremen Senate demanded an increase in aid from the federal government from 12.5 per cent to 17.5 per cent of the cost of a ship for those owners who ordered ships from German yards. On March 31 1982 the four governments of the coastal states agreed to support the Bremen proposal and with this the 'strange coalition' was re-established. When the new proposal was considered in the first chamber of the federal parliament in Bonn (the *Bundesrat*, consisting of representatives of the *Länder*) it was blocked and Social Democratic Saarland and Hessen, where car and steel production were located, were among its opponents. Regional, or more precisely trade, solidarity proved more important than political hegemony.

During the discussions about the Bremen proposal, it became known that the Lord Mayor of that Hanseatic city, Hans Koschnik, had baited his application with an inquiry about a merger of the shipbuilding companies in Bremen. This inquiry about merger was intended to make the demand for federal money easier for Bonn to swallow. It was a continuation of earlier talks between the owners of the two yards in 1979[34] and it was widely realised that such a merger could hardly mean anything but a reduction of the total labour force. Consequently 3,000 shipyard workers rallied in a spontaneous demonstration.[35]

The proposed merger was a collectively experienced threat, because all workers involved feared that their own workplace was at risk. The works councils of AG Weser and Bremer Vulkan rejected any idea of a merger, and they had full backing from the shop floor. The workers of the two yards were traditional rivals and this was possibly an additional cohesive factor. The will to remain separate unified the two works councils.

The political temperature in Bremen rose when the date of publication of the inquiry approached. In June 1982, Hans Koschnik and the IG Metall *Bezirks* leader Otto vom Steeg were invited to a heated union meeting, where they both came under attack. Before the meeting began a small Marxist group which had interrupted the opening were 'immediately seized by the collar by union members and thrown outside the doors'.[36] There then came a heated discussion. The Social Democrat Lord Mayor, who had a reputation as a People's tribune, was reproached for all too often having represented the interests of the capital owners and for an anti-union policy. Von Steeg was also pressed hard. He argued in vain that IG Metall would not accept any redundancies and that the union had not yet decided on its reaction and failed totally to appease the angry shipyard workers. The chairman of the work council of AG Weser, Hans Ziegenfuß, was applauded for his attack on Koschnik. His colleague at Bremer Vulkan, Fritz Bettelhäuser, called the proposal of IG Metall to present a plan of its own later on in August 'a placebo before the holiday period'. One worker supported this verbal attack with a threat of physical violence: 'If you come to Vulkan today you should bring a bodyguard.'

The collectively experienced threat produced action and the consequent grass roots protest created a wide division between the works council and the industrial and political leadership. The offensive integration of IG Metall in the 'strange coalition' was about to turn into a defensive integration challenged from below.

The report of the inquiry was presented in July 1982.[37] Possibly on account of the massive popular protest, it was moderate. It considered three possibilities, and the one it recommended required a closer co-operation between the yards rather than a full merger. The works council were not appeased. They saw it as just the first step towards a final merger. Moreover, even in its moderate form the plan recommended a cut of some 500 jobs. The unions maintained their negative attitude.[38]

Koschnik was squeezed between the incompatible federal demands for a reduction of the size of the industry in exchange for financial support and the workers' resistance to job losses.

Koschnik tried to escape from this impasse by a letter to the two works councils.[39] He argued that he was not to blame for the crisis in shipbuilding, nor could he be accused of not having done everything in his power to alleviate the effects of the crisis:

To foster the illusion that appeals to the Senate and the federal government is the only real way to get out of the shipbuilding crisis must be deceitful for those hit, and avoids the real causes and responsibilities. To compress complicated contexts into simple demands on the state does not correspond to our social and economic reality.

The employers were responsible, not the politicians:

> . . . the growing impression is that increasingly — at least in public explanations — the appearance is given that the Senate [the *Landes* government in Bremen] or the federal government have responsibility for the enterprise, and the enterprises, who are really responsible for business decisions, for instance, for miscalculations in contracting, are lost sight of. If our economic system is weakened in such a way in the argumentation, not only the start becomes wrong but also the order of battle. In our economic system employers have the responsibility . . .

To say this was not to deny political responsibility for the structural conditions of economic regions or industries, Koschnik continued. The coastal *Länder* and the federal government had never denied such a responsibility. He went on to enumerate public subsidies since the 1960s, in all some DM 12 bn. The goal of the aid was clear: the maintenance of jobs. This was, of course, not the same as arguing that all jobs had to or could be maintained.

> Only in this context is it to be understood that the Senate has been interested in an investigation of the yards and of their production drain.

For a long time the Senate had wanted a common structural plan for the coastal region which would be presented to the federal government. He did not say so openly, but such a plan was a prerequisite for more federal contributions. And in the context of such a plan the Bremen merger study had to be undertaken.

The works council had another perspective. They urged the Senate to use its capital share in Bremen Vulkan to oppose every merger and every employment cut. (The *Land* Bremen was a minority shareholder in Bremer Vulkan after an urgent rescue operation in 1981.) Their efforts were almost exclusively directed towards politicians. Little was said about the role of private enterprise.[40]

For the works councils the only relevant question was that of employment: how could work be created and how could it be financed? They realised that a merger would imply a reduction between 1,000 and 2,000 men. They also realised that only the Senate and the federal government had the money required. However, the politicians were not prepared to spend any money before the yards had a structure which gave them a fair chance of survival. It was for this reason that Koschnik demanded the inquiry. The merger idea was the platform which was intended to allow room for political manoeuvre.[41]

The idea also gave managements room for manoeuvre. The merger was tentatively accepted, but different models for ways of handling the Bremen shipyard situation were discussed in tentative talks. The managements' report over the merger inquiry was published in December 1982 and this considered the different alternatives.[42] Not unexpectedly they all cost money. The sum was not specified but the figure mentioned in all the alternatives was DM 150 m.[43] But the companies had no money for shipbuilding: they wanted the Senate to pay. The alternative, by implication, was bankruptcy.

To obtain any federal assistance Koschnik had to present a reasonable merger plan[44] but this would mean deepening the chasm between the Social Democratic Mayor and the yard workers in Bremen, since resistance to any merger plan continued to be the policy of the works councils.[45] And after massive criticism at the meeting in June 1982 IG Metall itself opposed (or had to oppose) every idea of a merger.[46] But in the long run resistance was impossible. In the winter of 1983 Bremer Vulkan was again insolvent. At least DM 200 m was said to be required. The managements of the two Bremen yards presented a plan to the works councils and asked for a prompt answer. It involved a reduction of 1,000 men. Shipbuilding capacity in Bremen had to be reduced and this reduction had to be co-ordinated between the yards. This required additional capital which Krupp and Thyssen Bornemisza were not prepared to provide. Thus without public support Bremer Vulkan would be finished.

Koschnik was obliged to go to Bonn for federal government money and in these circumstances continued works council and IG Metall resistance[47] would undermine Koschnik's efforts. The pressure from the federal government and from the owners on the Senate resulted in Senate pressure on the workers.

Koschnik's immediate response was to attempt to get the workers to agree to a merger. He brought the works council and IG Metall representatives together in the Senate on Saturday 12 February 1983, after the management had presented its DM 200 m plan. The meeting was described as a 'sudden week-end attack to prevent the works councils from calling the workers together'.[48]

At a meeting attended by almost all the 4,000 workers of Bremen Vulkan on 14 February, Koschnik said that some DM 200 m had been requested for the rescue action. Two-thirds of the sum would be spent on the merger and on a social plan for the 1,000 men who would have to go. He told the meeting that he was prepared to go to Bonn and seek financial support from the federal Minister of Economics. But a necessary prerequisite for public support was a forward-looking plan supported by all concerned.[49] In other words, he needed the approval of the works councils before he would go to Bonn.

The resistance of the works councils was broken. At a meeting on 15 February they agreed to a merger with only minor reservations. They insisted on joint ownership of the new company involving the federal government, *Land* Bremen and private capital; the retention of both yards; and a guarantee of 'optimal' employment.[50] The first demand about state ownership was never seriously pushed and was perhaps intended rather to cover their climb down. The remaining demands served to conceal the extent of the defeat.

The development of the crisis in the summer of 1982 broke down old loyalties and created new ones. Pride in one's own enterprise and rivalry between the two yards had long existed in Bremen. A shipyard worker did not willingly move from one yard to the other. For decades there had been something of an imaginary barrier between AG Weser in Gröpelingen, an old working-class district of Bremen, and Bremen Vulkan in Vegesack, some 15 miles down the river in more rural surroundings. However, the importance of this old rivalry should not be exaggerated. It provided a general background, but the crisis situation *per se* probably was of much more immediate importance. So were the tensions between the workforces of AG Weser and Seebeck where there was no tradition of rivalry.

There had been tension between the two Bremen works councils as the crisis developed but the merger inquiry by Koschnik united them. This was a collectively-experienced threat. A merger not only affected individual employment but could be a threat to the whole workplace: this threat broke down old barriers. However, this outcome was only of temporary importance. The new solidarity and the resistance it created could delay but not prevent the subsequent development.

With the support of the works councils, Koschnik went to Bonn. Before the journey he met the works councils and the local branch of IG Metall. They all now realised that an employment cut was necessary. The discussions dealt with the question of the extent to which such a reduction could be attained by early retirement and natural wastage.[51] Pressure from Bonn had created unity in Bremen.

But the federal government rejected Koshnik's compromise. The merger plan in Bremen was not sufficiently far-reaching for federal intervention. The Minister of Economics, Otto Graf Lambsdorff, argued that reorganisation in Bremen was not enough; a plan for the restructuring of the whole German shipbuilding industry had to be elaborated before he was prepared to consider any assistance.[52] The promise of financial assistance from Bonn acted as a powerful incentive to search for a solution and this pressure provided the backcloth to the conference in Hamburg.

PRESSURE FROM BELOW

The pressure from the federal level on the *Länder* government was obvious.[53] However, the developments in Bremen also demonstrated very distinct pressures from below. The four coastal governments had to act but had little space for political manoeuvring. They were caught between the conflicting interests of the industry and the federal government and, moreover, could not agree with each other. The Senate of Hamburg wanted an agreement which left the location structure of the industry intact, with large yards at Bremen, Hamburg, Kiel and Emden. The government in Schleswig-Holstein wanted concentration of new construction in Kiel with repair work in Hamburg, which in effect meant a long-term death sentence for Hamburg. Consequently it rejected the Hamburg proposal.

In the talks before the April 1983 conference, Hamburg struggled vainly for a share in the new construction. Behind the scenes Lower Saxony and Bremen, for obvious reasons, passively supported Schleswig-Holstein. Hamburg was faced with an impossible choice: to torpedo a common strategy would be to reject every hope of federal money, and to support it would be to agree to the eventual closure of the HDW yard in Hamburg.[54]

In this framework of diverging and conflicting interests VDS, the federation of the shipbuilding industry, had the most room for manoeuvre. Quite logically it was they who had to present to the conference the plan — described above — which the four governments accepted or had to accept but which it was impossible for IG Metall to support.

The losers in April 1983 were the Social Democratic governments in Hamburg and Bremen together with IG Metall, Hamburg quite obviously and Bremen because they had to agree to a reduction of 3,000 men instead of the 1,000 discussed some months previously. The logical consequence, though not one spoken about, was that one of the Bremen yards would also have to close. The fact that two of the three losers remained in the 'strange coalition' meant new strains in the labour movement. The Social Democratic Mayor of Hamburg, Dohnanyi, was criticised violently by exasperated party members at an extraordinary party meeting[55] 'I was thrashed and beaten up', Hans Koschnik said after a party meeting in Bremen.[56]

During the preliminaries to the Hamburg conference the Senate in Bremen had made an attempt to secure financial support from the private sector after the federal government's refusal to Koschnik during his visit to Bonn in February 1983. Although Krupp and Thyssen-Bornemisza had already earlier refused to make any further financial contributions, there were other possibilities. The banks with interest in Bremer Vulkan were approached. The DM 200 m contribution considered necessary in February before Koschnik's visit to Bonn was reduced in order to make this more attractive. For the immediate rescue some DM 80 m were now said to be enough. In long and intense meetings the Senate discussed the subject before they decided on their bid: DM 40 m from the banks and the same from the Senate.

The situation was tense and few seemed to know what was going to happen to the yard. The manager of the yard, Norbert Henke, then made a new move and announced discreetly that DM 68 m would be enough for the moment. The banks agreed to contribute DM 28 m. On 1 March Henke could communicate that the crisis was over.[57]

As the intense negotiation between the Senate and the banks went on, the manager Henke played a key role in setting the sum of money which would suffice, the works councils and the metal workers' local branch demonstrated their new-won unity in Bremen and gave Koschnik full backing. Their object of attack was the federal government which had rejected any involvement in the problems of Bremen when Koschnik visited Bonn in February 1983.

However, contemporary with the new-won unity in Bremen the old split with Otto vom Steeg and the *Bezirksleitung* in Hamburg reopened. At a heated IG Metall meeting in Hamburg, the Bremen representatives wanted IG Metall to apply for federal financial support on the Weser. The representatives of the smaller and the medium-sized yards had long been suspicious of public sums spent on the large yards which they claimed distorted competition. Supported by the people from the smaller and medium-sized yards, vom Steeg rejected the proposal whilst the representatives of the other large yards abstained.

The discussion was hot-tempered and several people walked out. Without support from their colleagues the Bremen local branch and the two works councils decided to continue on their own. They hired 86 buses and on 3 March 5,000 shipyard workers from Bremen went to Bonn where they rallied in a protest against the federal government.[58]

IG Metall was hard pressed and could do little but withdraw from the 'strange coalition'. The grassroots protest in the summer of 1982 and in February-March 1983 made the proposal in Hamburg of a cut of 9,000 men unacceptable to the union.

THE CLOSURE OF AG WESER

In Bremen the hope of a breathing space after the decision in April was short-lived. In August Thyssen-Bornemisza sent a confidential communication to Koschnik. They were no longer ready for a merger implying further financial involvement. They wanted to withdraw from shipbuilding.[59] This meant that the Senate was invited to take over the ownership of the bankrupt enterprise.

At the same time it was clear that the federal government, despite the decision in Hamburg in April, was still not prepared to intervene. The four coastal states had requested an increase in the aid to shipowners of from 12.5 to 17.5 per cent of the purchase price of orders placed with German yards, but this was refused. No federal assistance could be expected *before* capacity had been reduced. The Conservative-Liberal coalition went further and demanded practical plans showing how the *Länder* governments and yard owners proposed to finance and run viable operations. It was not only a matter of contraction and concentration. Prospects of profitability also had to be demonstrated.[60] The ball was again in the Senate's court. The smallest *Land* of the Federal Republic had pumped DM 200 m into its shipbuilding industry since 1975. Now its resources were exhausted. In a last desperate attempt to win over the federal government, Koschnik presented a sensational plan, less than one month before the elections to the *Land* parliament. Koschnik himself informed the works councils, to whom his message came as a bombshell. After months of wrangling about plans, after mutual accusation and endless discussions, the Senate and the two yard managements now saw only one economic solution: AG Weser with 2,200 employees was to be closed. This decision was a logical consequence of the fact that the Krupps concern wanted to get out of shipbuilding and of the fact that two yards would be too much for the Senate.[61]

AG Weser was a yard full of tradition for the people of Bremen and a monument as important to them as the statue of Roland in the market-place. It was here after World War I that the revolutionary movement in Bremen had its headquarters, and where the city's *Räterepublik* was finally destroyed. It was also the scene of the legendary post-war Mayor Wilhelm Kaisen's announcement in 1951 that restrictions on German shipbuilding, introduced in 1945, had been abolished. The yard which less than a decade before had been the object of admiration throughout the Federal Republic when it launched the largest tanker (383,000 dwt) built in Europe up to that date, was now doomed by bankruptcy.

Koschnik's announcement was made in the middle of the election campaign. It smashed the fragile political alliance. Outside the city hall 3,000 shipyard workers rallied in the market-place in a protest demonstration. Koschnik was met by boos and shouts of 'yard murderer' when he tried to speak. The Social Democratic People's tribune was suddenly in an election campaign being opposed by an important section of the working class. This was quite a new experience for the Mayor, who had held office for 18 years. The attack from the yards hit him hard. Having grown up in very working-class area of Gröpelingen where AG Weser was situated, and as the son of a famous union leader, Koschnik was deeply upset by the imputations of being a traitor to the workers.

On 20 September the Liberal Economics Minister, Otto Lambsdorff, visited the yard to tell the employees that the federal government could not commit any funds for any restructuring plan until after the elections. Koschnik had wanted DM 115 m from Bonn to hold a merger scheme. Less than an hour after Lambsdorff had left the meeting with the employees, the works council announced that the plant was occupied until further notice. Foremen acted with the full backing of the 2,200 member workforce and sent lookouts to take up position at crucial gates. Workers hung up a flag bearing the symbol of Poland's banned Solidarity labour movement. Signs announced: 'occupied day and night'. The works council declared that the length of the occupation would depend on decisions by the Senate. The occupiers singled out the Senate, because the federal government and the private owners were out of reach of their influence.

One week after the start of the occupation the Social Democrats who had generally been expected to lose heavily in the election, won an absolute majority. From 49.4 per cent in the election of 1979 and 48.7 per cent in the federal elections in the spring of 1983, they now increased their share to 51.3 per cent. The occupation had backfired. Spending money on shipbuilding did not bring with it the gains in the political market. Indeed, Koschnik had his biggest success in Gröpelingen. There was a mobilisation in the housing areas close to the yard the days before the election. By means of intensified efforts the party apparatus and its many canvassing workers managed to convince people that Koschnik was not the one to blame. The federal government had that responsibility. The pressure on their own *Land* government was turned into mobilisation against an external threat.[62] It is obvious that the action of the yard workers did not influence public opinion in the desired direction. When the works council's chairman, Hans Ziegenfuss, threw away his membership book (SPD) two days before the election in front of the TV cameras, it symbolised a split in the labour movement, but it did not have the intended political effect. In an interview Hans Koschnik illustrated the difficulty of his position:

Had Bremen belonged to Lower Saxony and had I been Lord Mayor in the *City* of Bremen instead of *Land* Bremen, I would have led the yard workers' march on Hanover [the capital of Lower Saxony].[63]

The occupation was a desperate undertaking with no prospects. As a means of political influence it failed, as had been clearly demonstrated by the outcome of the elections. When it had failed there was nothing more to be done.

Of course, such a judgement is the retrospective interpretation of the historian and has nothing to do with the prevailing mood during the occupation, when there was a zest among the yard workers and a conviction, or at least a hope, of being able to win the fight. So it was never, from their point of view, a fight without prospects. Or, as they put it in a later booklet about the occupation: *Wer kämpft kann verlieren, wer nicht kämpft hat schon verloren*, he who fights can lose, he who does not fight has already lost.[64]

THE POLITICAL PROPENSITY TO SPEND

The tensions inside IG Metall and between the union and the SPD were quite clear. The leaders were sensitive to the pressure from below, and there was no question of the movement being out of touch with its members. Neither was it a matter of top-level co-operation over plans. The tripartite coalition was characterised by a power struggle where the decisive question was to get somebody to pay. The coalitions changed constantly during the struggle, which grew more intense as the supply of money decreased.

The decreased supply of money can be regarded as a decline in political propensity to spend money on shipbuilding, resting on the growing awareness that the crisis was structural and lasting and could not be countered by cyclical measures. This realisation was further prompted by the gigantic budget deficits. However, in Bremen, the elections demonstrate that it was probably not only a matter of economic factors but also of the political market. The long period of general economic stagnation and the enormous sums spent on industries which never recovered, resulted in a change of attitude: as a bent for spending freely no longer automatically yielded a return in the form of more votes. In addition, the national struggle should be seen in the wider context of the international restructuring of shipbuilding and developments in the market for ships.

This change in thinking makes it difficult to compare Social Democratic and Conservative government politics before and after October 1982. Such a comparison is made no easier by the fact that the Liberals were a coalition partner in both governments and that Otto Graf Lambsdorff remained the Minister of Economics until the summer of 1984. However, the differences were probably much smaller than the political slogans suggest. Indeed, many public pronouncements reflected the individual views of the speaker rather than party policies. For instance, consider the case of Gerhard Stoltenberg as Minister President in Schleswig-Holstein and as federal Minister of Finance. In 1981, in the former role, he criticised the federal government emphatically for not continuing the subsidies introduced in 1979. The steps and measures taken by the

45

federal government were 'completely insufficient'.[65] As federal Minister of Finance a year later, he took a different view. Of course the change of opinion could theoretically be based on new insight. But then the new insight must be related to the new role. Social Democrats at the federal level were no more prepared than Stoltenberg to spend money on the yards without asking further questions. The Bremen Social Democrat Claus Grobecker in the budget committee of the Bundestag in a letter to the Social Democratic Minister of Finance Hans Matthöfer, reassured him that he was trying to keep the costs down:

> Heinrich Müller and I are at the moment working on a programme for the yards which, as far as the federal budget is concerned, is close to cost neutrality.[66]

Quite apart from the question about differing interests in spending money on shipbuilding (possibly more varied between levels of government than between political parties), is the question about the actual possibilities of gaining practical support. Both the holding of power and the need to be responsive to public opinion (the political market) affect the practical relevance of one's own opinion.

The difficulties of IG Metall increased with the deepening of the crisis and as the industry became more and more dependent on state intervention. It had only two weapons: the mobilisation of its members and its influence on public opinion, which became increasingly problematic as a structural perspective gradually replaced the cyclical one. Furthermore, IG Metall had to consider the interests not only of the shipyard workers in one or other of the large yards but also those of the small and medium-sized shipyards and more generally the workers in all other crisis-hit industries, which often meant a balancing act between conflicting interests in a zero sum play. Furthermore the importance of the local level in the organisational structure of the union did not make the problems of IG Metall any easier.

INDIVIDUAL AND COLLECTIVE THREATS: THE BREMER VULKAN CASE STUDY

> If a 'social plan' is elaborated, 70 per cent of the people prefer it to other options and hope they won't be on the list. (Karl Schönberger, vice chairman works council of Bremer Vulkan, interview April 1983.)

How then was overall stability brought about despite the obvious tension in the labour movement and between different political levels? Viewed rationally such tensions would have been destabilising. This question will be the main theme in this section. There are two points of departure: one we have already explored in looking at local character of union policies; the other is Schönberger's remark in the quotation above about 'social plans', which underlines the importance of individualising the sacrifice.

The advantage of using the twin concepts of collective and individual crisis consciousness is well demonstrated by the workers' actions at Bremer Vulkan in October 1982, some months after the outburst of protest against the merger inquiry discussed in the previous section. On 21 September the manager Norbert Henke in a letter to all the 3,000 employees abruptly announced that immediate measures had to be taken in order to avoid bankruptcy. Five hundred employees had to be fired immediately, and the piecework part of the wage was to decrease by 20 per cent (or the work-pace had to increase by 20 per cent if the payment was to be maintained). The letter ended: 'We have chosen this form of communication [instead of communicating with the works council] because all will be hit'.[67]

The management posed a collective threat but had reasonably reckoned upon individual reactions out of fear for the existence of the whole enterprise.[68] But the collective threat provoked collective action and a spectacular demonstration of opposition. The employees at the yard had so far been relatively unaffected by the economic crisis. With much more diversified production than for instance at AG Weser, there had been enough orders to guarantee employment. There had been no serious talks about planned reductions, although the merger talks had caused some worry. The suggested contraction was said to be necessary to create a profitable yard and enable the company to increase efficiency and survive. The change in wages and the proposal that 500 men had to be sacrificed to that end constituted a collectively-experienced threat: nobody knew if he was to remain or would have to go.

The 3,000 workers stopped work for an hour and a half and rallied outside the administration building of the yard in an overwhelming demonstration against the management under the motto of 'no sackings'. A delegation of 25 people — works council representatives and shop stewards — told the manager that they would resist the plan.[69] The backing from the shop floor was total.

On the third day after the announcement, an unofficial strike started. The Lord Mayor Hans Koschnik intervened and declared that there would be no political decisions without preceding talks between the management, the works council and the unions. The management reacted promptly, without changing their plan. Six days after the first announcement, a list announcing those who were to be fired was published.[70] Before the presentation of the list to the works council, the workers again rallied in the morning and decided unanimously by a show of hands to go home and continue the strike.[71]

When the list was published the threat was no longer collectively experienced. The threat became personalised and collective solidarity evaporated. Indeed, 800 workers demonstrated to pressurise the works council into starting immediate talks with the management to expedite the redundancies. By identifying individuals to be sacked, management converted the redundancy from a collective to an individual problem. Those not affected abandoned the protests, and German employers learned a valuable lesson in the technique of managing redundancies.

THE 'SOCIAL PLANS'

'Social plans' involving early retirements and voluntary redundancies with compensation had meant that threats of unemployment were individualised, affecting only the elderly and those less capable of work. For the others, the gradual slow-down has not implied any immediate threat, but rather been regarded as a necessary step to guarantee long-term survival. For a long time there was no basis for collective action and protest.

At the beginning of the 1980s the climate became harsher. Instead of social plans, the closure of whole enterprises and mass sackings were proposed. The political propensity to spend money on an industry whose problems were structural rather than cyclical had decreased.[72] Moreover, the previous gradual contraction process within the framework of social plans had considerably reduced the protest potential, which made the tougher stance of the governments easier to accept.

When the crisis deepened, the target of union politics became the state much more than the employers. This policy, supported by local collective actions, was at first successful, as for instance in Bremen in 1980 and 1982. But it could not stop a new attitude developing. 1983 brought more planned reduction in capacity and it was obvious that the goal was to close one yard in each of Hamburg and Bremen. But AG Weser and HDW Hamburg failed to co-ordinate their fight and there was no talk of support from other yards. The protest was local and dispersed. After having been on the retreat for years, it was not possible to develop offensive dynamics (especially as the potential for protest had decreased during that retreat). Moreover, public opinion had become less favourable towards huge subsidies of tax-payers' money to industries which, however, much was spent, never recovered, which in turn made it easier or necessary for politicians to resist yard workers' demands.

Union attempts at co-ordinating resistance to the progressive run-down of shipbuilding was hampered by power at the local level. The union structure has strengthened local forces, and the works councils system also worked in the same direction. It has been difficult for IG Metall to raise the problems from the local level and create a successful national union strategy. Certainly IG Metall developed a strategy — no reduction in shipbuilding which was not balanced by planned increase in employment elsewhere — but this strategy was continuously undermined by local agreements which did not involve the development of new industries. Local power caused obvious tensions within IG Metall, but it would be wrong to call this a crisis of legitimacy. It is rather that the members have realised how limited is the union's scope for action.

These social plans have individualised reaction and the local structure of the union movement and the works councils have dispersed collective protests. In addition, whatever resistance could be mounted have been decreasingly effective, as the state has been increasingly prepared to resist demands for subsidies, being supported in this not only by changing economic realities but also by a change in the political market. The elections in Bremen in 1983 dramatically demonstrated the increasing difficulties for the ship-yard workers.

The social plans concentrated the unemployment effect of run-down on the old, the disadvantaged and the young. The old and disadvantaged had left the enterprises and the young ones were not offered jobs there. Despite the highest total unemployment figures since the Weimar Republic and for a short period after World War II (around 10 per cent in Kiel and just below 15 in Bremen),[73] the gradual slow-down and the concentration of the effects on certain groups have given the whole process a relatively low profile both industrially and politically.[74]

WEST GERMANY: CONCLUDING REMARKS

In the turn-about from growth to contraction, union action has been directed against federal and, above all, the *Länder* governments rather than the employers, even at the local level. This is especially true for the period since 1982. Up to around 1982–3 the perspective was predominantly cyclical. A gradual adjustment of capacity to the market in a context of social plans paid for by government subsidies occurred without major friction. Both the industry and IG Metall at a regional/national level, and employers and works councils at a local level, turned successfully to the *Länder* and the federal governments to get money to weather the crisis and to stabilise the situation.

By 1982–3 it was obvious that any hope of a cyclical recovery had more or less vanished. Moreover, a point was reached where from the management's economic perspective further gradual reductions yard by yard became impossible. The political will or capacity to spend public money decreased. This is above all true of the federal government, for the sensitivity to local opinion and to the local effects of continued contraction was greater in the *Länder* governments. There, as in Bremen, continued financial support became a matter more of economic resources than of political will.

Officially, IG Metall has always agreed to necessary reductions in shipbuilding, but argued that for every job lost a new job in another production field has to be created. However, in reality they had to accept a local 'social plan' for gradual reduction which took no consideration of overall regional or national strategies for developing alternative production. There were no problems for the organisation involved so long as social plans could individualise the threat. But when it became much more collectively experienced, the tensions inside IG Metall forced its withdrawal from the 'strange coalition'.

The insight that capacity in shipbuilding had to be reduced and the hope that the crisis could be bridged by government support was the basis of a strange coalition. A prerequisite was that the reductions could be carried through by social plans which marginalised possible grassroots protest. When the federal government demanded much more swingeing cuts, and when for economic reasons management found the gradual contraction yard by yard became more difficult, the room for manoeuvre of the members of the tripartite coalition became small. In order to get federal support at all, the four *Länder* governments and VDS agreed on a scheme which IG Metall, exposed to local protests, could not accept.

The 'strange coalition' should not be mistaken for a body with total harmony of interests. It was rather a matter of traditional lobbying by pressure groups with conflicting interests, but which nevertheless had a shared interest in the future of shipbuilding. Internal tensions were visible all the time, although much more so by the end of the period. Unions and industry never or seldom acted together in their lobbying in Bonn. Empirically, the case of shipbuilding in Germany demonstrates an interest group influencing events more by virtue of the backing of local opinion, and by virtue of pressure on the political system, than by their integration into that system, as would be predicted by corporate theorising. Thus the state, although influenced by the interest groups, had the power to operate with a certain degree of autonomy.[75]

In this latter respect a special feature of West Germany is its federal structure, which has meant that shipbuilding has been a matter of relatively small concern in Bonn but of much more importance in the coastal *Länder*. Thus the intensity of the conflict has been more according to political level between tiers of government (*Bund-Land*) than political parties.[76] Apart from this question of relative influence at different political levels the decisive question has been: who has had the money to buy political and social stability and how much money has been regarded as necessary?

The local bias has also been very important for what IG Metall could and could not do. The most significant feature is the works council system which functions in parallel to the union and often centrifugally. Direct elections at workplaces have meant that every representative who wants to be re-elected has had to promote the best interests of his own enterprise.

> Above all you are works councils representatives. The union comes second. Solidarity ends where it involves one's own existence.[77]

This structure has also meant a slight tendency to 'japanisation' i.e. an identification more with one's enterprise than with the workers in rival enterprises. The works councils have enforced this bias within IG Metall. The shipbuilding crisis has been much more the affair of the Hamburg *Bezirk* than of the national board in Frankfurt: and it has been a local affair rather than a regional affair when it came down to practical policies. The possibilities for IG Metall to carry through a national strategy were limited.

51

A much greater general belief in the market economy adds features to the West German picture, an attitude historically produced by the experiences of the spectacular economic recovery and growth after World War II (*das Wirtschaftswunder*), and sharply contrasting with the ruins of the war and the slow economic development in East Germany. The Social Democratic post-war programme from 1959 (Bad Godesberg programme) illustrates this. The cautious approach of the higher echelons of IG Metall who have had to take wider member groups into consideration has been one of its effects and in this respect it should not be forgotten that white collar workers make up an important group in the union. The strong demands for government intervention at the local level, where the crisis has been more immediately experienced, have been 'mentally diluted' higher up in the hierarchy, which also has had to consider the problems of many industries other than shipbuilding.

One outcome has presented itself: the crisis has not produced grassroots pressure for collective action. The developoments in 1982 and 1983 hardly change this conclusion. The state has been the object of hopes and expectations. The union has in this context been regarded more as a pressure group than as a body which was able to do anything in its own right. However, expectations about the real possibilities of state action, amongst others, have not been unlimited. There has hardly been any crisis of legitimacy despite obvious tensions within the union movement. Local collective protests have been dispersed — thereby becoming more divisive than unifying — or the threats of unemployment have been individualised and mainly experienced by marginal groups lacking the possibility of political action. The individualising impact of the social plans, and the split between different workforces, have prevented workers' mobilisation above the enterprise level, and so have guaranteed the relative stability of the political system.

The prior role of the state rather than of the interest organisations, the tensions inside the tripartite coalition and inside the labour movement, and the local/regional focal centre are some main observations which should remind us of how oversimplified are corporatist and other equilibrium models of the harmony of interests at the levels of the elite in industry, union and the state.

3

France: National Decisions with Local Protests

CONCENTRATION: A LENGTHY PROCESS

Merchant shipbuilding in France has been concentrated in three regions: Dunkirk in the north, Nantes and St Nazaire in the Loire estuary, and La Ciotat and La Seyne in the Mediteranean east of Marseille. Naval construction is based in Lorient (Brittany), Brest, Cherbourg and Toulon.

The yards are part of large industrial conglomerates as in Germany, but the formation of two main groups was the culmination of a long process of concentration that started after World War II and was encouraged by the government. These two industrial groups are Empain-Schneider and the Compagnie Général d'Electricité (CGE), the latter having been nationalised by the Socialist government in 1982.

In 1982–3, the five large merchant yards merged to produce two groups. The large yards in La Ciotat, La Seyne and Dunkirk merged to form Chantiers du Nord et de la Méditerranée (Normed) under the aegis of Empain-Schneider.[1] The second group was formed by the CGE subsidiary Alsthom-Altantique which had already by the mid-seventies absorbed Chantiers de l'Atlantique in St Nazaire and made it a shipbuilding division within the company. In 1983 it took control of Dubigeon-Normandie in Nantes. Thus there were two yards within the shipbuilding division of Alsthom-Atlantique. However, Dubigeon remained a separate legal entity within the division.

In 1983 the two groups employed 11,000 and 7,000 people, respectively. In the 1950s the shipbuilding industry in France had employed 45,000 employees in new construction. This figure was reduced to 25,000 in 1970, although it rose to 32,000 during the boom years of the early seventies (*les années d'euphorie*).[2]

Most naval construction in the post-war period has been undertaken by the naval yards. Employment in these yards has remained steady at levels of between 30,000 and 35,000, of which some 25,000 are in new construction and the remainder in maintenance and repair.

It has been claimed that after the mid-seventies crisis the French government did not help private yards by placing naval contracts with them. But in 1976 three export orders for submarines were placed with Dubigeon-Normandie, and in 1980 three frigates, also for export, were ordered from merchant yards. In 1984 the government announced further plans for placing contracts for the French Navy in these yards.[3]

In any case, during the process of concentration, there has been considerable reduction in the numbers employed (Table 3.1).[4] But these figures do not include the job losses experienced in the peripheral industries. In France the net of subcontractors is institutionalised and widespread. These workers belong to the less-skilled sector of the labour market, and can be classified into two groups: the *intérimaires*, hired and fired as circumstances dictate, and the *sous-traitants*, who have more regular employment conditions. Inevitably these workers suffer most in lean periods, when they are the first to lose employment. This fact is illustrated by labour force figures from the Dubigeon yard in Nantes. In 1976 there were 3,900 employees including subcontracted labour and of these 2,635 were employed directly by the yard. In 1983 the respective figures were 1,745 and 1,545.[5] The general pattern of reaction to the crisis has largely followed the *sauve qui peut* principle, and the yard workers have fared the best, with the subcontracted workers becoming something of a crisis regulator.

Table 3.1: Employment in French shipbuilding, 1975–1984

	1975	1980	1984
Alsthom-Atlantique, St Nazaire	7,900	5,100	5,500
Dubigeon-Normandie, Nantes	2,600	1,800	1,600
Chantiers de France, Dunkirk	3,700	3,600	3,300
La Ciotat	6,100	3,700	3,700
Le Seyne (CNIM)	6,000	4,900	4,200

The role of subcontracting in protecting the directly-employed labour force was demonstrated by a study of the phenomenon in the naval yards at Toulon.[6] The subcontractors had lower wages, less job security and were the first to be laid off. They also had a lower social status and were less well unionised than the direct employees of the yard. This 'vertical sectionalism' into the direct and subcontract labour force had divisive consequences for the workforce and meant that the contraction process of the shipbuilding industry has not been experienced as a collective threat by the yard workers in Toulon. Relatively safe employment for direct employees has meant that wages rather than the employment question have been the main area for dispute. Generally, industrial relations have been non-conflictual, but when there was a lengthy strike in the summer of 1979 it is significant that the issue in contention for the regular shipyard workers was wages, whereas for the subcontracted workers it was employment. The shipyard workers were well mobilised: 'for the exclusive defence of their protected status; it doesn't matter much that the others are eating hamburgers. Their goal remains not to let the size of their entrecôte steak decrease, but if possible to increase it' (Gallon, p. 30).

GOVERNMENT INTERVENTION

In 1951 French shipbuilding order books were empty, the war losses had been made good, and the yards were less efficient than other Western European yards. In this year Gaston Defferre, Minister of the Merchant Navy, presented his Aid Act, which led to government subsidies totalling FFR 4.9 bn by 1964.[7] The naval dockyards (Lorient, Brest, Cherbourg, Toulon) had for a long time been used only for the maintenance of warships and it was not long after World War II that they undertook new construction. In addition, for employment reasons naval orders under the Aid Act were given to certain merchant yards, and with these measures the overall situation improved. The government also used the subsidies to exert pressure to restructure the industry. As a result, Chantiers de Penhoët and Les Ateliers et Chantiers de la Loire merged into Chantiers de l'Atlantique.[8] A novel aspect of the Aid Act was the subsidisation of shipbuilding not only for the French market but also for export, and this protective device provoked protest from other European countries.

The Aid Act and the subsequent restructuring measures did not

55

bring long-term profitability. When naval construction finished in the late 1950s the government intervened again. The *White Book* (*Livre Blanc*) of 1959 stated that the production capacity of the yards was not to exceed 400,000 gross register tonnes (grt) per year, large ships would be built by four or five yards and 12,000 redundancies were planned.[9]

The Gaullist government had two ways open to it for enforcing the contraction. It could either force the conversion of some yards, or it could withdraw financial aid and allow market forces to eliminate the less competitive yards. It chose the first alternative. In July of 1960 a list of six yards was presented where support would not be given if it involved the construction of ships over 3,000 tonnes.[10] The future structure of shipbuilding in France was thus laid down, though these measures were only a first step. The redundancy plan outlined in the *White Book* of 1959 was carried out during the 1960s. This and other measures of the 5th Five Year Plan led to massive local protest. This unrest will be dealt with in a later section of this chapter.

An important consequence of this renewed government intervention was a concentration of the industry: several mergers took place which led to the closure of some yards. In Nantes, Dubigeon-Normandie was established after a merger of two companies and the closure of one yard. Also in La Ciotat, La Seyne and Dunkirk there were mergers which finally ended with the closure of some yards. But even contraction on this scale did not make the industry viable. In 1968 the government presented an Industrial Agreement (*Contrat Professional*). This expressed the need for continued support for the yards, linked to a continuation of the restructuring process.[11]

The boom years of the early seventies temporarily concealed the long-term difficulties. This was especially true of Chantiers de l'Atlantique in St Nazaire which together with the yard in La Ciotat were restructured to increase building capacity, especially for supertankers after the Yom Kippur War in 1967.

The specialisation and standardisation encouraged by increasing concentration from 1960 onwards had increased the market power of the remaining yards. As a consequence of the *Livre Blanc* and the *Contrat Professional*, standard or near standard vessels were being built by each yard. The scale of production increased, in an approach similar to that pursued in Japan and Sweden,[12] and comparable to the concentration of German shipbuilding by the end of the 1960s.

Direct subsidy decreased in 1970 but was almost fully compensated for by offering the yards low-premium insurance against inflation. However, increasing output by the rationalised yards operating in a growing market meant in the period 1966–70 a decreasing subsidy per individual contract.[13]

On 1 January 1976 help under the Aid Act ceased as a result of the 10 July 1975 EEC directives regarding subsidy policies. But in other respects the French government continued to intervene.

On 23 July 1975 the government made a proposal to regroup the yards into two large groups.[14] Resistance by the CNIM in La Seyne was particularly strong, and the government had to postpone the scheme. Seven years were to elapse before the Socialist government implemented the plan at the end of 1982. However, during the mid-seventies some minor steps were taken to merge the yards into larger units. The CGE subsidiary Alsthom and Chantiers de l'Atlantique merged and created a new company, Alsthom-Atlantique, with different divisions. The Chantiers de l'Atlantique yard in St Nazaire constituted its shipbuilding division. In July 1977 the government proposed a new merger scheme. Alsthom-Atlantique were to merge with CNIM in La Seyne and Dubigeon-Normandie to form one group. The other group would be created by merging the two yards in Dunkirk and La Ciotat.[15]

In March 1979 the Minister of Transport stated that the ship-building policies of the government had three aims. First, a reduction in capacity from 700,000 to 500,000 tonnes by 1981; second, the development of diversified production in order to create 1,500 new jobs by the end of 1981; and, finally, placing orders in such a way as to help weather the crisis. The details of how these policies were to be implemented was left to the yards; the government merely guaranteed financial aid on a scale which the industry itself regarded as 'important'.[16]

The Socialist government of 1981 maintained these objectives and the necessary aid was noticed and appreciated by the ship-building federation (*Chambre Syndicale des Constructeurs de Navires*, CSCN).[17] The only difference was that the 1975 plan for regrouping could finally be implemented as part of the nationalisation programme which followed the elections. This regrouping was the logical consequence of post-war developments in shipbuilding and the related political discussions. However, it did not have the desired effect: it failed to stop the decline of the shipbuilding industry.

Tripartite meetings took place in February and March 1983 to discuss the government's modernisation programme. The industry's

57

fortunes reached crisis point in 1983 and were still critical after the rescue operation in January 1984. The new programme had involved the loss of around 5,000 jobs and a 15 per cent improvement in productivity during the following three years. A 30 per cent reduction in capacity was planned. Within such a general framework it would be up to the employers and the unions at the local level to negotiate the shrinkage, yard by yard. Yards would specialise in certain products; for instance, Dubigeon-Normandie in Nantes and La Seyne were to be the bases for military production. This meant that France finally went the same way as, for example, Great Britain: military orders would maintain overall capacity and employment. The Secretary of State for Naval Affairs, Guy Lengagne, emphasised that the cut in employment would be implemented by means of early retirement and retraining.[18]

The unions which participated in the tripartite talks that preceded the presentation of the plan certainly announced opposition to the planned job cuts, but this reaction seemed almost like a token gesture.

By the beginning of 1984 the orders of the five main yards had fallen from 200,000 tonnes in 1982 to 105,000 tonnes[19] compared with a total production capacity of 350,000 tonnes per year. But at this point the Secretary of State for Sea stated that the government was prepared to support orders during 1984.[20]

Financial support to the shipbuilding industry had been an integral part of the system since 1951 and had been part of the overall government strategy of concentration. Apart from rescue handouts in 1977 and 1984 it was always a well-calculated operation. These government policies should also be situated in the more general framework of intervention in French industry. These interventions were all outlined in the Five Year Plans which began in 1945. In the 1950s in general, industrial activity was largely protected from international competition.[21] It was in this spirit that Gaston Defferre signed the Aid Acts in 1951: subsidies and naval orders to resist foreign competition and to allow new investments to raise productivity.

In the 4th Plan (1960–4) the aims changed. The liberalisation of trade and the creation of the EEC formed a reduction in government influence. The private sector became exposed to international trade, which revealed the vulnerability of French manufacturing industry. The *White Book* of 1959 is an example of this change of attitude. The contraction and modernisation policies outlined in it reflected the EEC directives, and resulted in stong local unrest. The *Contrat*

Professionel fits the same pattern. The shock produced by the exposure of the industry to competition required swift stabilising action by the end of the 1960s. The fifth (1965–9) and sixth (1970–4) Plans outlined increases in the size of industrial units, and laid down precise production goals for entire industrial sectors such as steel and shipbuilding.[22]

The period of stagnation in the late 1970s resulted in a more selective approach. Projects in expanding industries, such as space technology and electronics, were to subsidise declining sectors, such as steel and shipbuilding. The policy of the Socialist government, to 'reindustrialise' in order to recover the home market, is a continuation of these policies, which resulted in the establishment of large industrial conglomerates and the reviving of plans with clear and ambitious goals. The shipbuilding contraction and concentration process of 1982–3 can thus be regarded as a logical consequence of overall industrial strategies.

The participation of the unions and the shipbuilding firms in the government-inspired restructuring of the shipbuilding industry during the post-war period provides the subject matter for the next section.

NEGOTIATIONS WITH THE UNIONS AND THE INDUSTRY

The French trade union movement has several distinctive features. In the shipbuilding industry only around one-fifth of the workforce is unionised. However, even this low proportion overstates the representative strength of shipbuilding unions because the membership is divided between competing organisations. The blue collar workers are split between the CGT (*Confédération Générale du Travail*) which has close ties with the Communist Party, the CFDN (*Confédération Française Démocratique du Travail*) established in 1964 by a majority of the Christian Union CFTC who decided to secularise it, and the FO (*Force Ouvrière*) which has no particular political affiliation. White collar employees mainly belong to the CGC (*Confédération Générale des Cadres*), although in fact very few are unionised. Some white collar workers are also to be found within the blue collar unions.

The CGT is strong in the north and the Mediterranean, but is relatively weak in the Nantes-St Nazaire area, which is where the CFDT is strongest. At the Dubigeon yard at the beginning of the 1980s CFDT obtained more than 60 per cent of the votes in the works council election. The CGT obtained some 40 per cent and the FO only a few per cent. At Alsthom-Atlantique the FO holds nearly a quarter of the votes, CGT 40 per cent and CFDT some 30 per cent. At the national level CGT represents approximately 45 per cent of the unionised workers in shipbuilding, CFDT around 35 per cent and FO approximately 10 per cent.[23]

The CGT has maintained a consistent ideological position since 1947 (when the non-Christian union movement split into the Communist CGT, and the FO). It has an overall strategy of gaining political power which is applied with flexibility in day-to-day matters. The FO has no wish to take any responsibility for running industry. Its view is more pragmatic, and includes no general social design. The CFDT argues for workers' influence, but not from the point of view of parity of power. They would like a more decentralised system with a large amount of employee self-management (*auto-gestion*),[24] a view increasingly shared by the CGT.

Employees elect their representatives to the works council (*Comité d'entreprise*). In the first election round the unions have the exclusive right to nominate candidates. If none of the candidates obtains more than 50 per cent of the votes, there is a second round in which any other candidates can also compete. Unlike their German counterparts, the works councils play only an informative and consultative role. They have no right to proclaim strikes, and have little influence in running the enterprise.[25] Legislation introduced in 1966 detailed the items on which the council should be consulted (matters such as vocational training, and the general running of the industry, specially when employment was affected). In the case of redundancy, the labour code only states that 'qualifications, seniority and family charges' have to be observed. As a rule the workers do not know how the lists have been drawn up. In a system such as this the unions have the advantage of being able to refuse responsibility for such decisions.[26]

Before 1968 the unions had no legally recognised function in the enterprise. They nominated the candidates for the works councils, to which they also appointed a representative. In addition they signed the collective agreement of the enterprise. After 1968 they were given the right to appoint shop stewards, who were protected against redundancy, who could undertake union duties in working hours (up to 200 hours per year), and who could also hold one meeting per month with the other union members.

Union strength rests on its shipyard organisation and local rivalries between the various unions increase the propensity to conflict.[27] Strike decisions are taken by local unions. The federations do not have any effective means of influencing decisions, their role being limited to providing information and making proposals for action. The small membership also means that they are financially weak and the CGT is the only union federation with significant resources.

UNION STRATEGIES

In the late 1970s the three unions formulated a co-ordinated reaction to the shipbuilding crisis. They had of course expressed their views during the fifties and the sixties, but in a less unified form. As early as 1964 the FO was speaking of the necessity for product diversification.[28] From 1964, when redundancies in the wake of the publication of the *White Book* began, the three unions united in a demand for reduced working hours and early retirement.

In a national shipbuilding report in November 1978, CFDT argued for the development of the French merchant fleet. More goods should be transported in French holds to increase demand for French ships. But that alone would not solve the problem. The CFDT admitted that a degree of overcapacity existed and that some diversification of production at the yards was therefore necessary. Furthermore, a reduction of working hours to 35 hours per week without wage cuts, voluntary early retirement at 55 years, a fifth holiday week, and the suggestion of overtime were proposed.[29] The demands were reported and elaborated on at later conferences. In 1983 a general modernisation of the French merchant fleet was requested together with retirement at 55 years with 70 per cent of the wage (in 1981 the demand had been for 75 per cent) offset by new recruitment.[30] The government was also asked to formulate a national plan for shipbuilding.[31]

CGT argued for a nationalistic and protectionist strategy,[32] echoing the CFDT calls for an increased use of the national merchant fleet for transporting French goods, a scrap and build scheme, and a reduction in hours and early retirement programme.

A slogan was created to express this strategy: Build French, transport French and repair French.[33] In 1983 the scrap and build proposal of 1978 had been expanded into a detailed plan for the construction of 75 ships.[34] The Communist newspaper *L'Humanité* summarised the CGT shipbuilding policies in the headline 'CGT keeps the national flag flying'.[35]

The FO was less inclined to call for protection and demonstrated an understanding of the need to restructure the shipbuilding industry. Like the CFDT, it requested a national plan from the government. Its aim was to develop new technologies to maintain or to increase employment at the yards instead of maintaining obsolete production methods. The FO also emphasised the need to pay attention to the social consequences of any restructuring of the industry. Thus it elaborated a plan for shipbuilding which included early retirement at 55, with favourable conditions, a 35 hour week which was not subject to wage cuts, and an additional week's holiday.[36]

To sum up, CGT has been protectionist to a much greater extent than FO. CGT has been more eager than the others to defend existing production structures in shipbuilding, whereas CFDT and FO have argued for the development of production in new fields.

UNION INFLUENCE

The three union federations recognised that they had little influence on the government decision-making process. They had been isolated before the crisis. In December 1970 CFDT had left the preparatory talks concerning the 6th Plan and somewhat later FO and CFDT in a common declaration stated that the talks only dealt with problems that industrialists found interesting, ignoring all social questions.[37] Again in February 1976 the CGT and the CFDT resigned from the committee preparing the seventh Plan. FO remained in the committee but its representative refused to endorse the conclusions of the final report.[38] The refusal of the employers to answer union questions concerning the employment situation increased union alienation.[39] Somewhat later, FO demanded tripartite negotiations under government auspices,[40] but both the government and the federation of the French shipbuilding industry refused.

The unions regarded the government and management as hand in glove and felt themselves to be excluded from the decision-making process. In this respect the new Socialist government of 1981 brought little change.[41]

There was within CFDT a general dissatisfaction with the steps taken by the new government. The regrouping at the end of 1982 was considered to be only a technical solution. What was lacking was any social programme for the national restructuring. The Socialist government was accused of co-operating with the industry on the closure of some yards and the progressive slimming down of the whole shipbuilding industry.[42]

Similar complaints were voiced by the FO:

> It is both useful and necessary to recommence talks with the Ministry of the Sea on the subject of an agreement which was once proposed to us, but which seems to have been forgotten in the bottom drawer of some Ministry filing cabinet.[43]

However at the same time the FO wanted to demonstrate its independence of all parties by solemnly reaffirming '. . . its absolute independence of employers, governments, state . .' The CGT also had misgivings on too close co-operation between the industry and the Socialist government.[44]

Representatives of all three federations have told the author that the government does not intend to give the unions a more important role. Suspicion of the government increased in the autumn of 1983 when, after significant losses in the local elections, the government announced a policy of general contraction. Shipbuilding, which had been previously the responsibility of a Cabinet Minister, was to be transferred to the duties of a State Secretary. This decision implied a lower priority for the industry.[45]

The rescue operation in January of 1984 stands out as diverging from the general trend. This time the government complied with the unions' demands, but only after the shipyard workers had been mobilised, and 3,000 of them demonstrated in the streets of Paris against a reduction in capacity.[46] The readiness to respond should be seen in the context of massive protests in other contracting industries like steel, protests which threatened the whole credibility of the Socialist government.

In February Guy Lengagne, Secretary of State for Sea, invited the shipbuilding unions to formal tripartite talks at national level for the first time since 1968. The government had already formulated its strategy. There were to be no closures of whole yards as in other countries and modernisation would not result in compulsory redundancies. During this process the unions would be kept fully informed (which, of course, is not the same as having influence).

At two meetings in February-March 1984 there was little negotiation but rather communication between the government, the industry and the unions. Thereafter there were some tripartite meetings, in smaller groups, to discuss details and points of importance (*petits sujets*)[47] but as protests petered out the old order was re-established. The continued tripartite talks over details could not conceal this fact; rather, they underlined it.

Therefore the judgement remains that during the crisis the unions were generally left out of talks at national levels: a position reaffirmed by the Socialist government. It should be borne in mind that nationally the French labour federations are weak and divided. Only at local level were there frequent inter-union contacts.[48] Apart from this lack of co-ordination, there was no inter-union agreement on general policy; for example, the FO were opposed to more protectionist policies of the other unions, specially that of the CGT.[49]

THE INFLUENCE OF THE SHIPBUILDING INDUSTRY

The shipbuilding industry has had much closer contact with the government than have the unions, but this does not necessarily mean that it exerted a much greater influence. It is rather that government strategy has been more in tune with opinion in the industry than with that in the unions. The views of the industry include those of individual shipbuilding companies and their branch organisations, *La Chambre Syndicale des Constructeurs de Navires* (CSCN). This organisation is a coalition of the different interests of the various enterprises, which are not always in agreement. This reduces the effectiveness of the CSCN action and means that the disunity between the union has to a certain extent had its counterpart in the industry. Very seldom have the employers presented a unified strategy, nor has there been any real attempt by the industry to establish a national policy.

Nevertheless, the representatives of the industry have had much easier access to the government decision-making process than have the unions. In turn there has been greater government interest in consulting the industry, both through the individual firms or the CSCN.

In 1977 the CSCN stated: '. . . last year's policies for French shipbuilding have been formed with close collaboration between the government and the industry'.[50] This collaboration, in which the government was the motive force, was in existence before the crisis. A typical expression was the Industrial Agreement (*Contrat Professionel*) between CSCN and the government published in 1968. It merged the yards in Nantes, St Nazaire, La Ciotat, La Seyne and Dunkirk. The industry undertook to increase the level of production from 400,000 to 500,000 compensated gross register tonnes (cgrt) (gradually increasing to 750,000 cgrt towards 1975) without increasing employment, and to work for restructuring of shipbuilding in two groups. There would be no lay-offs or declassification of employees. In return the government agreed to maintain financial support. The contract was negotiated between the government and the industry and the unions had no substantial influence on the talks.[51]

In 1978 relations between the government and the industry became strained, when the effects of the abolition of the Aid Act on 1 January 1976 became apparent. The rescue operation in the summer of 1977 was a response to demands formulated by the industry, but the resulting subsidies were, according to the industry, too small to be of any value.[52] In March 1979 more financial aid was allocated in the budget and harmony was restored.[53]

The Socialist government had no intention of abandoning a policy supported by the industry. In fact, the new government was praised by the CSCN for continuing the old government policies:

> These policies are a continuation of those which have always been pursued by the government. In this respect one can only congratulate oneself . . . thus one can imagine that the new guiding authority will have the means to follow through the actions previously undertaken to help industry.[54]

Since 1951 shipbuilding has been an industry *sous tutelle*, under the wing of the government with permanent contracts between the government and the industry.[55] Relations have been close but in its contacts with the government, CSCN have pointed out the consequences of different actions but, even if it had its own preferences, has left it to the government to decide. 'It is the government who pays'.[56] For its part the goverment has never been prepared to let the unprofitable industry collapse, and the long-term process of mixing private and state capital has been welcomed by CSCN.[57]

NEO-LIBERAL PLANNING

What has been said about shipbuilding can also be placed into a wider context. One scholar of post-war France, Stephen Cohen, has described France's traditional economic policy as being oriented, not towards the market, but towards the state, a tradition of planning rather than of *laissez-faire*. Of all the West European countries, France has the longest experience of elaborate industrial planning.[58]

65

The Monnet Plan in 1945 began a new era for this old tradition. The plan involved a new kind of sectorally-selective, industrially-oriented economic planning acting as an agent of economic growth, rather than a step towards socialism.[59] The idea of an *économie concertée* gained widespread acceptance throughout the government administration. The state was to maintain harmony and order among competing interests but also to ensure that the technological and economic process did not lose momentum. For this reason the planners preferred large firms and oligopolistic industries for the ease by which they could implement the plan.[60]

Trade unions only participated marginally. The 'concerted economy' was better suited to the needs of adminstration and business than of labour. Initially Monnet tried to involve the unions, but within a few years of 1946 they had disappeared from the central areas of decision-making.[61] After the widespread militancy in 1968 the government stepped up its attempts to engage the unions in a national dialogue but the essential framework of a divisive industrial relationals system remains.[62]

Planning has been concentrated directly on the organisation of particular industries, both modern industries including aerospace, telecommunications and biotechnology, and traditional industries, like coal, steel and shipbuilding.[63] In these industries there has been more dramatic and open political manoeuvring, especially by labour.[64]

Examples from shipbuilding and steel demonstrate that restructuring and contraction were the main plan objectives, although they were intended to happen in two stages. The regrouping in 1984 in shipbuilding was relatively painless but the subsequent redundancy talks were interrupted at the beginning of 1984 by the protests of workers worried about their jobs. In these circumstances the government demonstrated that it had both a long-term economic strategy and sufficient flexibility to tackle the problems resulting from this strategy.

The examples from the steel and shipbuilding industries show the importance of focusing attention on the grass-roots level in developing an understanding of the paradox of weak unions at national level and their surge of strength at local level. This will be discussed in the following section.

COLLECTIVELY EXPERIENCED THREATS AND LOCAL UNREST: ECONOMIC GROWTH AND THE CASE OF ST NAZAIRE

In the chapter on West Germany the difference between individually and collectively experienced threats of redundancy was discussed. In this section these same concepts will be used for two French case studies, one from the 1960s, when a climate of economic growth perhaps created conditions favourable to government intervention, and one from the crisis period, which is more immediately reminiscent of the German case. As in the German chapter the discussion will centre on government and union policies and how the two inter-related over the issue of redundancies.

The first yards in the Penhoët peninsula were built in the 1860s and from that time St Nazaire, some 35 miles west of Nantes on the northern side of the Loire estuary, was increasingly dominated by shipbuilding. M Barbance's description of St Nazaire and its industry and workers in 1948 was still valid in the 1970s, before the crisis and the threat of unemployment.

> With no pleasant scenery, no monuments, monotonous under the chequered regularity of its streets which inexorably intersect at right angles, with no natural resources, no families of long-standing, with no traditions, and no past, St Nazaire has really always been the modern town which only lives off and from its work. The rhythm of life of its inhabitants has been almost totally determined by the siren of its yard.[65]

From the earliest period a symbiotic relationship existed between industry and the surrounding countryside. In the 1960s only 30–40 per cent of the workforce lived in St Nazaire. 60–70 per cent came from the nearby villages, especially La Brière.[66] In the rural settlements almost all of the 20,000 inhabitants belong to families in which trades or crafts have been passed down from generation to generation. Whole families live in small enclaves a mile or two from each other. Industrial work was, and is, eked out with some agriculture.[67]

This rural-industrial socio-economic pattern has meant that the shipyard workers are very attached to their land, very resistant to social change and extremely sensitive to redundancy.[68]

As a prelude to employment contraction at the beginning of 1964, lay-offs became increasingly frequent amongst shipyard subcontractors

There were rumours about a redundancy proposal at Chantiers de l'Atlantique where 8,000 people were employed and some short warning stoppages occurred in February and March.[69]

On 10 March Jean Pinczon, the head of the company, told the works council, meeting in Paris, that in three days time he was going to fire 246 workers and that on 1 April he would dismiss another 354 who were 62 or over, giving them early pensions. Twenty minutes after the communication the three unions, taking joint action, decided to stop work at the yard. The following morning the postman distributed the letters to the 246 workers. The workers downed tools. The three union leaders, Paul Malnoë (FO), Joel Busson (CGT) and Yves Thoby (CFTC), delivered their sharp protests to the yard manager while the workers waited outside the adminstration building. However, it was not a matter of *general* collective action. The force behind the action was the workers who had been dismissed. It was a collective action only among those workers hit. The others remained rather passive and, as events showed, soon withdrew their support. As in Bremen at the Vulkan yard in 1982 (pp. 46–8), solidarity was fragile. The difference was that in St Nazaire the men hit were capable of fighting whereas those in Bremen remained passive and disillusioned. This difference was probably conditioned by the special geo-economic structure and political tradition in the St Nazaire area.

While a meeting between the yard manger and the three union leaders was still in progress, some 50 of the fired workers invaded the management offices, smashed some 20 windows and threw documents outside. Having continued 'tidying up', they lit smoke bombs. The yard's fire brigade came on the scene but did not intervene. The vast majority of workers remained outside the office waiting for the outcome of the talks.[70] Malnoë realised how serious the situation was:

> If the men want to take such and such action you have to lead them — of course — but you must be sure to take account of what they are thinking. At that time, what they cared about was keeping their jobs and the assurance of having a job, and the rest, they did not understand![71]

What they did not understand, according to Malnoë, was the general economic framework in which the contraction process occurred and the nature of the economic forces they opposed; only their jobs counted. In the split between conflicting interests the range of alternatives open to the union leader was limited: they had not only to listen but also to lead.

A vote by show of hands revealed that many workers refused to take part in any action. The redundancy scheme did not pose a generally perceived collective threat, and only those workers who had been made redundant demonstrated any collective spirit.

The unions' goal was to get the company to agree to early retirement at 61 years of age instead of 62, which meant that no younger workers would need to be compulsorily redundant. But in order to be able to put pressure on the management at all, they had to lead and channel the workers' spontaneous reaction.

After midnight Pinczon arrived on the scene, flown in with his staff from Paris. During the night he met the union leaders in the *sous-préfecture* (local government offices). Pinczon made it quite clear that continuation of the riot would bring closure of the yard. He refused to consider early retirement at 61 and added that if there were no dismissals now there would be 800 by October. Asked about the criteria for the selection of those made redundant, he announced that the basis was the workers' industrial value and that there was no question of returning to the *status quo*. Against the unions' solidarity as far as the early retirement scheme was concerned was set Pinczon's efficiency criterion for the reduction of capacity. Faced with Pinczon's tough attitude the three union leaders had to limit their goal in the negotiations. They backed down from the idea of early retirement from 61 and directed their energies towards maximal compensation for the redundant workers, whom Pinczon described as being victims of a necessary surgical operation.[72]

On the following afternoon all metal workers in St Nazaire downed tools. A rally carrying banners like 'For the establishment of new industries', 'Work for the young' and 'No redundancies' marched on the *sous-préfecture*. The union leaders at the front of the demonstration had been tipped off that a large contingent of police had barricaded all access to the *sous-préfecture*. Sensing the explosive feelings of the metal workers, the leaders chose to avoid probable confrontation and halted at the town hall for an improvised meeting.

Thoby (CFTC) urged the workers not to let themselves be provoked: Busson (CGT) said that 'They want to crush the unions, but we won't fall into the trap'. But a number of demonstrators set out for the *sous-préfecture* and a battle with the police took place there. The workers bombarded the police with missiles and they answered

69

with teargas and smoke bombs. After an hour the union leaders acted as go-betweens in the no-man's-land between the forces, trying to calm the agitated workers and to obtain permission to march off. The rally was by now almost dispersed, and the workers had begun to follow their leaders to the Labour House whilst the *Préfect* ordered the police to clear the ground.[73]

The planned march on the *sous-préfecture* was a sign of the union leaders' awareness that the government, rather than the employer, played the key role. At a meeting with several thousand workers two days after the encounter with the police, the union leaders censured the government for its lack of interest and for so far having reacted by sending nothing but policemen. The union leaders were eager to have talks with the government. They had their eyes principally on the National Employment Fund. They hoped that the fund would make retirement pensions from 60 onwards possible — i.e. that the government would take over where Pinczon had stopped short. On the afternoon of 13 March they met two representatives from the Ministry of Labour in the *sous-préfecture* but nothing was promised. The workers there occupied the shipyard, an act which was followed by a progressive increase in social tension which extended from the workforce to the entire population, reaching such a pitch that the government was forced to intervene. The Minister of Labour, Gilbert Grandval, then received a union delegation and shortly afterwards announced the government's proposals.

On 26 March the government declared its intention to use the National Employment Fund to guarantee to those made redundant 90 per cent of their wages during a retraining period.[74] Those taking early retirement were guaranteed 85 per cent. In a TV speech the Premier, Georges Pompidou, talked about the immediate establishment of a subsidiary company of the Renault concern in the Nantes-St Nazaire region. However, he also underlined that the only lasting weapon against unemployment in the area was mobility of labour.[75] The government's intervention was a one-off response to the worsening political and social situation, and was never intended to be a permanent ingredient in any plan for the declining region.

The victory for the workers over 62 occasioned a general celebration, with the whole yard following the 354 pensioners in a long procession, accompanied by accordians and guitars, to the cafés in the neighbourhood.[76] But the problem of the 246 younger redundant workers remained.

The unions continued the talks with Pinczon to obtain re-employment for these men. However, on this point the employer was unyielding.[77] Compared with the vehement show of strength in March, the situation after the pensioners' victory was very different. In April there was certainly a short work stoppage, lasting 45 minutes, by the employees at Chantiers de l'Atlantique, but this was nothing compared with the scale of the action in the previous month, and Pinczon was unmoved. Defeat was recognised by implication when a special committee for the redundant workers was established two days after the April stoppage.[78]

Thus whilst there was solidarity with the elderly, when it came to those workers identified as being selected for redundancy on the grounds of their relative inefficiency that solidarity broke down — a perhaps understandable reaction when the threat of unemployment was real and compliant behaviour an important efficiency criterion. It is difficult to interpret in any other way the dramatic change in mood within the three weeks.

Malnoë has commented on this change in mood:

> Every redundancy scheme encompasses several phases. First, general disquiet. Then the collective response, the revolt, and finally diminishing solidarity. From the moment when the worker feels that it has nothing more to do with him, he goes his own way.[79]

The unity between the three unions during the action is worthy of note. It is as if they were welded together by the small room for manoeuvre left between the furious workers on the one hand and the unrelenting Pinczon and the government. No attempt was made by any of the union leaders to provoke rivalry or exploit the situation. The lowering of negotiation goals was agreed during the fierce meeting with Pinczon, and the three unions collectively agreed to back down.

The unity between the three was all the more surprising when account is taken of their personalities. The style of Busson, representing the CGT, who had experiences from Buchenwald and was a maker of rousing speeches, was in stark contrast to Malnoë's cool and logical exposition of the FO doctrine. There was also Thoby, the leader of the Christian union, who was younger and, unlike Malnoë and Busson, not established.

The concord between the three and their unions must be understood in the context of the pressure of conflicting interets to which they were all exposed. In March the situation was too explosive to be exploited for selfish advantage. However, by 1 May they had returned to old habits. FO, with a strong and long anarcho-syndicalist tradition, held its own rally, whereas the Stalinist CGT and the Christian CFTC marched together in another demonstration. For the anarcho-syndicalist like Malnoë any other order was impossible.

> It was traditional and it was a basic condition. I wasn't going to celebrate the 1st of May with people like CFTC who ignored the 1st of May before the war, and who went to Mass at Whitsun side by side with the bosses.[80]

There is a long tradition of workers' outbursts such as the one in 1964 in Basse-Loire, but they have not usually had any particular political orientation. But St Nazaire was the town where Fernand Pelloutier grew up. He was one of the instigators and impelling forces behind the anarcho-syndicalist movement. He had planted a strong anarcho-syndicalist tradition in his home town before he died in 1901, only 33 years old. The strike as a means to power and political independence was a pillar within that tradition.

For some time there has been a kind of class consciousness which has been expressed, independently of political and union allegiances, in frequent outbursts of militancy aimed at direct action without any specific political leadership. The eruptions have had their cause in the immediate interests of the workers and, often enough, in their particular need for job security. There has been class consciousness in the sense that the workers as a collective have known well their immediate interests which they have tried to take care of themselves.

The special mentality of the area has been summarised in this way:

> Direct action is that which, discounting all outside assistance, and without relying upon any influence of the powers that be or of Parliament, is exerted by the interested parties themselves with the aim of obtaining satisfaction, which may be either partial or complete, but is at any rate absolutely clear.[81]

COLLECTIVELY EXPERIENCED THREATS AND LOCAL UNREST: DUBIGEON-NORMANDIE DURING THE 'CRISIS'

The example of the local reaction above was in the context of the politics of authoritarian restructuring in the 1960s when there was general growth, and when the metal worker was still at the core of the labour movement. The potential for protest was still considerable, and the shipyard workers had massive support from the local population. The 1960s were crisis years for shipbuilding in Basse-Loire, but at that time it was a question of an obsolete production structure needing modernisation. After 1975, however, it was a matter of the survival of the whole sector, and the metal workers no longer held the same key position within the labour movement.

The questions which arise are: What effects did the change of general context have on the workers and unions? Has there been a move towards more defensive union strategies? What has the change of general framework meant as regards the support of other groups in the population, and what possibilities has it presented for exerting pressure on the government or for the mobilisation of the grassroots? What unity has there been in the patterns of reaction? These questions will be addressed by means of a second case study.

In 1977, 12 years after serious labour market conflict over redundancy in the shipbuilding industry in Nantes of the same kind as in St Nazaire, there was only one yard left in Nantes: Dubigeon-Normandie with 2,500 regular employees and employing some 700 subcontracted workers. There were two blue collar unions, CFDT with 52 per cent of the votes in the works council election in 1975, and CGT with 41 per cent; CGC, the white collar union, had 7 per cent. FO had no effective representation.[82] The dominant position of the CFDT on the Loire differs from that in shipbuilding on the Mediterranean and in Dunkirk, where the CGT dominates. Whereas CGT's main support in the yard came almost exclusively from the blue collar workers, CFDT also had an important white collar backing.

Marcel Guiheneuff and Yves Jallier personified the two unions, Guiheneuff to such an extent that CFDT was called 'Marcel's union' by certain workers. A shipyard worker from the age of 15, and an early member of the Christain union CFTC, Guiheneuff became the Secretary of the yard works council in 1977, was responsible for shipbuilding at the national level in CFDT, and had an outstanding knowledge of the problems of shipbuilding which he demonstrated at meetings of the works council. He participated in many national and European committes on shipbuilding. Jallier had been shop steward in the CGT union for 15 years and was the welders' foreman at Dubigeon.

At the works council meeting in January 1977, the director of the company, Grenn, gave an account of the world market situation.[83] Faced with general problems, he suggested that diversified production could be a possible solution. At the end of April the management proposed to cut employment from 2,450 to 2,000. All those over 56 years 8 months would be dismissed. 90 per cent of their wages would be guaranteed for the first year, and thereafter would be reduced to 50 per cent until the age of 60. For those over 60, pensions would be 70 per cent of their wages. CFDT said it would consider early retirement on condition that, for each pensioner, a new employee would be taken on, but it would not countenance the sacking of younger men.[84]

Throughout the talks from January to May there were disruptions to production. The social climate, which generally had been strained for at least two years, since a four-week conflict over the wage agreement, deteriorated further.

It was above all the social plan which provoked union reaction. 289 workers over 56 years 8 months would be fired and 200 supervisors, draughtsmen and technicians, and all elderly workers who had risen within the company hierarchy, would be downgraded, in order to take the place of those workers who had received an early retirement pension. This was to rectify the imbalance between blue and white collar employees but to those concerned it brought a cut in wages, and a reduction in status.

The two unions agreed to reject the plan but they differed both in their analysis of the situation and also as to strategy.[85] According to CGT, the fight had to be continued in those companies where actions on the wage question would be a pivot for mobilisation of the workforce. They obviously realised that the social plan in itself did not represent a collective threat great enough to produce collective action. The Dubigeon battle could possibly be a springboard for challenging the whole contraction scheme of the Barre government within the framework of the seventh Plan. Consequently CGT proposed tough action at Dubigeon — if necessary a strike and occupation.

For CFDT, the wage issue did not seem a suitable basis for a fight. Rather, the employment question should be exploited, but not at a company level. Their experience of employment struggles was that they tended to be long and hard. It was therefore necessary to find new and less expensive means of fighting than striking within the company. CFDT proposed selective action in order to influence public opinion.

The CFDT strategy was quite new compared to the example taken from St Nazaire above. Its analysis of the shipbuilding crisis made public opinion (and, indirectly, the political power) a more productive target than the local employer. It was a strategy akin to that used in Bremen and discussed above. It was in fact a strategy based on the realisation that the difficulties of Dubigeon were much less a management problem than part of a more general crisis. Consequently, only the state could resolve the crisis. This realisation was becoming common in most West European unions and it seems reasonable to locate its source in Guiheneuff's wider involvement in European shipbuilding. CGT maintained its old-fashioned conventional Marxist labour-capital approach which implied that the problems were to be found and solved at the yard.

A vote was taken on the two strategies, and an overwhelming majority, 1,200 out of 1,500 voters, were in favour of the CFDT approach.[86] However, this was a vote on principles. In practice, the deteriorating social climate and the increasing uneasiness about employment prospects throughout the spring brought about a gradual slide towards the CGT strategy. There were short work stoppages and go-slow tactics, and, on 4 May, just after the social plan had been presented, the management office was occupied. In these actions it was CGT which was active, and CFDT hardly had any alternative but to go along with them.

Just before the holiday period, the management made a move which finally and ironically was to tip the balance towards the CGT. At the same time as the management announced a modification of the clocking-in system, some of the white collar employees were informed of the declassification system.[87] The approaching holidays could only delay the riposte, not prevent it.

On returning from holiday the employees found that the time-clocks had been moved from the entrance gates of the yard to where they actually worked. They were notified that there would be a time check four times a day instead of twice. The large size of the yard implied that for many it took a quarter of an hour to move from the entrance gate to their workplaces. The working day was considerably prolonged and the time for the lunch break cut short.

The social plan scarcely hit the blue collar workers. Neither the early retirement scheme nor the declassification scheme posed a collective threat to them. But the clocking-in decision, which was considered to be a major step backwards, did. The joint decision to refuse to clock in had full backing. When the management responded by threatening to withhold wages the workers backed down somewhat by only refusing the lunch check, but when the management then escalated the conflict by announcing that it was prepared to fire those who obstructed the new system, worker action, and with it the full triumph of the CGT strategy, could no longer be prevented. All work stopped at the yard and a strike which was to last eight weeks began. The collective threat against existing privileges provoked immediate collective action, an impetus which was not provided by the declassification scheme with its sectional effect.

The strike which started on 7 September was a spontaneous 'that's far enough' reaction. One hundred and fifty welders stopped working and invaded the offices and the CGT immediately called for a strike of the whole yard from the following day. CDFT was more hesitant, and at first prompted a return to work and negotiations with management. However, pushed on by grass-roots pressure and by the strategy of CGT, they reluctantly joined the movement which went against the analysis of the situation and its general strategy.

The clocking-in decision by the manager of Dubigeon, Grenn, and his yard manager, Bavary, demonstrated how prepared they were for a decisive trial of strength at company level. Although the time-clock decision was on the face of it aimed at an increase in productivity, the management can not have been unaware that the decision was a controversial one and that in the prevailing climate it would spark off a collective reaction. During the talks in April, Grenn had made it clear that he thought it would be possible to solve the problems at that level. No additional state subsidies would be required during the lull until the market recovered in three or four years, if the social plan were carried through. Adjustment to the market by contraction and increased productivity would secure Dubigeon's recovery.

The management 'helped' CGT gain popular support for its analysis based on class conflict. Grenn and Jallier agreed with each other in that definition of where the problem was located. The time-clocks became a symbol on which the protests could be focused. Clear cut and easy to understand, they stirred up emotions and concealed more complicated causal connections. Throughout the two-month-long struggle, the newspapers spoke only of the time-clock conflict. They portrayed the long and hard contest as a fight for control: other and more profound problems were hidden.

Faced with this local escalation and its logical consequences, CFDT could do little but admit that its own strategy had failed. It was a strategy which identified the problems at quite a different level, and which sought a remedy at that level. Their strategy had no symbols which could effectively mobilise the enterprise: it was much easier to fight the movement of time-clocks than to fight the restructuring of the world shipbuilding industry.

After one week, pickets at the gates controlled traffic in and out the yard. Dubigeon was in effect occupied. The staff, which had been keeping things running all this time, moved out to premises in Nantes.

It was a strike of blue collar workers. CGC, the union of the white collar employees, the group really hit by the social plan, remained aloof. The time-clocks were not their problem, and many of them even set up a committee of non-strikers. In September, 350 of them demonstrated outside the Town Hall demanding the right to work.[88] On the afternoon of 3 October there was a violent confrontation between strikers and non-strikers who had forced their way through the gates in cars, and were bombarded by stones, scrap iron and eggs. The strikers tried in various and quite spectacular ways to appeal to public opinion. However, the longer the conflict lasted the harder public opinion found it to understand why the shipyard workers were fighting so intensely on the time-clock issue when the whole shipbuilding industry was suffering from a severe economic crisis.

The support from other shipyard workers was also patchy. The time-clocks in Nantes were never perceived as a common threat and did not produce collective action outside Dubigeon.

Given the different periods of departure, the increasing tension between CGT and CFDT is not surprising. After seven weeks of strike, the CFDT strike leaders increasingly felt the mood of their membership to be moving towards settlement. Finally they found it necessary to take the unusual step of calling for a strike vote without having obtained anything at all from the bosses. Out of 2,400 employees only 710 voted. Of these, 543 voted for an immediate return to work. CFDT interpreted the outcome as a demand to end the strike. CGT argued that only a minority, less than one quarter of the employees, wanted to end the strike. At least, 1,600 workers had participated in the strike meeting before the poll, but only 700 of them had voted. According to CFDT, only 1,000 workers attended the meeting, and from among those attending the majority was for a return to work.[89]

At an interunion meeting two days after the poll, nothing could conceal the breach between Guiheneuff and Jallier. They could not agree on how to proceed. CFDT was determined to propose a return to work. This time CGT has to follow CFDT, for they could not go on alone. This would have been as impossible for them then as it would have been for CFDT to remain outside the strike eight weeks previously.

So after this long campaign they were faced with total defeat. Grenn and Bavary had made no concessions whatsoever during the conflict. Not until one week after the strike finished did talks with the unions recommence. The talks dealt with the social plan, of course, not with the time-clocks.[90] At the negotiating table everyone was aware of what the real problem was: there was no need for symbols.

In the short term, CFDT regarded the CFT offensive with some bewilderment. In retrospect, Guiheneuff summed up that bewilderment. 'What was the conflict about? We didn't know . . .'[91] In the long run, the challenge from CGT strengthened the position of CFDT. Six months after the conflict it increased its share in the works council elections by almost 4 per cent, to 55 per cent. The CGT share decreased by 3 per cent, to 38 per cent. It is not clear, however, how much of the CGT loss can be attributed to its role in the strike, since during the spring of 1978, CGT suffered a general defeat in the works council polls in the wake of the Left's failure in the parliamentary elections in March 1978.

In any case, the works council elections at Dubigeon-Normandie in 1981 brought continued progress for the more moderate CFDT. They got 63 per cent of the votes, as against 33 per cent for CGT. The further reduction in jobs, from 2,000 in 1977 to 1,600 in 1984, took place gradually and without any major protest. There were never any grounds for a repetition of the events of 1977. The gradual shrinkage failed to produce a collectively-experienced threat, and the longevity of the crisis in shipbuilding demonstrated that the problems could not be solved at the yard level. CFDT had argued this constantly since 1977.

The role of symbols in 1977 in producing motivation and mobilisation was obvious. In 1964 in St Nazaire the very employment issue had been enough to create this mobilisation. By 1977 the employment situation was perceived in more general terms as a political question. The 'time-clock' symbol targeted the employer and this was of major significance in mobilising support, but the pressure on the employer rather than on political power had little relevance to the prospects for success on the broader issue of jobs. Moreover, compared with 1964 the employees of Dubigeon-Normandie in 1977 had to fight much more in isolation. There were major divisions between different groups of employees of the yard, and little support from other shipyard workers.

The differences between the conflicts in the 1960s and in 1977 could be regarded as a consequence of the diminishing potential for protest, the decreasing role of the metal workers (and among them the shipyard workers) within the union movement, as well as a result of the increasing rivalry between different social groups and different regions with increasingly stagnant or declining industries.

It could be disputed just how total the union defeat was in 1977. It could be argued that the fight, after all, had prevented total closure and had prolonged the life of the yard. This was also said about the workers' defeats in Bremen and Hamburg. But in this respect the historian's hindsight should be distinguished from the prevailing mood of the workers before and during the fight.

In any case, the erosion of union power in 1977 meant that there were no real protests against the continued contraction process. Since 1977 protests in the shipbuilding industry have been concentrated mainly on the Mediterranean and Dunkirk. There they have not yet had their 1977.

FRANCE: CONCLUDING REMARKS

Since the early 1950s French shipbuilding has been an industry under the wing of the government, an industry *sous tutelle*. There has been a national shipbuilding strategy within the framework of a generally planned economy. The *économie concertée* and its neo-liberal planning has meant a conscious contraction process carried through with close co-operation between the government and the shipbuilding industry, rather than the *ad hoc* provision of subsidies. This was especially obvious during the 1960s. Although privately owned, at least up to 1982 when large sections were nationalised, it is justifiable to speak of French shipbuilding as a national industry. Its attempted reconstruction has been a concerted effort under state control. On the whole, the unions have not been involved at the national level, particularly when compared with the union integration in the 'strange coalition' in Germany before 1983. This observation is in accord with Rolf Torstendal's conclusion in his study of industrial development strategies in Western Europe. He considers France close to the so-called organised capital model.[92]

Moreover the French unions have not been able to co-ordinate their protests at the national level. This is a result not only of the fact that they are, historically, organisationally weak, but also of the fact that they have followed different strategies. So, for instance, CGT has been much more protectionist and nationalistic then CFDT and, above all, than FO, for which free trade and European economic co-operation have been important.

The difference can possibly be explained by the fact that CGT has had its greatest strength in the old basic, so-called sunset industries with a high proportion of blue collar workers, whereas CFDT and FO have had substantial member groups in the new sunrise industries which are much more dependent on export and consequently adherents of free trade. A blunt neo-mercantilist protectionist strategy in shipbuilding would have jeopardised internal cohesion much more in CFDT and FO than in CGT.

Union co-ordination has been far more in evidence at local level, as was shown by the two local case studies. At that time there was a pronouncedly local agreement in the Basse-Loire based on opposition to the government's merger and contraction drive after the establishment of the Common Market. In Nantes in 1977 the combination of pressure and the resolute attitude of the employer faced co-operation between the assertive CGT and the reluctant CFDT. But then, even at the local level, there were tensions within the labour movement and the mobilisation was not primarily caused by the employment issue.

At the local level in France militant action was more directly focused on the employer than in Germany. The state has, paradoxically enough, remained much more in the background and consequently the possibilities for 'passing the buck' between industry and the state and between the different levels of government has been less in France. Moreover, at the national level the unions have been unable to convert local protests into pressure directed at the government. Local protests have been widespread, but they have not presented an overwhelming threat to the government. The outcome has been a contraction process under local protests which has never posed a threat to overall stability.

The state was the co-ordinating and directing institution. This does not mean that it was set completely apart from the social groups which attempted to use it. There has been a readiness to absorb protests when they have tended to grow too strong. The state in France is a powerful force in political life, and it has long been an instrument of centralising power.[93] In Germany, as we have seen, the federal state in providing finance and in mediating conflict acted as a framework within which interested groups, including the local state, competed. The centralisation of the French state provided the conditions for government *action* rather than *reaction* to pressure.

In France there have been, of course, elements of government reaction as well as action. Shipbuilding policy has not been exclusively a long-term strategy to renovate and rebuild. It has also been a social policy to preserve. This was obvious in 1951 with the Aid Act and in 1977 and 1984 with the rescue operations. This summing up can be compared to the paradoxical conclusions of a study about the textiles industry in France.

> . . . policies of reorganisation and modernisation of industries were used as 'vehicles' for politically willed survival of the non-competitive traditional industrial sectors . . . What was originally designed to renew has in fact preserved . . .[94]

Whereas the state and the industry in their long-term strategy concentrated on the supply side, the short-term policy, particularly affecting demand, remained the domain of traditional politics.[95]

There is yet another outstanding feature of French shipbuilding which has contributed to its stability. The system of subcontracting has produced a buffer which absorbed much of the redundancy before it hit the core of shipyard workers. It is a system which in its application has obvious signs of the personnel strategies used in Japanese shipbuilding, where key groups of employees are closely bound to the enterprises (or, rather, to the whole concern or conglomerate), and where marginal groups whose security of employment is much less certain have served as a cyclical regulator.

When the threats of unemployment have also reached the core of shipyard workers, these threats have been largely individually dispersed by schemes for early retirement such as were used much earlier in Germany. The use of early retirement has made it possible for the unions at the local level to accept reductions, since a lower retirement age has been a union goal since the 1960s.

Union politics have had a marked local focus in both Germany and France. In Germany, the target of local union politics has been the political power rather than the employer, whereas in France this target has been difficult to aim at, both because of the structure and weakness of the union movement and the centralisation and strength of the state. Therefore the target has been more the employer, at least up to 1983–4. This corresponds to the different degrees of integration and to the different industrial relations structure in France. Another difference has been the weaker contacts between local and central levels of the unions. In Germany there has been much more continuity in play between the different levels of the union hierarchy.

This conclusion differs from the commonly held opinion that strikes in France are of a basically political nature.[96] The very ability of the state to remain distant and reserved made the accessible employer at the local level much more of a target and safety valve. In federal Germany the political system was much more immediately the object of employees' action. There it is justified to talk about political action. It is quite another matter that conflicts in ship-building in France have been politically *exploited* and that state intervention, on some occasions, has been crucial.[97] This does not mean that the immediate aim of the conflict or the mobilising reason have been political as was demonstrated by the local case studies.

How then is the distinctively French mark to be understood?[98] The French industrial relations system is basically conflictual, lack-ing high union density and effective systems of collective bargaining and procedures through which disputes can be channelled. The conflicts at the shipyards were necessary to provoke state action. The state is an important actor not only in the French economy but also in the industrial relations system. As the French unions are weak, although they tend usually to direct pressure against the management their inability effectively to represent their members means that their ultimate target is the state. Generally the union strategies have been defensive ones, again because the unions are not very strong. The final objective is to bring the state to arbitrate social conflicts, by using its influence as an important economic actor in certain branches (like steel, shipbuilding or automobiles) or by means of public funding of social programmes.

In France, mobilisation starts at the local level. Attempts to enlarge it to the national level have been unsuccessful; even at the local level mobilisation was more successful in the 1960s than in the 1970s. In the 1970s the economic situation made the state less prepared to satisfy the union demands for industrial assistance or funding for early retirement in the shipbuilding industry.

Compared to West Germany, shipyard workers in France have had less representation in, and influence on, the process of contrac-tion and have been less disciplined. In the next chapter the focus will be on where Sweden lies with regard to the parameters of influence and discipline. The connection between them will also be discussed.

4

Sweden: Union Participation and a Peaceful Passing

THE TANKER IMPASSE

Historically, the Swedish shipbuilding industry has been concentrated in Gothenburg on the west coast and in Malmö-Landskrona in the Sound region of the south-west. In Gothenburg during the mid-nineteenth century, the three yards of Götaverken, Lindholmen and Eriksberg were established as engineering workshops on the island of Hisingen in the Göta älv estuary. During the 1910s they expanded to become more streamlined shipyards. Kockums in Malmö developed along similar lines. Öresundsvarvet was established after World War I in Landskrona on the Sound coast, and it became a subsidiary of Götaverken during World War II. The sixth largest yard, Uddevallavarvet, some 50 miles north of Gothenburg, was established after World War II.

Before the period of government intervention all the yards were centres of strong local culture. Each had its own market segment, within which business was influenced by personal contact between management and owners. The nationalisation of the debt-ridden industry during the late seventies was the culmination of a lengthy process of concentration, which had as one consequence the steady decline of the once-strong local cultures. This process started in 1957, when Uddevallavarvet collapsed and was finally taken over in 1963 by the government and Eriksberg.

During the 1960s, with a market share of approximately 10 per cent, the Swedish shipbuilding industry was the second largest in the world. This position was reached thanks to investment in cranes, welding equipment, computerised systems and large docks capable of berthing very large vessels.[1] More than any other country in Europe, Sweden responded to the Japanese challenge and restructured its yards. As a result productivity and competitiveness increased rapidly. The yards were now designed for the mass production of large bulk ships.[2]

In Gothenburg, Götaverken had remodelled the Arendalsvarvet yard by 1963. It was built under the inspiration of Volvo production techniques: the plant resembled the conveyor belt factories used in the car industry, hull sections being produced in huge prefabricated units. Unfortunately this yard was built too early, and the docks were to prove too small for the VLCCs to come.

Despite heavy investment and rapidly increasing productivity the industry experienced increasing difficulty in meeting Japanese credit competition, and by the end of the 1960s it requested an inquiry to investigate the problems of credit. The government was also concerned about the threat of over-capacity and the inquiry committee was given the additional task of presenting a scheme to co-ordinate shipbuilding. The industry was completely opposed to any such plan and the only outcome was an improvement in export credit guarantees (which had been in use since 1963) and a very loose agreement for co-operation between the major yards.[3]

These problems were largely forgotten during the bonanza years of the early 1970s when the Swedish yards could exploit fully the investment in new production technology. Between 1967 and 1972 the Kockums yard in Malmö was able to improve on its mass production techniques. It created an efficient production line for large batches of standard-sized ships, so that it was better placed than any other Swedish yard to exploit the rapid increase in demand between 1971 and 1975. They built 30 tankers in 210,000–255,000 dwt series and 13 tankers in the range of 350,000 dwt, taking 40 days to produce a 255,000 dwt tanker — a world record at the time.[4] Kockums was an extreme example, but the idea of organising a shipyard as an industrial system dominated the major yards until around 1975. But this system, developed at Arendal and refined at Kockums, placed Sweden in a vulnerable competitive position by the mid-1970s.

Even in the prosperous period prior to 1975 there was stagnation and closure of individual yards. In 1971 the decision was taken to close Lindholmen which Eriksberg had taken over two years earlier, and in the same year the Götaverken Group in Gothenburg was saved from bankruptcy by government intervention.[5] However, as late as 1973 a decision could still be taken to make a large investment in the government-owned Uddevallavarvet. The first stage of the investment programme was completed in 1977. Six hundred million

Swedish crowns had been spent; and 800,000 dwt tankers could be built in the large dock yard; but there was no longer a market for the supertankers that the yard was designed for.[6] Between 1975 and 1980 the Swedish shipbuilding industry collapsed. By 1974 new orders had ceased to arrive. There was still an order backlog until 1976–7, but after that the books were empty.

In Gothenburg, in 1974, 25 per cent of all employees in industry worked at these shipyards; in Malmö the figure was 19 per cent, in Landskrona 39 per cent and in Uddevalla 52 per cent.[7] The importance of the yards for the labour market in the shipbuilding centres can scarcely be exaggerated. In Gothenburg there were 14,300 shipyard employees, in Malmö 5,600, in Landskrona 2,800 and in Uddevalla 3,000.

The number of people in Swedish shipbuilding (new construction) declined from some 28,000 in the peak years to 5,500 in 1984. In 1980 it was decided to close Öresundsvarvet in Landskrona, and since 1981 no new ships have been constructed in the shipyards in Gothenburg, where at the beginning of 1976 there were still three large new construction yards in operation. In 1984 it was decided to close Uddevallavarvet and in 1986 to close Kockums, so that Sweden was left without a single large yard. The state-owned Svenska Varv still operated, employing some 18,000 people. But of these 3,000 were in offshore services, 1,800 in energy, 3,200 in ship repairs and naval construction, 7,500 in other types of industry, and only 5,500 in the construction of new ships.[8] By the end of 1986 there was nobody left in this latter group.

The reduction in employment since 1975 at the large yard is as shown in Table 4.1:[9]

Table 4.1: Employment in Swedish shipbuilding: 1975–1986

	1975	1980	1984	1986
Götaverken (Cityvarvet Arendal)	9,500	7,000	5,000	3,000[a]
Eriksberg	5,000	closed		
Kockums	5,300	4,700	3,000	under closure[b]
Öresundsvarvet	3,300	2,900	closed	
Uddevallavarvet	3,400	3,000	2,000	closed

Notes: a. off-shore, repairing. b. 700 will be left in a new company dealing with submarine technology.

The concentration on bulk tonnage in series in the 1960s had its price. The 26,000 employees at the larger yards in 1975 were reduced to

4,000 in 1986. Questions remain to be asked as to the role of the industry, the union and the gigantic budget transfers during the contraction process, and about the extent to which this was achieved by co-operation or conflict. These questions will be discussed in the following sections.

INCREASED GOVERNMENT INVOLVEMENT

Eriksberg in Gothenburg with 4,000 employees was the first casualty of the market collapse of Swedish shipbuilding. In the spring of 1975 it faced bankruptcy and the government had to step in.[10] In 1976 the government intervened to save another yard, and acquired 51 per cent of the shares of Götaverken to add to the 9.5 per cent it already held after an intervention in 1974. Eriksberg was integrated into Götaverken, which meant a gradual close-down, accomplished by 1979.

In 1976 it was also decided to cut down employment within shipbuilding by 30 per cent from the 1974 level. The reduction was to be completed by the end of 1978. Around 8,000 employees including a few thousands subcontractors would leave the industry. Gothenburg was hardest hit, with a loss of 4,500 jobs. A year later it was obvious that more had to be done. In April 1977 the new centre-right government elected in September 1976 (interrupting 44 years of Social Democratic government) proposed a further cut in capacity combined with massive financial support of around Sw Cr 4 bn and an additional 10 bn in credit guarantees. At least 5,000 jobs were to disappear before the end of 1979, and all the large yards except Kockums would merge into the state-owned group Svenska Varv.[11]

This scheme was a typical rescue operation lacking any long-term strategy. It was said explicitly that a financial decision had to be made by the end of 1980 regarding yard closures. Thus the nationalisation of the Swedish shipbuilding industry was not the product of long-term political considerations as it was in Britain (p. 128). There the establishment of British Shipbuilders at about the same time was a goal the Labour government had long fought for; an element of an offensive Labour strategy to be driven through against bitter political opposition and resistance from the shipbuilders, and designed to secure a long-term future for the industry.

The situation was quite different in Sweden. At a government meeting in May 1976 the Social Democratic government discovered that the state had gradually acquired 'an important owner interest in Swedish shipbuilding'.[12] The concept of nationalisation was not even mentioned. The Social Democratic shipbuilding policy in 1976 aimed at rationalisation rather than nationalisation. There were other more general differences in shipbuilding strategies between the British Labour and Swedish Social Democratic governments by the middle of the 1970s. Socialisation of key industries was a major element in Labour politics after World War II, whereas the Swedish Social Democratic government was more inclined towards increased public consumption and a redistributive income policy in a Keynesian framework. When the Swedish centre-right government nationalised Swedish shipbuilding in September 1976 it was because nobody else wanted to put more money into an unprofitable industry.

The new state concern Svenska Varv had only been in existence for four months when its management announced that another Sw Cr 1.2 bn was required immediately to cover the losses of the year under review. They had already received 2.6 bn when the group was established on 1 July 1977. For each of the following three years an additional 1.5–2 bn were demanded and further employment reductions were anticipated. At the same time the only remaining private yard, Kockums, accounced that it too was in financial difficulties.[13]

At the same time a political process began aimed at a drastic slimming down of yard capacity. It was clear that the Social Democrats were not prepared to countenance the closing down of a whole yard. This emerged in official talks between the Ministry of Industry, Nils Gunnar Åsling, and his counterpart in the Social Democratic (unofficial) shadow cabinet, Thage G. Pettersson. But despite the anticipated protests from the opposition, Åsling's goal was to close Arendal and Öresundsvarvet.[14] In September 1978 preparations had been made for a government bill proposing a 30 per cent reduction in employment and the closure of Arendal and Öresundsvarvet. However, Åsling never got the opportunity to carry his plan through. The government resigned on the contentious nuclear energy question and a Liberal minority government took over.

The new Liberal Minister of Industry, Erik Huss, modified Åsling's draft bill considerably. Instead of a 30 per cent reduction, a 20 per cent was proposed, without any closures. The 'cheesecutter' principle would be followed, meaning an even reduction over all yards.[15] The Social Democrats were still critical, although they considered the Liberal bill to be an improvement. With the support of some Liberals they modified the bill in parliament, and shipyard employees were given a guarantee of employment until the end of 1980.

The parliamentary elections in September 1979 returned a centre-conservative-liberal coalition and Åsling was again Ministry of Industry. In January 1980 the Board of Svenska Varv (which had included Kockums since 1979) presented a structural plan involving the loss of 7,000 jobs and the closure of Öresundsvarvet. Åsling adopted the plan when some months later he submitted a new shipbuilding bill to parliament. The only difference between the bill and Åsling's bill of 1978 was that Arendal, now specialising in offshore structures, was to be saved.[16]

In April 1983 a bill by the Social Democratic government (which had succeeded the non-socialists after the elections in September 1982) proposed a Sw Cr 6 bn support programme combined with the loss of 1,300 jobs. The political debate on the bill revealed an increasing readiness in all parties to close more yards if the new gigantic support package did not restore profitability. The Conservatives and the centre party demanded that one yard should be marked out for closure. (This readiness may be compared to the increasing disinclination to continue with subsidies in Germany at that date, discussed in Chapter 2.) In May 1984 the Social Democratic government decided to close the Uddevallavarvet yard and in 1986 reached the same verdict on Kockums. There was opposition only from those immediately concerned.

The outcome of the Swedish contraction process has been a greater cut in capacity and employment than in other West European countries (Table 1.4, p. 8). By 1983 new construction capacity was only 20 per cent of that in 1975; however, in the autumn of 1977 there had been signs of an even more ruthless and deliberate contraction strategy.

THE INTERESTS REPRESENTED IN SWEDISH SHIPBUILDING

As a prelude to an analysis of the mangement of the demise of the Swedish shipbuilding industry it is necessary to describe the interest groups involved. The Swedish unions organise industrially so that there is only one blue collar union in shipbuilding in Sweden, the Swedish Metal Workers' Federation (*Svenska Metallindustriarbetareförbundet*, known as Metall). The white collar employees are organised by the *Svenska Industritjänstemannaförbundet* (SIF). In this study attention will be focused on Metall.

At each work place there is a local union (*verkstadsklubben*), which in shipbuilding was strong and well-organised, often with 2,000–3,000 members. The workplace unions in one locality constitute the local branch, *avdelningen*.

Metall is in many respects a hierarchical and centralised organisation with an important administrative apparatus in Stockholm. However, this does not mean that it is controlled from above. The strong local unions mean that there is considerable influence upwards through the union hierarchy. The metal workers have been represented on all major government-appointed commissions and inquiries in shipbuilding since the 1960s, and the union membership of these bodies has included both central and local representatives. Metall is one of the most influential member unions in the federation of Swedish blue collar unions, Landsorganisationen (LO), which traditionally has close ties with the Social Democratic Party.

The 1960s saw the end of the development brought by post-war economic growth. Structural rationalisations ensured by encouraging the mobility of production factors had meant rapid technological and economic progress. The reverse of this development, increasingly apparent by the end of that decade, was enterprise closures, redundancies and transfers. People were increasingly forced to move from their customary workplaces, and labour processes were being transformed. A wave of unofficial strikes followed in the engineering industry after a long strike in the iron ore mines in Kiruna. This was not a specifically Swedish development but part of a more general West European pattern of political radicalisation.

There was an obvious pressure at grass-roots level which activated union and political leaders, not least in Metall which was pushing for job protection and co-determination — i.e. for equal rights with employers in formulating industrial policy. When it proved impossible to reach long-term agreement with the employers, the Social Democratic government used legislation. A set of laws was introduced in the 1970s: the laws regarding board representation in 1973, job protection in 1974, and co-determination in 1976 are just a few examples.

This development towards increased employee participation in the running of the enterprises occurred within the existing organisational framework, i.e. the traditional system of representation *via* the union was maintained. No parallel system was developed, as in Germany (*Betriebsrat*) or in France (*Comité d'Entreprise*).

The shipbuilding employers were organised into a federation. *Varvsindustriföreningen*, which still exists, although it is of much less importance since the nationalisation of the large yards. Even before 1977 it was relatively weak. The conflicting interests of the individual members were too strong for it to match Metall's organisational strength. In dealings with the government it was the managing directors of the individual yards rather than the Federation who spoke for the industry. Thus Varvsindustriföreningen cannot be compared with CSCN in France, with its close contacts with the government, or with the German VDS, with its tight organisation.

TRIPARTITE POLICIES

The financial difficulties of the yards at the end of the 1960s provoked the formation in 1971 of a loose tripartite arrangement which was to be led by a steering committee consisting of the presidents and the managing directors of Kockums, Götaverken, Eriksberg and Uddevallavarvet (Öresundsvarvet as a subsidiary of Götaverken was not involved) and two representatives of the Ministry of Industry.[18] The ten members of the commmittee and ten union representatives from the four yards constituted a consultative group with no powers of decision.[19] The Ministry of Industry was satisfied that the unions had achieved a forum where they could influence development but little was said about the functions of the consultative committee.[20]

The unions were invited to participate in policy-making during a difficult period of restructuring in Swedish shipbuilding industry, but it soon became clear to them that their role during the prosperous years which followed, at the beginning of the 1970s, was to be very limited. The consultative group was more or less forgotten, and the unions formed the impression that the employers regarded the group as a necessary evil and a forum only for one-way information from employers to employees.

However, the union was not yet ready to withdraw and consideration was given as to how to change the group or infuse fresh life into it. At a meeting between the union representatives of the group in March 1974, it was agreed to try out a smaller committee of employers and employees from the five big yards, i.e. including Öresundsvarvet. The committee would replace both the steering committee and the consultative group. In addition the unions would establish a so-called reference group with representatives from the unions of all the yards and from the national leadership.[21]

This proposal has to be seen in its wider social context. It was launched at a time of intense debate and legislation about employee co-determination. It had nothing to do with the threat of unemployment in shipbuilding, which was still a prosperous industry. The issues the unions wanted to bring to the fore concerned the workplace environment and so called 'grey' labour. In the prevailing 'overheated' labour market the yards increasingly hired subcontractors to do jobs where there was a labour shortage (for instance, welding). The subcontracting firms quite often operated between black and the white economies, hence the name *gråfirmor*, grey firms.[22]

In the autumn of 1974 the first signs of a financial crisis at Eriksberg appeared and the union proposal took on new significance. From then on the question of employment and the union's demands for co-determination in these matters take on a quite different importance. The union proposal was a factor in the government's treatment of Eriksberg.[23]

In 1975 the consultative group was transformed into a tripartite organisation in accordance with the union proposal. The Chairman of the new shipbuilding council became the Under Secretary of State in the Ministry of Industry. An extensive information system covering production, employment, investment and financing was instituted.[24] The contraction talks which were to follow in the subsequent years of crisis had an institutional framework which included union participation. The new organisation could be seen as a part of the general transformation of industrial relations in Sweden at this time but also as an indication of increased insight into the desirability of greater union participation in decision-making in an industry facing difficulties. The long-term employment prospects of the shipbuilding industry were discussed in conjunction with the Eriksberg crisis and the government's acquistion of the majority shareholding in Götaverken. The crisis brought government influence to bear on the industry and the shipbuilding council became the forum for tripartite contraction talks.

The government's interest in getting the unions to agree on a reduction scheme was clear. In 1975–6 there was unanimous agreement in the council not only to close Eriksberg but also on a 30 per cent reduction in employment in shipbuilding. Some 8,000 people, including a few thousand subcontractors, were to leave the industry (Gothenburg was the hardest hit with the loss of 4,500 jobs). But the redundancies were to be carried out within the framework of a 'social plan'.

Metall was keen to avoid tension and division between the workforces of the different yards during the contraction process.

One essential means of eliminating or decreasing such tension would be to handle all employment questions at firm level. There the members could be guaranteed equal influence on the distribution of employment in line with the policy of the Metall board, which in 1976 made no objection to employment reduction in shipbuilding.[25] When in February 1977, during the preliminaries to the establishment of Svenska Varv, a new redundancy scheme involving 7,000 jobs, of which 5,500 were in Gothenburg, was presented, Metall was certainly 'extremely hesitant' but it raised no objection.[26] The fact that the new scheme was discussed with the non-socialist government which had succeeded the Social Democrats after the elections in September 1976 meant nothing.

At a meeting with Åsling in May 1977, Stig Malm, in charge of shipbuilding in Metall, emphasised that 'union influence' in Svenska Varv should be 'considerable'. A special 'reference group' with union representatives should be 'linked directly to the management', which would have to 'contact' the group 'over all questions concerning the employees'[27] Åsling agreed to the reference groups, which consisted almost exclusively of representatives from the yards. There was only one Metall secretary from the national level.[28]

The local union leaders should negotiate, as a body, over employment questions with the Svenska Varv management and not with each separate yard management, and in these discussions, local antagonisms and differences should be set aside. The grouping of the local spokesmen into a formal unit would make it possible to meet Svenska Varv's management as a single body. Centralised decisions by local decision-makers would reduce local antagonism and potential tensions in Metall. A prerequisite for the success of such a stragegy was even-handed reduction in all yards, following the 'cheese-cutter principle'; closure of just one or more yards would threaten the *status quo*.

It is obvious that interaction between the central and the local levels was crucial for Metall. Therefore I am now going to move the spotlight from the central to the local level and to this interaction. The Eriksburg yard will be the focus of the next section, keeping in mind all the time the interaction with the central level.

THE CLOSURE OF ERIKSBERG: A DIFFERENT PATTERN OF REACTION

The collapse of Eriksberg in 1974 and the subsequent closure of the yard came at the same time as the intense debate on co-determination which resulted in legislation in 1976. The example of the yard provided the unions with arguments for the need for co-determination in the running of the enterprises. In these circumstances more union influence could also be in the interests of government and the employer: more influence meant more responsibility for the decisions made. Thus the content of co-determination and the areas where it should operate took on new significance.

In retrospect, the Eriksberg crisis was the first sign of the more general stagnation, but in 1975 it was not interpreted as such. Rather, it was seen as crisis in management. In the 1960s Eriksberg had begun to re-finance their dollar contracts in Swiss francs, tempted by the very low interest rates on Swiss loans. Götaverken also followed the same policy, both yards acting on the advice of leading bankers.[29] At a time when the dollar was still rising, successful financial speculation concealed the structural problems of the industry. In fact it could be argued that banking rather than shipbuilding earned a substantial part of the profits in what was thought to be a healthy and wealthy industry during the bonanza years.

At the beginning of the 1970s, when the Swiss franc more than doubled in value relative to the Swedish Crown, Eriksberg was subjected to a severe currency squeeze (see Figure 4.1).

Figure 4.1: Buying rates of Bank of Sweden for US $ and Swiss francs, June 1971–May 1975.

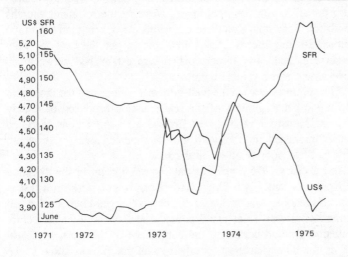

Source: 'Varv i Kris', Supplement 1–2. Kristian von Sydow's private archives.

The Metall representative in the company board, Bertil Levin, realised by May 1974 that the enterprise was in economic difficulties, but he did no realise how precarious it was or why. In August the managing director Bengt Eneroth was suddenly dismissed, thus underlining the seriousness of the situation.[30]

The unions asked the personnel manager, Leif Molinder, for information on the economic situation of the yard but after the sacking of Eneroth, the yard management was also ill-informed. Three times Molinder asked Ingemar Blennow, managing director in the Broström shipping group which owned Eriksberg, to brief him about the economic situation of the yard and about what to tell the unions, but to no avail. Three times he had to see the unions without having anything to say to them.[31] However, in an inquiry held by the Metall federation in Stockholm, the working party of the union gained enough information to brief the Minister of Industry in the Social Democratic government, Rune Johansson. This took place in September 1974. Rune Johansson was also having frequent talks with the owners and a group from the Ministry of Industry received permission to see the company's books. This information was subsequently passed to the unions, who were then better informed about the economic situation of the yard than was the yard management. Only Blennow and Kristian von Sydow, the president of the Boström group, on the owners' side had detailed knowledge of the situation.

In November a delegation of eight union representatives from Eriksberg saw Rune Johansson and in December he went to Gothenburg for talks with the local union.[32] During the following months he visited Gothenburg on three occasions for briefing talks with the unions. By this means Metall was able to put the case for state ownership, and early direct contact was established between the government and the local union.

The contrast between the well-informed unions and the ignorance of the yard management of the real situation produced extremely strained industrial relations at Eriksberg.[33] The unions were no longer interested in talks with the yard management, with whom they had had poor relations in the past.[34]

In February 1975 a government commission under the direction of Kockums' chief Nils-Hugo Hallenborg began work on a rescue plan. Hallenborg was the leader of a competing yard but one that had a more progressive personnel policy than Eriksberg and therefore Hallenborg could command the confidence of the workers. Bertil Levin, the union leader at Eriksberg, said that he was known to be a director who listened to the workers.[35] When the commission was introduced, the press conference indicated there were new power constellations as compared with the previous prosperous years. On the raised podium Rune Johansson, Nils-Hugo Hallenborg and the union representatives Bertil Levin and Arne Johansson formed one group, and the two Tirfing (the holding company of Eriksberg) directors Ingemar Blennow and Kristian von Sydow formed a second group. As von Sydow put it: 'We were treated like small boys in the commission'.[36]

For Hallenborg it was an Eriksberg crisis, not a general crisis in shipbuilding. His criticisms of the Eriksberg management and of Broströms were severe and formed a part of the report of the commission:

> The owners' running of Eriksberg is a long story of how to sink an enterprise. One first starves it of investment and then one gets into a situation like this, where there is no competitive capability. It does not matter how clever the workers are, they have to have equivalent tools.

The proposals by the owners to save Eriksberg (e.g. to reduce employment by 40 per cent and to continue under the same ownership) the commission regarded as 'piling of words on each other . . . resting on completely unrealistic assumptions'.[37]

The commission's proposals for Eriksberg required the holding company Tirfing to make a cash injection of Sw Cr 225 m, to order two bulk ships for 237 million from the yard, and relinquish their shares in Eriksberg for Sw Cr 1,000. The state had not only taken over the yard, as the union claim had demanded, but had also forced the shipping family of Broström which dominated Tirfing to pay a considerable amount of money for the transfer.

The package also included a reduction of 2,000 jobs to be achieved through voluntary redundancy. This the union agreed to without too much difficulty, as it avoided a collectively experienced threat.

THE MERGER OF ERIKSBERG-GÖTAVERKEN

The government's intention for the yard was obvious from the very outset: it would be closed.[38] Co-operation with sections of the industry could be helpful in achieving that goal. After the shipping company of Saléns had taken over in 1971, the new manager at Götaverken, Hans Laurin, and his personal manager, Bengt Tengroth, brought in from the metal workers' union, seemed to be pursuing a progressive personnel policy. Götaverken was generally considered a social laboratory, in striking contrast to the old-fashioned and harsh capital-labour relations of Eriksberg.

The merger talks between Götaverken and Eriksberg had been taking place behind the scenes at the same time as the Eriksberg crisis, but became of immediate significance only after the rescue decision in May 1975.

A merger between the Gothenburg yards would be a pretext to close Eriksberg. A merger would be the logical final consequences of long-standing policy. The diary of the managing director of Götaverken, Hans Laurin, illuminates how the government's long-term aim was achieved. In retrospect, knowing that outcome it is all too easy to imagine that this was the result of a linear process of high-level rational and technocratic decision-making. In fact, it was a process of incessant trial and error, in which the shifting balance of power between different interests was decisive. The object of this power struggle was the government's money: how much was available and on what terms?

Whereas there were obvious signs that the Social Democratic government saw the old idea of a merger of the Gothenburg yards as one solution, very early during the Eriksberg breakdown Hallenborg, as chairman in the commission, got the 'definite feeling' that the same government considered Uddevallavarvet to be central to the contraction operation. Thus the government kept its options open.

At the end of November 1975 the Premier, Olof Palme, the Minister of Finance, Gunnar Sträng, and the Minister of Industry, Rune Johansson, met Hans Laurin, the managing director of Götaverken, and Sture Ödhner, the managing director of Saléns, at a dinner in the home of Ödhner. Hallenborg was also present, as a member of the government's shipbuilding élite. Laurin has described the meeting in detail. This reveals an odd atmosphere for decision-making, with both antagonism between the different parties and an important degree of uncertainty on the part of one protagonist about the intentions of the others. The diary reads:

24/11 . . . Palme, Sträng, Rune Johansson and Hallenborg arrived at 1800. Sture [Ödhner] was expected to report on shipping for half an hour but it took one hour. It was rambling report. Sture doesn't like reporting and being stringent and decisive. Sträng blamed the tax which made the exaggerated need to level all benefits. I thus got some time [to think my own contribution over]. Hallenborg broke in and carped. [I] would have liked to speak more exhaustively. Dinner, [I] was dispirited over their reply: we shan't have time to get into this [merger scheme] until 17/12. Palme was interested in Venezuela. With the coffee Sture summed up the discussion, not especially well, somewhat aggressively and exaggerating in the wrong places. Then Sträng started. Götaverken-Eriksberg were to merge into one company, but we had to consider that a Götaverken worker and an Eriksberg worker always remained who they were, and he prattled that we had to get rid of local chauvinism. Some sort of an umbrella company with two yards, an [umbrella] company with another name, AB Göteborgsvarvet. (Something using the initials GV, Rune Johansson facetiously suggested to keep me quiet.) Discomfited, I don't fully remember the whole of this message. Palme sat grinning, somewhat embarrassed; Rune Johansson was mostly silent. We were confused; they had (earlier) said that we would close Eriksberg all at once. Over my dead body! I tried to make a stand for the name of Götaverken and said that one organisation had to be supreme. No support for this, but we would be the ones to do the job. Palme talked about politics as a matter of timing and that the unions had not hitherto been ready.

[A later amendment in the diary] This evening the government seemed completely prepared to pay Saléns Sw Cr 136 m for 41.5 per cent of the shares in Götaverken. Furthermore, Rune Johansson demanded that Saléns use these 136 millions to order ships at Götaverken. On the latter item I protested and said that it would imply big losses, but I was shut up.[39]

The uncertainty about the intentions of the other participants persisted after the agreement in December. In January, the manager of Eriksberg was still (according to Laurin) ignorant that Eriksberg was to be closed '[I was] rather frightened at the thought that the unions had as little information [as the Eriksberg manager] . . . double talk from politicians etc.'[40]

Laurin's reflections indicate that the unions receded even more into the background of the decision-making process, after the warding off of the impending threat in April 1975. Once the potential protest from Eriksberg workers had been circumvented, talks about the technical details of the merger/closure were taken over by the government and the industry. The union would agree with this interpretation.[41]

The redundant workers from Eriksberg were given jobs at Götaverken. Thus there was no compulsory redundancy, although there was substantial friction between the two workforces. The Götaverken workers complained that they had been downgraded by the Eriksberg people. Cityvarvet, for instance, was ordered to increase its capacity from 1.5 to 2.8 m working hours to absorb the surplus labour. But the market collapsed and the outcome was a huge surplus capacity and a tendency for the workforce to divide into an A and a B team.[42]

The Eriksberg case is an example of how government, industry and unions tried to reduce capacity gradually. It happened over a period of four years, and every attempt was made to transfer the knowledge, competence, skills and people to another major company. The costs for the Eriksberg operation including production losses, financial costs and social costs totalled Sw Cr 1.3 bn. This was borne exclusively by the Broström family.[43]

This case exhibits typical merger syndromes. Eriksberg and Götaverken had two completely different management and organisational cultures and they had been rivals historically. The difficulties this might cause was completely overlooked by the architects of the merger.[44]

The elimination of the collectively-experienced threats gave a political advantage to the government which, like the unions, could refer to 'a socially acceptable solution' of what was presented as a problem of private capitalist management. However, the disadvantages dominated, both economically and organisationally. Here are some comments from some of the people involved in the merger process:[45]

The integration of Eriksberg into Götaverken destroyed all former natural organisation in the shipbuilding company. People have been walking all over Gothenburg during the last years. The transfer of Eriksberg personnel meant an organisational mess in the whole Götaverken group. The integration severely wounded the Göteverken companies. (Managing director in one of the Götaverken companies)

If you have the ambition and objective to develop more efficient companies and strengthen your competitive position forget about the Eriksberg model. It is not the only reason for much lower efficiency and productivity but it sure is an important one. (Personnel director, Svenska Varv).

It was a tough thing for the unions to take part in the close down of Eriksberg. It was, however, done in a way that could be accepted by the unions and it was not totally in conflict with union policy, and some of the knowledge and competence for producing speciality ships could be tranferred to Arendal. The integration of Eriksberg was managed pretty well, but I don't think it is possible again. (Union leader)

THE ERIKSBERG CASE — A BALANCE

The Eriksberg issue led to a lively debate. Two contrasting pictures are presented. The Broström family which owned Eriksberg became a symbol of that form of private capitalism which is totally governed by the ideas of high profits at any price. In the 1960s Dan-Axel Boström's private amours were headline news in the popular press, giving the shipowning family a touch of capitalist decadence. Kristian von Sydow was the head of the family company when the Eriksberg collapse occurred. In 1966 he had been one of the promoters of a centre-right election coalition against the Social Democrats who lost their majority that year in Gothenburg, the leading labour city in Sweden. On TV he had expressed fears that the Swedish Social Democrats were about to develop an East European state socialism.[46] The picture of a decadent private capitalist family opposing social democratic politics was completed by the strained industrial relations at Eriksberg, which gave the union no role in the running of the enterprise.

The other picture was that of the progressive Kockums boss Nils-Hugo Hallenborg, who was in charge of the most successful Swedish yard and who was a union man with few serious objections to Social Democratic government politics. Hallenborg and the government succeeded completely in making the Eriksberg crisis one of bad management. This black and white picture of Eriksberg as a symbol of decadent private capitalism and of mismanagement, in sharp contrast to the well-run Kockums and Götaverken with a modern personnel policy, was arguably what was needed to effect the closure of Eriksberg.

The Eriksberg case is unique. Unions and government in close co-operation closed a yard, against the will of the owners, but supported or rather inspired, by parts of the industry, which thereby got rid of a competitor. For decades industrial relations at Eriksberg were much more polarised than at Götaverken. A union whose confidence had grown in confrontations rather than collaboration with the employer, was worried about the prospects of the yard. When it was given no information it started its own inquiry. The strained industrial relations at the yard and the chilly relations between the Broström family and the Social Democratic government made the politicisation of the bankruptcy inevitable.

The Boström family fulfilled the same function as the time-clocks in Nantes somewhat later (see Chapter 3). During the battle about Eriksberg, nothing was said about any more general shipbuilding crisis, just as nothing was said in Nantes in 1977. Eriksberg was and remained a private capitalist crisis. It was much easier to mobilise people for a fight against unsuccessful private capitalists than against the changing structures of world shipbuilding.

In the parliamentary debate about Eriksberg the Social Democratic MP Hugosson interpreted the feelings then prevailing:[47]

> Within the Broström concern and also in certain centre-right quarters people have wanted to assert that the situation the company has got into is a consequence of the international situation in shipping and the currency troubles. This is not true. The Eriksberg crisis is mostly a consequence of incompetent management.

His conservative colleague Bo Siegbahn represented a minority:

> The only right thing is . . . to consider the prevailing crisis a manifestation of the general problems which exist in shipbuilding. The fact that the problems have had their special character for different yards does not affect this general opinion.

Of course it can always be argued that it was not a condolence that the worse off and worst-managed Eriksberg was the first yard to fall, but in retrospect Siegbahn's statement makes much more sense.

METALL AND THE PROPOSAL TO CLOSE ARENDAL AND ÖRESUNDSVARVET

The Eriksberg crisis led to a building up of tripartite co-operation between the government, the unions (including the local level) and sections of the industry. The basis of co-operation was a concentration and contraction of the shipbuilding industry based on the principle of no closures (apart from the exceptional case of Eriksberg where those made redundant were transferred to Götaverken) and by an even reduction across yards by means of natural wastage within a framework of social plans enabling there to be no compulsory redundancy. The political process which started in the autumn of 1977 aimed at the closure of Arendal and Öresundsvarvet meant a deviation from that rule.

According to the law on employees' co-determination, negotiations with the unions were necessary for closing the two yards. The proposal, which departed from the principle of equality of treatment between yards, raised the sceptre of tension and division within the union, between the branches. It was considered necessary to maintain the strategy developed in the shipbuilding council and in the 'report-back' group of Svenska Varv: decisions to be made at the central level by local decision-makers acting as a body. When the unions' report-back group met in February 1978 to discuss the closure proposal it agreed to wreck the co-determination talks at the yard level and to bring them up to the holding company level where the group would negotiate with the central management.[48] The eagerness to avoid local conflict was the obvious motive behind the decision.

Metall was prepared to participate in a restructuring of the shipbuilding industry but in a way that avoided redundancy by diversification and the development of 'alternative products'. The union insisted that there should be no contraction before the new state-owned concern Svenska Varv had a fair chance. Capacity should be maintained until 1980 when the world market situation would be clearer.

In April 1978 a draft of a government bill was presented to the reference group which again opposed the plans to close the two yards.[49] The strategy that Metall developed meant that parliament and the Social Democratic opposition became more the target of union labelling than the government whose policy objective seemed determined. Instead of co-operative talks with the Social Democratic government as in the earlier Eriksberg case, the unions rallied for a battle to win over public opinion.[50]

The government was not interested in a conflict with the unions. After a meeting in the Ministry of Industry the Under Secretary of State complained of the 'harsh pitch' of the proposals. Stig Malm, in charge of shipbuilding in Metall, had talked about the bill as 'an assassination' of the shipbuilding industry. After the meeting Malm was told that the government was not prepared to change the decision to close the two yards, but that it could agree to a longer closing-down period under 'socially acceptable' forms. Malm found that modifications positive but the decision not to revise the closure plans incompatible with union participation.[51]

In September 1978, just before the government resigned, Malm developed Metall's policy about the future of Öresundsvarvet in a debate with Åsling and others in Landskrona. The government should convince shipping owners who were thinking of having ships built abroad to place their orders in Sweden.[52] 'Swedish ships in Swedish yards' was the cry. In a meeting at the Ministry of Industry 18 days later, Malm argued for subsidies for 'stock production' in case there was no orders. The notion of 'stock production' was politically unacceptable after a failed attempt in 1975 to bridge the crisis by such means, but Malm kept the option of producing for other than the direct orders providing another name could be found for it.

The Metall strategy deployed to prevent the closure of Arendal and Öresundsvarvet cooled relations with the government, although they were not broken off. Metall also used its historically close relations with the Social Democrats (now in opposition) to exert pressure on the government. This pattern continued under Erik Huss, the Minister of Industry in the new Liberal minority government, who in the autumn of 1978 revised Åsling's bill, reducing the planned cuts in employment to 20 per cent instead of 30 per cent and yielding to the request not to close the two yards.[53]

Resistance to plant closure was a reversal of earlier policy in Sweden. In the 1950s and 1960s restructuring of the industry was an important union goal. Then economists within LO, the federation of blue collar unions, developed a strategy which gained the support of both the employers and the government. The unions, seeking the most productive use of scarce labour, pushed for lay-offs and contraction in less competitive industries such as textiles, and encouraged in inter-regional transfer of labour. Union wage policy was a powerful instrument for structural change and for the transfer of workers to high productivity industries. Centrally-negotiated wage agreements were initiated by the employers in the mid-1950s. Thereafter the unions exploited the centralising approach to develop what they called the 'solidaristic' wage policy, meaning that the wage agreements in the most productive industries became the guide-lines for the whole labour market.

Wage policy was based on the LO's high productivity ideology, which they shared with the employers, and which had been developed as early as in the 1920s. From a union point of view efficient production was essential to promote rising wages.[54]

Union policy was matched by the labour movement's use of the political power to bring about economic growth on capitalist premisses. The Social Democrats held the political power almost continuously from 1932 until 1976.

The role of the government in this co-operative promotion of production beginning in the 1950s was to develop an active labour market policy, involving retraining courses, housing schemes and so on. This development went with economic growth and reached a peak in the 1960s. Structural rationalisation by stimulating the mobility of productive factors meant rapid technological and economic progress. The reverse of this development, increasingly apparent at the end of the 1960s, was enterprise closures, lay-offs and transfers. People were increasingly forced to move from environments they had got used to. The labour process was changed, especially in the engineering industry where the introduction of new piece-work systems was resisted at the local level. A wave of unofficial strikes followed and demands were made for worker-involvement in decision-making (co-determination) and job protection.

The dramatic political and ideological radicalisation in Western Europe at the end of the 1960s, together with pressure from the grass-roots, activated union and political leaders. Where such radical change proved impossible to achieve by agreement, legislation by the Social Democratic government was used. For example: laws were enacted between 1973 and 1976 which enforced employee representation on company boards, gave greater job protection and introduced co-determination. This development went far beyond previous Social Democratic commitments, which were mainly concerned with income distribution.

All the new laws had their origins in a period of economic growth. The increased union influence was intended to be exerted in the distribution of an ever-increasing pie and to overcome problems resulting from the very rapid pace of change.

The experiences of the union movement during both the area of growth and the period of stagnation from the end of the 1960s help to explain why the unions accepted restructuring with contraction but resisted yard closures and temporary redundancy. When in the 1970s growth in the whole of Western Europe declined, the unions' influence had to be exercised in a quite different economic situation than when it had been acquired.

It now became obvious that influence also meant responsibility. The traditional ideology of high productivity and the instruments provided by recent legislation made it possible for the union leadership, though not without considerable strains and considerable subisidies, to carry through a contraction process more drastic than elsewhere in Western Europe but with less protest and less unemployment.

Though the government maintained its active labour market policy which meant that unemployment never exceeded 4 per cent, there was simultaneously a development in sectoral industrial policy which responded to crisis by increasing subsidies to bail out non-profitable industries like shipbuilding. When growth abated the active labour market policy had to be supported by a sector-specific industrial policy. The stagnation revealed potential conflicts between the workforces of the different yard and, to prevent these divisions being open, Metall had hardly any other options than the proportional reduction principle. When the government tried a more drastic restructuring policy it met resistance from Metall.

The centralised decisions taken by local officials was a cornerstone of the Metall strategy. The policy worked when all the yards were more or less equally affected by cuts. Then support from below could be gained in the name of solidarity. The government's change of policy to yard closure concentrated the effect of closure and upset the balance of power in the union.

Åsling's intention to close Arendal provoked immediate protest in Gothenburg. The shipyard unions which earlier had agreed to close Eriksberg now disagreed. The transfer of redundant workers from Eriksberg to Götaverken had individualised the unemployment threat. The plan to close Arendal brought a collectively-experienced threat which provoked collective action and 6,000 blue and white collar shipyard employees rallied in a show of strength against Åsling's plan.[55]

The bill by the new Liberal government in the autumn of 1978 represented a retreat from this plan by reducing the planned redundancy and reprieving the Arendal yard. Moreover, in parliament the Social Democrats and the Liberals agreed on an employment guarantee until the end of 1980. Although the bill meant an employment reduction in Gothenburg of 2,300 jobs, it laid the groundwork for a lessening of the extent of the collectively experienced threat. Resistance could even be transformed into union participation in the contraction process.

The union leaders in Gothenburg were well aware of the surplus capacity there and realised that something had to be done. The problem was accentuated on the shop floor by the transfer of redundant Eriksberg workers to Götaverken and the hostility between the workers from the two yards further reduced the potential for collective action.

The employment guarantee made the reduction in the shipbuilding labour force possible within the framework of a social plan, which was decided by Parliament in December 1978. In January 1979 Svenska Varv was given the responsibility of getting unions agreement to a cut in the workforce coupled with guaranteed employment for 1979–80. It was recommended that a special organisation should be established, to be called Project 80. Under Project 80 those regarded as superfluous to production needs were put into a pool. They would remain in the pool until they got other jobs or took early retirement.

Immediately after the agreement there were numerous protests from the members and signs of a fast-growing rift between the leadership and the members. There was general dissatisfaction with the agreement on the grounds that it put efficiency before job security. According to the Employment Security Act those employed last had to go first. Project 80 circumvented this. However, the protest disappeared rapidly once the selection process began. Once individual workers were 'pooled', what had been a collective threat became individualised. The segregating effect of the pool was reinforced by the fact that Project 80 was an independent organisation outside Götaverken.

The dilemma which faced the union was how to accept this sidestepping of the Employment Security Act without being accused of conspiring with management and failing to protect the interests of the membership. They solved it by working closely with the management in the design of the plan but evaded formal responsibility by not signing it.[56]

Thus the strain in relations at the central level caused by the shipbuilding crisis from the autumn of 1977 was followed by the union integration at the local level, and the management of the crisis shifted from the national to the local level. There both management and Metall considered Project 80 successful. Management appreciated the role of Metall:

> We have been lucky that there are such strong local trade unions in Gothenburg. The unions have strong leaders who show a great deal of realism. Had we done it according to the Employment Security Act, it would have been the same thing as a gradual closing of the whole industry. The P 80 solution is a relative success.

We have a much better personnel mix and we have even started to recruit people again. The unions have accepted that.[57]

To sum up, in Gothenburg the local reaction to the government's tougher approach meant that the local union gave up the important principles of the Employment Security Law in favour of increased efficiency. Rather than defending a law it had long fought for it found itself co-operating with local management to improve productivity in order to survive.

To a certain extent it is justifiable to say that the strategy of closing one or more yards instead of following the 'cheese-cutter principle' formed the development of local pockets of concerted action which were effectively mobilised against each other during the contraction process. The personnel director of Svenska Varv, Bengt Tengroth, described it as a 'war of all against all'. The bitter Metall protests at the central level against the decision to close Öresundsvarvet did not happen in Gothenburg or in Malmö. Inge Karlsson, the chairman of the metal workers at Götaverken, expressed the local feelings in Gothenburg in terms which contrasted strongly with the central expression of solidarity:

> There was no use in us dying with our boots on. It was a struggle for survival. We realised that somebody had to fall and we thought, God forbid, it was going to be us. After all it was reasonable that Öresundsvarvet should disappear. It was the least competitive.[58]

Stig Malm was well aware of the problem. At a meeting with some 1,000 shipyard workers in Malmö in January 1980, he warned of the danger: 'It is important that we don't get into a situation where region stands against region.'[59]

The decision in January 1980 to close down Öresundsvarvet provoked immediate collective action. More than 2,800 shipyard workers were supported by the whole local population. In addition, the entire local management of Öresundsvarvet was on the employees' side and together they formed a local task force to fight the parent firm's management. In a spectacular torchlight procession, with more than 10,000 participants, union leaders and local management marched side by side.[60]

But local action in Landskrona differed from that in Gothenburg in many respects. The protest in Landskrona could be isolated. Employees and higher management were alone and could not do much. The verbal support of Metall in Stockholm and the Social Democratic opposition should not be mistaken for a general preparedness to take actions of solidarity in the other shipbuilding centres. In Gothenburg and Malmö they had enough problems of their own and were happy to have escaped a yard closure.

KOCKUMS: THE SMOOTH SLOWDOWN

Kockums in Malmö faced the crisis later than Eriksberg and Götaverken. They also faced the difficulties with a stronger tradition of social partnership than prevailed at Eriksberg.[61]

By the middle of the 1970s Kockums and Götaverken had much in common as regards industrial relations. But modern personnel management at the two yards did not mean complete concord and harmony. On the contrary, the forced growth and the adjustment to tanker production during the 1960s had caused considerable strains. The protest from below against the payment systems and other injustices were frequent, although small and sectional, because the systems always favoured some and not others.[62] Modernised industrial relations meant a willingness to discuss and to try to find solutions to problems together with the unions. These unconventional methods provoked protests from the employers' organisations.[63]

Continuity of leadership both in the metal workers union and in the management was essential for the development of industrial relations at Kockums. From 1945 to the nationalisation in 1979 there had been only three managers and three union chairmen. From 1968 Nils-Hugo Hallenborg was manager and John-Erik Olsson leader of the metal workers' union. As was seen from his role in the Eriksberg enquiry (above p. 94), Hallenborg had the confidence of the national federation of the metal workers and was regarded as an ideal manager.

Unlike the Gothenburg yard managers, Hallenborg never tried to build up the financial solidity of the yard by currency speculations, which may explain why Kockums was hit later than the Gothenburg yards. His strategy was to refinance in the same currency as the orders, i.e. US dollars. Kockums thereby forewent spectacular profits from currency transactions in the 1960s but was on the other hand protected from the adverse currency movements of 1973. In a difficult short period towards the end of the 1960s, Götaverken accepted many orders at lower prices while waiting for better times.

107

But Hallenborg only took one order at a time in order to avoid being caught with a heavy commitment to build low-price ships when the market turned. At Götaverken the strategy of accepting low-price orders led to the financial crisis in 1971 which brought Saléns into the company. But when prices increased after 1971 Götaverken without much surplus capacity could not exploit the situation as did Kockums. However it was only a matter of time before Kockums too had to face the crisis. Eventually the Malmö yard ran out of orders.

In 1977 the union and the management at Kockums together turned to government in order to get financial guarantees for the building of gas tankers. However, this attempt to exert pressure failed, and in February 1978 the answer from the government came: 'no'.[64] Before that in December 1977 the board of the Metall workers' union agreed to demand the nationalisation of Kockums. The common campaign with Hallenborg seemed to be lost and what the union had regarded as a threat until as late as October 1977 ('if we don't get the guarantees perhaps we'll be forced to join Svenska Varv')[65] now became a goal. In December there was discussion in the union at Malmö about the advantages and disadvantages of such a request. Hesitation as to how much influence they would have in a conglomerate of all the big yards was a factor against, but in the end the view that only the state could do anything for the survival of the yard dominated. Remaining outside Svenska Varv could mean less favourable treatment in the talks about the future of Swedish shipbuilding.

As a result of the talks with the government, notice was given that 900 employees would become redundant. This was in addition to the 30 per cent agreed centrally in 1976. The unions protested against the redundancy notices and argued that if a capacity reduction was necessary it had to be made in the same way as the 30 per cent reduction: by voluntary redundancies and natural wastage.[66] Though they did not deny the existence of the problems, they argued that they could be solved in other ways:

In our opinion the management should put pressure on the government and the society, of course must participate and take its responsibility . . . All the winter we have negotiated with the management about different alternatives. Finally it came with the notices which we wanted to prevent . . . Our claim was that everything should be done to put pressure on different authorities.[67]

Little consideration was given to such questions as: How much solidarity could they rely on from other social groups in a stagnating economy? What power did the bankrupt enterprise and its employees really have to put pressure on the authorities? They could mobilise the employees and public opinion locally, but what this amounted to in December 1977, although spectacular, had no lasting effects. Some months later the movement had lost momentum amongst the shipyard workers, and only about 50 people came to a meeting arranged by the Metall workers' union when Hallenborg issued the redundancy notices.[68]

The notices did not represent a collectively experienced threat. The union leaders at the yard realised that 'the suit was too big' and that it had to shrink. There were no new orders and morale in the yard was low. As soon as the size of the operation was known everybody knew who would have to leave: according to the law of employment security those last employed would be first to go and the law had its role in individualising the threat of unemployment.[69] Thus although in the spring of 1978 there was a good deal of unrest at Kockums, the situation was far from explosive.

The union was successful in delaying the execution of the redundancy scheme. A gradual reduction of the labour force was initiated by means of voluntary and natural wastage. Hallenborg had to yield to those who wanted Kockums, the last big private yard to be incorporated in the state-owned Svenska Varv. From June 1979 Kockums belonged to the group.

If the unconventional and independent Hallenborg was unusual among Swedish employers, the chairman of Metall at the yard, John-Erik Olsson, personified the reformist tradition of the Swedish labour movement. Together they step up a system of industrial relations which served as a model for all the unions in Sweden. It worked because in the interaction between Hallenberg and Olsson and the other union leaders all the different interests involved could be expressed, the claims of the workers and counter-claims from the management, the interests that converged and interests that diverged, both possibilities and limitations. The system of industrial relations at Kockums could admit a substantial amount of protest and criticism from below. Its strength was the way in which these protests could be taken on board by both the union and the management. What was developed at Kockums was a tradition of compromise resulting in co-operation.

The joint management and union campaign for money for the gas tankers was a logical consequence of this tradition. But it demonstrated that even the best of industrial relations systems could not solve the structural problems of the industry: if a solution could be found it would come from another level and any such attempt would cost a great deal of money. John-Erik Olsson realised this, of course. At a meeting in January 1980 he commented:

> I don't know whether Hallenborg will come, he is not invited. On the other hand the politicians in Scania [the provice where Malmö is situated] are invited and they do have responsibility for our jobs in the future.[70]

Exit Hallenborg. Enter the politicians.

Although Olsson's remark signalled the end of a certain way of thinking, the shift of regime did nothing really to change the balance between different interests for John-Erik Olsson and the other union leaders. Nationalisation did not mean a break in that development. The nationalised enterprise too argued that employment had to be reduced, and the new management also had increased productivity as a major goal.

In December 1980 the union had talks with the management about a new concentration plan. It was 'generally known' at the yard that job cuts were 'necessary'. If the management itself was allowed to select those who would be made redundant, between 100 and 400 people was said to be enough. If the job protection law was to be applied, the management threatened that as many as 1,500 people could be involved.[71] By implication it was understood that, if the management could select ineffective workers, productivity could be increased and the yard would be more competitive. It was said that the original plan for a capacity reduction from 3.1 to 2.4 million working hours could then be modified. The union was squeezed between different interests.

The solution to which both the union of the Metall workers and the management agreed was the establishment of a 'Kockums' resource' centre, a special department *within* the enterprise (unlike Project 80 in Gothenburg) to which 400 people would be transferred for retraining without being given notice.[72] Thus the last-in first-out rule could be circumvented and efficiency improved.

Kockums' 'resource' became a source of irritation among the employees. Those in it became familiarly known as the B or C production team and were regarded as failures or undesirable persons. Their selection was ostensibly governed by principles of efficiency, and there were long talks between the union and the management over their selection. The union leaders then had talks with all who had been put on the list and some were removed from it after having 'improved their behaviour'. This revealing expression indicates the true nature of the exercise, but when the board of the Metall workers' union discussed the criticism that they were involved in a 'speed-up exercise' it was rejected with the argument that: '. . . the union has undertaken to contribute to greater efficiency and consequently we also have to make it good.'[73]

A few months later in September 1981 there was another productivity agreement in a new emergency situation. This proved compatible with 'Kockums' resource' and there was also an agreement on a new bonus system.[74] Thus even after nationalisation the idea survived that workers and management had coincidental interests.

When the new Social Democratic government started to work on a new shipbuilding bill it soon became clear that Kockums would have to reduce capacity and 900 jobs would disappear at the yard. It also became obvious that 'Kockums' resource' would not be sufficient, and that people would have to leave the yard. In the new situation the union of metal workers quickly and resolutely decided to abandon the 'last-in first-out principle' of the job protection law. For efficiency reasons an early retirement system was considered better, a view shared by the management. The step was a logical consequence of earlier union strategy at the yard: early retirement would make it possible to maintain efficiency without making people redundant.[75] According to the bill 900 jobs would have to disappear at the yard.

In the bill nothing was said about early retirement. There were several reasons for the government to handle that question very cautiously. Early retirement in shipbuilding could also lead to demands from other groups in crisis-hit industries and ultimately demands for expensive general early retirement, i.e. a reduced pensionable age. For a Social Democratic government it would also be embarrassing to pay out money for the suspension of a law which had been introduced in triumph and seen as a symbol of Social-Democratic power and success. Therefore, politically, the early retirement proposal had to be circumvented. It was agreed at the yard that the unemployment fund would pay the early retirement pensions for the first 450 days after people had left their jobs.[76] The disadvantage for the unions with this arrangement was the 'pre-pensioners' could be forced to take a new job if one was offered by the employment agency.[77] However, in practice only a handful of the redundant were offered other jobs at all.

The common endeavour at Kockums to improve efficiency had its consequences. The crisis hit it later than the Gothenburg yards. From 1975 to 1984 the labour force had been cut by more than 40 per cent. The reduction was smaller than in Gothenburg and also more gradual. As in Gothenburg there has been no compulsory redundancies, and it was a relatively smooth process[78] compared with other yards investigated. There were never any collectively-experienced threats or mass reactions from the workers, apart from some protest rallies against the centre-right government. The grumbling about 'Kockums' resource' cannot be compared to the vivid and immediate protests against Project 80. The metal workers' union and the management had had the common goal of being about job cuts without lay-offs and of reaching a certain level of efficiency.

A NEW SOCIAL DEMOCRATIC APPROACH

After the elections in September 1982 the Social Democrats succeeded the centre-right coalition government. After their severe criticism of the closure of Öresundsvarvet in opposition, the new Minister in charge of shipbuilding, Roine Carlsson, had few options but to return to the 'cheese-cutter principle'.

However, he also had to take into account the increasing doubts among large groups of Social Democrats about a continued policy of subsidies. Since 1976 the yards had received Sw Cr 20 bn in direct support from the taxpayers with additional guarantees of some Sw Cr 22 bn by the end of 1982. This amounted to considerably higher state support for shipbuilding than had been given to other industries in difficulties. For instance, every employee in shipbuilding was subsidised about Sw Cr 320,000 whereas the figure for textile employees was Sw Cr 21,000.[79]

Thus the government had to steer its way between its commitment to shipbuilding and the growing criticism in its own ranks about both the scale and the efficiency of state intervention. During the elaboration of the shipbuilding bill Svenska Varv informed the government that the goal for profitability in 1985, established by the structure plan of 1980, could not be attained for Kockums and Uddevallavarvet. Under the terms of that plan unprofitable units should be disposed of, and therefore both Kockums and Uddevallavarvet should be closed. But for the Social Democrats this was impossible politically. The compromise was to delay the target for a return to profitability until 1986 and give another Sw Cr 6.1 bn to the yards.

Employment was to be reduced by 900 jobs at Kockums and 400 at Uddevallavarvet.[80]

In Parliament the Conservatives and the centre party argued for closing down one of the two yards.[81] It was a novelty for the opposition parties to be demanding a less far-reaching policy than the government. Of course, it was a continuation of Åsling's policy as Minister of Industry from the autumn of 1977, but it should also be regarded in the context of changing public opinion. In the 1970s massive support for shipbuilding was a sign of political strength; now it was increasingly regarded as a waste of taxpayers' money. The same change of attitude can also be observed in Germany and France at about the same time.

The new government and the temporary return of the 'cheese-cutter principle' restored the prerequisites for an integration of the local union officials into central-decision making.[82] However, the unions were increasingly aware that the days of the billion Sw Cr rescue packages for shipbuilding were over. If profitability was not restored by the end of 1985 Metall realised that there was an obvious risk that either Kockums and Uddevallavarvet, or both, could be closed.

In 1983, under its new chairman, Leif Blomberg, the Metall leadership began the elaboration of a new strategy, built on the premiss that subsidies had gone as far a they could and that the potential of employment in the industry had decreased. It was also a strategy based on the awareness that solidarity between shipbuilding workers and those in other industries was breaking down. According to Blomberg, not to recognise these realities would limit the union's influence on the outcome. Instead of a defensive rearguard action aimed at the hopeless task of saving all jobs, it was vital to develop an offensive policy the emphasis of which was not the opposition to the run-down itself but the pace and the methods used in making the reduction and the possibilities of transfers to other sectors. The goal would be a competitive industry, and research and technology development, the diffusion of new technologies to small and medium-sized enterprises and greater flexibility to adjust capacity to a new market conditions would be the instruments.[83] Implicit in such a strategy, although this was definitely not said out loud, was the long-term abandonment of shipbuilding in the traditional sense.

This new strategy by the Swedish Metall meant that, if carried through, it would be possible to continue the contration of operations in shipbuilding: a reduction in the readiness of unions to support non-profitable industries decreased the potential for protest and prepared the terrain for more radical change.

At the end of 1984 it was obvious that profitability would not return to Swedish shipbuilding by 1986. When the government consequently decided to halt the production of merchant ships in the two remaining large yards, Uddevallevarvet and Kockums, there were protests only from those shipyard workers directly concerned. The government had no problem in getting the bill through, and had at least the passive support of Metall.

SWEDEN: CONCLUDING REMARKS

Despite the length of the contraction period as compared with other West European shipbuilding industries, the process has been more peaceful in Sweden. There have been no strikes nor yard occupations. The only forms of collective protest have been demonstration rallies. The 'social plans' for the cut in jobs have implied natural wastage with few or no sackings. Moreover the unions have been integrated into the contraction process. They never objected to the slimming down of the yards but demanded only that the cuts be made according to the 'cheese-cutter principle'. However, this was not a case in which top ranks of the union dictated policy. On the contrary, a striking feature was the extent to which the unions at the local level have been involved in decision-making.

An important union goal in the 1950s and 1960s was the structural development of Swedish industry. The unions even pushed for lay-offs and contraction in the less competitive industries such as textiles, and they encouraged the inter-regional transfer of labour. Union wage policy was a powerful instrument for structural change and for the transfer of workers from low- to high-productivity industries.

This traditional co-operative Swedish model of structural change was based on a growing economy. However, many of its ideas survived in the new economic situation. The model has still worked in the context of slow growth and stagnation from the mid-1970s, although less well and not without tensions in regions dominated by one or two industries, as is the case with the shipbuilding areas. The unions have never wanted to defend obsolete structures at any cost: their policies have been concerned with how to achieve that reduction rather than with avoiding the reduction itself.

The experiences of the Swedish model, which included increased union responsibility resulting from its increased influence given by the industrial relations legislation at the beginning of the 1970s, the maintenance of an active labour market policy so that unemployment never exceeded 4 per cent, and the introduction of a sector-specific industry (subsidy) policy to mitigate the consequences of the collapse of shipbuilding, for instance, seem to explain the more far-reaching and less contested contraction process in Sweden.

The strategy of Metall was reminiscent of that of the German IG Metall. The different outcomes must be referred to a more unified political power centre in Sweden, where local union officials participated in central decision-making in direct talks with the government, and the generally greater union influence/responsibility there. All these factors have in turn their roots in the experiences of the union production ideology and the active labour market policy in Sweden.

Two union functions stand out. One is the problem-solving function, where the unions have faced problems jointly with management and have often co-operated in finding solutions. The other function is that of articulating members' interests, which often are in conflict with the interests of the employers. During the reduction process union politics balanced these two functions, but severity of the problems facing the industry has meant an emphasis on the first function. Correspondingly, there has been far less conflict than in Germany and France where the unions have to a larger degree exerted influence by mobilising their membership. Swedish unions have rather tried to justify their existence by influencing the shape of the compromise.

But what influence have the metal workers exerted? The fact that the reduction in Sweden has been larger than elsewhere makes this the crucial question.

The 'social plans' have been a union success. In the circumstances, the interests of the majority of union members could hardly have been better represented. The money spent on shipbuilding over and above the state budget is a much better measure of union influence than the number of jobs lost — in the end these were outside the control of the unions, employers and the state.

There seems to be a connection between influence and discipline. A prerequisite for influence is discipline (i.e. the capability to make necessary compromise without protests of such a magnitude that the final compromise is called into question). Sweden seems to have had more disciplined and more influential unions and shipyard workers than France and Germany. In France they have been the least disciplined and have had the least influence. Germany has been in an intermediate position.

5

The United Kingdom: A National Strategy and Local Co-operation

Shipbuilding in the UK has been concentrated in a small number of areas since the middle of the nineteenth century. By the 1870s the Clyde, the Tyne, the Wear and the Tees accounted for nearly all the ordinary tonnage launched in the UK. This concentration process took place alongside and as a consequence of the development of steam-propelled iron and, later, steel ships. Trawlers and other small and speciality craft were built on the Mersey, the Humber and the Scottish east coast. Other important building areas, such as Belfast, Barrow and Hartlepool, developed later. Roughly speaking, we can say that by the time of World War I, UK shipbuilding was practically confined to three major areas: the Clyde, the North East and Belfast,[1] and this geographical concentration has continued ever since. In the 1970s, only a few large yard existed outside this area: Cammell Laird in Birkenhead (Liverpool) on the Mersey, Vickers in Barrow some 70 miles north of Liverpool, and Vosper Thornycroft in Southampton.

The explanation for this geographical concentration can be found largely in the availability of cheap and plentiful labour, handy supplies of raw materials, and easy access to markets.[2] The supply of labour was more elastic in such areas, and rush orders could easily be met by taking on extra workers.

The history of British shipbuilding in the last hundred years is also the history of a dramatic decline.

THE PROCESS OF CONTRACTION: MARKET SHARE

Around 1890, the British share of the world's shipbuilding was 80 per cent. British dominance began in the decades after 1860, when hardly any other country had the iron, steel and engineering capacity to build steamers on a large scale. This advantage persisted up to World War I (although with a market share decreasing from 80 per cent to 60 per cent) because of Britain's access to a large market (providing the opportunity for 'mass' production and specialisation), its cheap supply of raw materials and the skills of both management and men.[3] The relative decline before World War I reflected the build-up of German, US and to some extent French and Dutch capacity behind protective barriers, rather than any British loss of competitiveness in a strictly economic sense.[4]

However, the British share of world production continued to decrease. Just before World War II it was 35 per cent, and the temporary increase in the years immediately after the war a mere interlude due to the special circumstances of reconstruction and post-war adjustment. The 1950s saw a sharp decline to 15 per cent, followed by spectacular collapse in the 1960s.[5] By then, countries like Japan, West Germany and Sweden had totally taken over Britian's earlier role. The loss of export markets took place even faster than the loss of production share. By the end of the 1950s, the British share of export markets was down to less than 7 per cent from 22 per cent at the beginning of the decade.

The rapid British decline in the 1950s must be understood in terms of the contemporary shift in world shipping towards larger and more standardised vessels. Welding and prefabrication techniques replaced traditional shipbuilding technology and production processes.

For British producers this development meant that their traditional comparative advantage — skilled labour — was undermined. British shipbuilding has traditionally chosen a much more labour-intensive strategy than the rest of Europe, exploiting the skills of its workforce and avoiding the problems of high overhead costs during the frequent cyclical downswings in the industry. Moreover, the size of the early markets allowed for inter-yard specialisation.[6]

The changing market for ships and the perfection of the new welding techniques developed in the 1930s favoured large-scale, capital-intensive yards of the type that dominated on the Continent. The transformation from a coal to an oil economy, and the subsequent shift from liners and tramps to tankers with their simpler, more standardised design, both had an obvious impact. And the steady post-war expansion in world demand also reduced the problem of high fixed costs during cyclical depressions which had previously worked to the disadvantage of Continental yards. The growing acceptance of standard designs among shipowners also worked in the same direction.

Britain's labour-intensive strategy, together with the British union structure (unionisation according to craft rather than industry), had long given British shipbuilding another distinctive feature: the numerous 'demarcation' disputes which characterised the industry in the period up to the early 1970s. Pride in their craft and, above all, anxiety over prospects for employment in an industry with unusually large fluctuations in the demand for labour forced the many craft unions to defend their hard-won concessions and privileges by insisting that particular tasks be done by particular grades of workers. When new techniques were to be introduced it was often a matter of dispute as to which union the new workers would join, and long-lasting disagreement between unions could prevent the introduction of new technology.[7]

The many demarcation disputes gave Britain the reputation of being the most strike-prone shipbuilding industry in the world, and to many contemporary observers demarcation disputes appeared as the cause of British shipbuilding's bad performance from the 1950s onwards. Modern research, however, offers a much more complex explanation. Lorenz, for example, argues convincingly that, although demarcation disputes did contribute to productivity problems, the decline of British shipbuilding was essentially the consequence of an outdated production structure which proved unable to cope with the changeover from a coal economy to an oil economy after World War II. The relatively much smaller British yards with much less capital equipment could not assert themselves in the changing market, where tankers became more and more important.[8] Demarcation conflicts were then but a mirror of these more general problems, an effect much more than a cause, deriving their driving force from the fight for jobs.

From the middle of the 1970s, however, despite a continued decline in employment demarcation disputes quickly ceased. It was not that there was no longer any anxiety over jobs. Rather, nationalisation of the industry in 1977, the debate that had preceded it, and other factors produced a new situation with different responses.

THE PROCESS OF CONTRACTION 1959–1985: EMPLOYMENT

At the end of the 1950s, some 275,000 people were employed in shipbuilding, ship-repairing and marine engineering. By the middle 1960s, the number was down to 220,000.[9] In 1977, when the industry was nationalised and British Shipbuilders was formed, only some 90,000 were engaged in shipbuilding, ship-repairing and warship production. Of this 90,000, almost 40,000 were engaged in the construction of new merchant tonnage, and 25,000 in warship production. At the end of 1984, the overall figure was 48,000, of which only 12,500 worked in new merchant-ship building. The number in warship production, however, has remained constant since 1977 or even increased slightly.[10]

For a long time the Clyde represented the densest concentration of shipyards in the world. There and in the North East half of the world tonnage was produced as late as 1914. Today, however, only two yards are left: Govan Shipbuilders (on the site of the old Fairfields), and Yarrows. No clues survive to suggest that shipbuilding was the distinctive mark of the city only a few decades ago. Further down the river the old, prestigious John Browns in Clydebank (today the French-owned Union Industrielle d'Entreprise) and Scott Lithgow in Port Glasgow have converted to the offshore sector.

The same is true in the North East. On the Tyne only Swan Hunter is left. But the backbone of Swan Hunter is not merchant production but warship production. This was also the case for Cammell Laird in Birkenhead on the Mersey opposite Liverpool and, of course, for the three 'pure' warship yards, Yarrows in Glasgow, Vickers in Barrow, and Vospers in Southampton. Indeed, any comparison of merchant and naval yards confirms the superior staying power of the latter (see Table 5.1).

THE GEDDES REPORT

In the mid-1960s the acute crisis facing the British shipbuilding industry had brought about the bankruptcy and closure of seven yards in four years. In February 1965, the Labour government appointed a shipbuilding inquiry committee under the chairmanship of Reay Geddes, which set vigorously to work, producing its final report after only one year, in March 1966.[11]

The Geddes Report suggested two ways of turning the industry round: these were recommendations for improving industrial relations, and a programme of mergers and reorganisation among the leading shipbuilding companies. In the area of industrial relations the report proposed organisational changes in the unions with the

Table 5.1: Employment 1977–84: merchant, naval and composite yards

Naval and composite yards	1977	1980	1984
Vickers	9,500	8,300	8,400
Vosper Shipbuilders	4,800	5,000	4,100
Yarrow	5,300	5,500	5,400
Swan Hunter	11,500	9,500	7,500
Merchant yards			
Cammell Laird	5,300	4,000	1,800
Govan Shipbuilders	5,600	4,500	2,200
Austin and Pickersgill	2,900	2,800	1,800
Smith's Dock	3,700	2,200	1,500
Sunderland Shipbuilders	4,600	3,800	2,000
Harland & Wolff	11,000	6,500	4,100

explicit aim of putting a stop to demarcation disputes, which were seen as one of the main causes of the situation facing British yards. Geddes recommended that there should be fewer collective bargaining agreements and predicted that as a consequence inter-union disputes would decrease. Moreover, the report stated that labour had to become more flexible, and this too, it was thought, could be achieved by fewer agreements. The proposal about union organisation was remarkably blunt, coming as it did from a Labour government committee. This was more than an invitation to change; it was an insistence that the unions transform their organisation and attitudes.

The Geddes Report recommendation should also be seen in the context of the general drive by Labour to improve the performance of British industry. The Wilson government's preoccupation with reshaping industrial relations to reduce strikes occasioned by inter-union and 'unofficial' disputes found its most dramatic expression in the 1970 Industrial Relations Bill, which met with opposition from the Labour movement and never became law. The likelihood of governments intervening directly in union affairs varies of course from country to country and period to period. It has, however, been relatively unusual in the countries discussed here in this period with the exception of Britain and Denmark — in Britain after unsuccessful attempts under previous Labour and Conservative governments — such intervention has become commonplace following the election of a Conservative government under Margaret Thatcher in 1979 and 1983.

The Geddes Report relied on economic and social engineering in its proposals for recovery, demonstrating a basic belief in the manipulation of social problems from above. It proposed a phase of 'planned contraction', on the assumption that, if this contraction were carried through there would be a 'potential' market for British shipbuilders.[12]

THE FAIRFIELD EXPERIMENT

In October 1965, when the Geddes committee was only half way through its work, the famous Fairfield yard in Glasgow collapsed financially. The collapse was seen as one more dramatic reflection of the serious situation of British shipbuilding, and the Labour government intervened to save the yard.

To George Brown, First Secretary of State at the Department of Economics, Fairfield was a social laboratory. As he said in the House of Commons:

I am sure the House will welcome our actions as a quite new partnership not only between Government and private enterprise but now between Government, private enterprise, and the trade unions, the motive being not only to save a recently modernized Scottish shipyard from extinction, important as that would be, but in addition to provide a proving-ground for new relations in the shipbuilding industry which would change the whole image of our country.[13]

The political background to the intervention was important. The Labour government, with a very small majority in Parliament, was exposed to job protection arguments from shop stewards and trade union leaders in the collapsing industry. Though responsive to their demands to defend jobs it knew there was little support within the Labour Party for full-scale public ownership as a means of keeping the yards open.[14] Thus the recovery plan also had to include private capital. Without government capital, on the other hand, private capital would never have considered becoming involved.

Iain Stewart, a Scottish businessman, played a key role in what happened next.[15] He had for some years been campaigning for better industrial relations in shipbuilding, and when Fairfield went bankrupt was already involved in discussions with local business and trade union leaders in shipbuilding and engineering on how to create more secure jobs and incomes, as well as better training, in return for greater flexibility among the workforce. He realised that a mass redundancy of 2,500 at Fairfield would destroy any credibility his scheme might have, but also that the workers might be willing to change their attitudes and labour practices in order to avert a shutdown.

With such thoughts in mind he let it be known that he would be prepared to play a part in the reconstruction of the yard. For different reasons, both he and the politicians were anxious to avoid majority government ownership. Stewart declared his political sympathies to be Tory, and was unwilling to be party to any 'backdoor nationalisation' arrangement. The government, with its delicate parliamentary majority, was keen to avoid a nationalisation debate.[16]

Thus the enthusiasm of George Brown and the interest of the unions and local business converged. The stated aim of the reconstructed company was to improve industrial relations by providing high and stable earnings. These were to be achieved by a combination of modern management techniques — full use of channels of communication, better utilisation of labour, manpower planning and extensive retraining — as well as the erosion of restrictive practises and the voluntary abandonment of the strike weapon. Two scholars on the Fairfields experiment conclude that remarkable successes were achieved in most of these respects.[17]

Strikes did not disappear completely at Fairfields but they were considerably reduced. The most manifest expression of the experiment was the creation of a joint council embracing management and all unions, which met regularly to consider all major developments within the company. This was an entirely new departure in the traditional confrontational industrial relations of British shipbuilding. In an industry where inter-union frictions had contributed so substantially to disruption and conflict, the creation of a unified negotiating machinery and a new approach to training and apprenticeships — one which accentuated the notion of 'shipyard workers' rather than 'plater', 'boilermaker', 'joiner', 'plumber' and so on — were marks of considerable progress.[18]

The experiment, however, failed. Some have argued that it never got the time it needed,[19] that developments in internal communications were interrupted by the merger with other yards on the Clyde proposed by the Geddes committee and that, as a result, it is impossible to judge how successful the experiment could have been. The speed with which modern techniques were introduced inevitably created difficulties, and Fairfield is a testimony to the fact that absorbing change is often more difficult than initiating it. Despite a general atmosphere of common effort, there were considerable fluctuations in yard morale,[20] and there were many who saw disadvantages in the change.

The Fairfields experiment and the Geddes Report had aimed at improving industrial relations and with them British competitiveness. But the period from 1966 to 1971 saw instead a fairly constant increase in total losses from industrial action in shipbuilding, although this was also true for industry as a whole. From 1965 to 1970, shipbuilding lost five times as many days through strikes as the national average. Only three industries — docks, cars and coal mining — had higher records. The number of stoppages, however, did not increase as fast as the total time lost. The change was due more to the size and length of particular disputes.[21]

UNION STRUCTURE

The trade union structure in British shipbuilding resulted in demarcation disputes. As a rule, the boundaries between unions organising skilled workers were the outcome of a long historical process and were relatively well defined. Disputes arose when new techniques were introduced. The lines of demarcation between semi-skilled and unskilled workers were less well drawn and were always a source of potential conflict. Around 1970, there were eleven manual workers' unions in shipbuilding. although there was only one yard (Cammell Laird) where all of them were represented. The largest unions were the Amalgamated Society of Boilermakers (ASB) and the Amalgamated Union of Engineering Workers (AUEW), both for skilled workers. The two general unions, the General and Municipal Workers' Union (GMWU) and the Transport and General Workers' Union (TGWU), organised most of the semi-skilled and unskilled workers, who consituted just over one-third of the manual workforce in shipbuilding. However, several of the craft unions also organised ancillary workers in any one yard. The division between the two general unions varied (and varies) from district to district. In Scotland, on the Tyne, on the Wear and at Barrow, for example, the GMWU was by far the stronger.[22]

The Confederation of Shipbuilding and Engineering Unions (CSEU or, colloquially, Confed) is an umbrella organisation for the unions in shipbuilding and engineering dating from as early as 1890. Around 1970 it was a bargaining organisation but without much power, as most collective bargaining was the responsibility of individual unions and within them of local shop stewards. There were at this time more than 100 collective bargaining agreements in force in shipbuilding.

THE WOODCOCK COMMITTEE

With the increasing number and length of strikes after 1965, the government decided in 1969 to appoint a new committee of inquiry under George Woodcock, the main purpose of which was to seek ways of reducing demarcation dispute, and, like the Geddes inquiry, to improve industrial relations in shipbuilding.

In its report of August 1971 the committee suggested: (1) that joint shop steward councils should be established at company and district levels (they already existed at yard level); (2) that arbitration procedures should be strengthened (a new national demarcation dispute procedure had been signed in 1969; replacing an inefficient one dating from 1912); and (3) that full-time union officers should be more closely integrated into the system of industrial relations in shipbuilding. However, the main responsibility for day-to-day industrial relation on the union side would still fall to the shop stewards, and the unions were said to have a special responsibilty to see that their shop stewards were able to operate effectively.[23]

Finally, the committee was keen to strengthen the position of Confed. It was a crucial part of the philosophy of the committee that there should be a strong representative body for the shipyard workers at the national level. The committee was well aware that there was a spread of opinion on the subject within the union movement and that the constitution of Confed prohibited its involvement in such matters as wage negotiations, working practices and productivity bargaining. The role of Confed was to negotiate national 'general agreements' concerning wages and working conditions, which were to be filled out in detail by the different yards and craft unions. The eagerness of the committee to give Confed another and more responsible role was obvious: another example of the Labour government's readiness to interpret the constitution of a private organisation such as Confed, and to argue that this was easily compatible with the aims of the government:

> In fact the key clauses in the constitution are in the statements of one of its objectives as being 'to negotiate general agreements concerning wages and working conditions on behalf of the

workers in the said industries . . . subject (to the rule that) piece work agreements and prices, either national or local, should be negotiated by the union or unions concerned.' We think this should give CSEU ample scope to enter into the sort of negotiating agreements we propose . . .[24]

The strategy of the committee was obvious: the integration of responsible and representative unions into the decision-making process from the local to the national level. Bodies where all unions were represented had to be strengthened or established, and in this way inter-union disputes could be absorbed and transformed into responsible claims on the employers. This was a strategy of integration from above.[25] The proposal was an extension of the Fairfields experiment and the suggestions of the Geddes committee.

In 1971 the joint shop stewards committees existed in almost every yard, but they were less common on a company or group basis. The Woodcock committee produced its report in August 1971. One month later the work-ins started on the upper Clyde. They were to mean much for the dismantling of craft barriers and segmentation between the workers, but this took place as part of a historical process in the yards, not as a result of a plan imposed from above.

THE WORK-IN ON THE CLYDE

In 1971 Upperclyde Shipbuilders (UCS, formed in 1968) collapsed financially. The group had always been short of working capital. Under the Labour government there was a four-month moratorium on credit between October 1970 and February 1971, and in January 1971 the new Conservative government agreed to a capital reconstruction. At the same time the owners agreed to pay 5 per cent more for their shipping. But the reconstruction was not forthcoming, and in 1971 the company was liquidated.

Liquidation was not the result of an empty order book but of poor cash flow. (There were orders for two years' worth of work, and the liquidator soon decided to continue operations.) The collapse was also much more a consequence of the technical and economic structure of the company than of the poor industrial relations which government inquiries had identified as a key problem ever since the Geddes Report. With full order books, the shop stewards had difficulty in seeing why there was no work and argued for the right to work. Thus the work-in from September 1971 to April 1972 meant that work continued with the support of the liquidator, whose decision also made it possible for management at different levels to participate in the action.

Much has been written about the long work-in, often with romantic overtones.[26] A new and united working class was seen to be rising up on the Clyde like a phoenix. Shop stewards are said to have forged and maintained a new solidarity among the workforce. Observers quite close to the events, forgetting the role of the liquidator and of management, have argued that the work-in demonstrated 'the latent managerial capacity of the working class', and that the workers 'most certainly can run industry'.[27] It is not my intention here to try to re-write the history of the work-in, but I would like to agree with a recent student that 'the real level of support for the work-in should not be exaggerated'.[28] The proportion of those made redundant who joined the work-in was at the most 69 per cent and by the end only 14 per cent.

The concept of a *work*-in instead of a *sit*-in was something quite new. The full order book meant that the shop stewards faced a situation quite different from that of an occupation with no work. More than ten years later shop stewards who played a major role in the action unanimously stress the importance of the mass media and their public relations, which gave an image of responsible people prepared to discuss with the government.[29] This image and the general support it created was essential for the continuing operations.

The liquidator certainly had to sack people but it was also he who made continued operation possible. Everybody from senior management to the youngest worker worked normally. Senior shop stewards formed a co-ordinating committee of some 40 people, acting in close co-operation with the liquidator. Jimmy Reid and Jimmy Airlie were the leading people in the committee, which undertook to re-employ those people who had been sacked, making use of the monies raised in support of the work-in from the Labour movement and the public at large.

The work-in was never an example of workers' control. It was rather a reaction to a collectively-experienced threat of unemployment. All five yards in UCS risked being shut down, and the action began with the slogan: 'No closure'. But the work-in had important political consequences. In October 1971 the Minister of Industry, John Davies, ordered a study of how UCS could be reconstructed, and the Hill Samuel Report, published in March 1972, discusssed the possibilities of forming a new company, Govan Shipbuilders, on the site of the old Fairfields Yard. (Govan Shipbuilders was the name of the company the liquidator operated.) The report argued that it was out of the question for such a company to attract commercial support,[30] and the decision was therefore made to use government funds. Govan Shipbuilders Ltd., wholly owned by the government, formally acquired the Govan, Linthouse and Scotstoun yard from the liquidator with government funds, and began trading in September 1972.[31] The massive aid this entailed and the assistance given to Marathon (see below) were the *first* major concessions to a new more interventionist style of economic management,[32] albeit one that the Conservatives were to abandon after losing the next election. They bear witness to the massive political pressure that the work-in had succeeded in bringing to bear.

Besides having political importance, the work-in changed many things. It saw the dwindling of craft barriers, although much rivalry remained.[33] Possibly more important was the new climate of industrial relations which existed after the action. Barriers between unions and management were declining. Management had participated throughout the work-in, and if industrial relations had improved before 1971, after the work-in they were altogether better. Indeed, strikes almost disappeared from shipbuilding on the Clyde.

The unions were more directly involved in shipbuilding politics than ever before, i.e. involved from within rather than as a pressure group. The best evidence of their changing role was the Marathon affair. In the aftermath of the work-in, different proposals were put forward. One was that Connells and John Browns should be closed down, and Fairfields and Stephens retained, although with cut-backs in the labour force. Later on, the government hinted that it was prepared to save Connells but that John Browns had to be shut down. It is still uncertain why John Browns was singled out, but it seems likely that the government simply shrank from saving all the yards since this would have meant that the demands of the workers in the work-in would have been met completely. The closure of one yard meant that workforces could still be played off against each other. The way out of the deadlock was to bring in a private company. However, as the Hill Samuel Report had clearly demonstrated, shipbuilding on the Clyde would not attract commercial support, and the solution was to bring in private capital for other purposes. Eventually, the American multinational Marathon, with government support, took over John Browns for offshore production.

Given the delicacy of the situation, the government found it impossible to act openly, and called upon to the unions to help. Two union leaders, Daniel McGarvey, President of the Boilermakers, and Jack Service, General Secretary of the Confederation, were sent to the US to start talks with a company interested in taking over John Browns. The idea of two British union leaders negotiating on their own with big business in the US might seem too fantastic to be true. Written documentation is still inaccessible and McGarvey and Service, as well as the then Minister of Industry, John Davies, are dead. Interviews with some people in the circles around McGarvey, Service and Davies throw some light on the event, however.[34]

In April 1972 they were first directed to the offshore company Brake Sea. Talks there came to nothing, and they went on to another offshore concern, Marathon in Houston, where they met its president, Wayne D. Harbin. This was the first time people in Clydebank had ever heard of Marathon. McGarvey and Service made a 'gentlemen's agreement' that there would be no strikes at the yard providing Marathon guaranteed jobs. Marathon moved into Clydebank in August 1972, when the Heath government produced a £12 m subsidy. It had also been clear during the talks that the shipyard had the wrong labour mix for offshore production. There were too many engineers, joiners, plumbers, and other finishing trade workers. An agreement on retraining was therefore reached whereby they would be retrained and transferred to the Boilermakers. McGarvey's and Service's journey to Texas was a sign not only of a new role for the unions about also of new industrial relations on the Clyde.

TOWARDS NATIONALISATION

Tony Benn, the Secretary of State for Industry in the incoming Labour government of 1974, has borne witness to the impact of the work-in on the Labour Party, especially for its views on nationalisation:

> The first great example of change in the thinking of the Labour Party on this question [nationalisation] was undoubtedly the work-in at the UCS . . . I haven't forgotten the impact that it had even in the Parliamentary Labour Party. As a result the Parliamentary Labour Party adopted ahead of the party conference — and that's saying something — a resolution to bring public ownership to the shipbuilding industry, which was a complete reversal of Labour Government policy in 1964–70.[35]

The move within the Labour Party and the TUC towards nationalisation had begun during the work-in. The new strategy was referred to in terms of 'a partnership between the trade union movement nd the Labour Party'. This was a step away from the old planning from the top since the unions were to be involved on a tripartite basis from the outset. Such a tripartite body was established in February 1974.

The minutes of the talks held at that time reveal that the unions (represented by Confed) were taken seriously and that they were prepared to fight for their opinions. In the autumn of 1974, when they felt that the nationalisation question was not being treated forcefully enough, they threatened to leave the tripartite talks, and the Secretary of State for Industry intervened. Confed felt that this 'gave new authority to Confed'.[36] In the spring of 1975, when Benn presented his Bill on nationalisation, the Shipyard Negotiating Committee of Confed was satisfied that: 'The proposals were in line with points which had arisen in our earlier discussions with the Secretary of State for the industry.'[37]

If the Labour Party and the unions were unaminous about nationalisation, the Bill aroused much political resistance among the Tory opposition and within the industry. The government, finding itself in a delicate parliamentary situation with its small majority, had great difficuly in getting the Bill through,[38] but nationalisation was accomplished on 1 July 1977. This was the culmination of a long political process, which had started with pressure from below within the Labour Party and the unions. As such, it can be distinguished from the situation in the Swedish shipbuilding industry, which was nationalised at the same time by a Centre-Right government, suddenly faced with a bankrupt industry and seeing no other solution. In Sweden, nationalisation was much more a means to an end: in Britain, it was for many the prime goal.

The decision to nationalise British shipbuilding did not, however, represent a simple accord between the government and unions. Jimmy Airlie, the leader of the work-in on the Upper Clyde, warned the Labour government:

. . . [The unions are] preparing the workforce of Govan Ship-builders for any steps that might be necessary to defend their jobs if the situation worsened . . . [They are] disappointed and angry at what they see as the Government's failure to respond to their appeals for State assistance.[39]

At the same time, disagreement between unions and employers on the nationalisation issue did not prevent local co-operation between them to exert pressure on the government for more money. One of the most active lobbyists on the employers' side was Ross Belch, managing director of Scott Lithgow. He co-operated willingly with the unions, and in a spectacular visit to London was escorted not only by the shop stewards, the local Labour MP and other local politicians but also by priests of the Church of Scotland and the Roman Catholic Church in a campaign to persuade the Minister of Industry, Gerald Kaufmann, to make it possible to go ahead with more building 'on spec', since there were no orders.[40]

Before his journey to London, Belch talked about the need for an immediate short-term policy to get more orders:

> . . . There is no longer time to develop medium or long-term policy for the industry. The only policy that matters now is one of survival. If we don't take emergency measures there will be no industry left to operate.[41]

Belch's lobbying was contemporary with pressure from Marathon on the government, and there are obvious parallels with the local battle order in Bremen (Chapter 2, pp. 36–40).

PHASE 1: A UNIFIED WAGE BARGAINING AGREEMENT

In 1977, when British Shipbuilders was established, there were 168 different bargaining agreements. In 1978 there was only one bargaining group. The new company undertook to level out differences between the yard and between staff and non-staff — a process that started 'very well' according to Confed.[42]

In March 1979 the so-called Phase 1 Agreement on wages and salary restructuring, harmonisation and productivity was signed.[43] This was an important step in the building up of very close contacts between management and unions, and had as its cornerstone a very strong and centralised union. Confed signed the agreement for all workers within British Shipbuilders, and from now on all wages were determined nationally for the whole concern. This created a completely new situation for the union movement, since before nationalisation each yard and each craft had had their own agreement. One important outcome of the Phase 1 Agreement was that shop stewards in the yards found themselves controlled by and

130

reliant upon national officials. It is true that local bonus schemes were allowed, but only within the framework of one of two national models to increase earnings through self-financing productivity schemes.[44]

Still another factor in this strategy of centralisation was the appointment of Ken Griffin as Deputy Chairman. After a career in the unions and as a civil servant, he was seen as Labour's man who would make something out of nationalisation. With his close contacts with both the government and the TUC, his position in personnel matters was in reality much stronger than that of the board personnel manager.

The centralisation of wage bargaining was in turn strengthened by the so-called 'social contract' of the Labour government, which implied centrally-agreed maximum wage increases, though in reality this meant a pay freeze. Shop stewards lost their power as yard managements refused to exceed the recommended level.[45] These developments in the reorganisation of the representation of labour, the depression of workplace initiatives on pay and effective wage cuts, took place in spite of the long history of opposition to both throughout the Labour movement. They were both an index of the seriousness of the crisis in shipbuilding and a foretaste of things to come.

THE BLACKPOOL AGREEMENT

In September 1979, only half a year after the Phase 1 Agreement, British Shipbuilders and Confed signed the Blackpool Agreement. Confed accepted a cut in jobs if there was no compulsory redundancy.[46] The crucial problem during negotiations, however, was not compensation for voluntary redundancy but how to allow for the transfer and flexible use of skilled grades.

The agreement envisaged 6,000 redundancies to be achieved in the first place through paying-off the long-term sick and natural wastage, together with the inter-yard transfer of surplus labour and a ban on adult recruitment. The Blackpool Agreement was at once the culmination of the centralising process and of the integration of the national union into decision-making. At the same time it spelled out the collapse of any idea of an industry in which the workforce could count on government support. Indeed, the Blackpool Agreement was a prime example of a concerted action for contraction resulting in a social plan which individualised every threat of unemployment.

131

A DECENTRALISED MANAGEMENT STRUCTURE

Forty-odd companies, in various stages of decay, had been brought together in 1977 with no common financial system, plan or organisational structure, and, although attempts were made by senior management to create a viable centralised structure, each company management retained its own ideas about what to do. The situation had been described as the beginning of 'guerilla warfare between subsidiaries and centre'.[47]

In order to increase centralised control direct-line reporting to the chief executive was introduced on a line management basis, but it did not help much. The better-off warship yards continued to tell top management to keep away.[48] In 1979, production and marketing remained decentralised and, in spite of the introduction of centralised wage bargaining, there was still no overall system of financial control. The yards all had different accounting systems, and the lack of cash flow control was particularly serious since shipbuilding finance is complex (contracts being long and control of production much weaker than, for instance, on the conveyor belt in the car factories).

Sir Robert Atkinson, who in 1980 became new chief of British Shipbuilders, set out to increase central management power. His means were *centralised* financial control and a *decentralised* production and productivity responsibility, and the yards were brought together in five divisions according to their product profile. Within the new organisational structure and under the new leadership a decentralised productivity campaign was initiated at the same time as centralised market efforts were made.

Atkinson's policies had an important impact on industrial relations. As the new Conservative government appointee, his approach was tougher than that of his predecesors, and this was underlined by the fact that Maurice Phelps from British Leyland was appointed as a new board member for personnel relations. Forty-five years old and with none of the labour background of Ken Griffin, Phelps can be described as a 'professional manager'. In this context, moves to centralise management power by transferring it into the hands of the board indicated the beginning of a development that would ultimately deprive the unions of any role in the shaping of the industry. In the short term local managements would be put under pressure to gain the greatest possible concessions from labour, and labour, given the ever deteriorating market situation of the industry, would find itself pushed ever more to cooperate with local management and to compete with other yards.

The tougher approach of the new regime in combination with certain decisions by Atkinson (that were inconsistent with earlier promises he had made) suddenly sharpened the industrial relations climate. And under Graham Day, who succeeded Atkinson in September 1983, there was a further hardening of approach. Before Day, British Shipbuilders approached policy making in what a senior civil servant in the Department of Trade and Industry has described as 'an astonishingly independent way'. The tighter control of the Conservative government, in particular from 1983 onwards, meant 'a clarification of the relationship' between the group and the government. It has since then become 'much clearer what money British Shipbuilders can expect and what the government expects from British Shipbuilders'. The government now sets the framework: 'We are the bankers and the owners. British Shipbuilders are the managers.' A four-year plan was introduced, and where earlier there tended to be a yearly battle about the money, since 1983 have been more 'realistic targets' and 'better knowledge or insight about the economic framework'.[49]

This new approach did not pay much attention to the unions, and the unions were not represented at high-level financial discussions. Whereas Maurice Phelps in an earlier phase felt that 'it was vital to get the unions involved',[50] there now seemed to be much less need for them. This new configuration of forces, with the government in the driving seat, is reminiscent of the situation in France.

As the unions were pushed away from decision-making, Confed found itself in a fundamentally weak position. For example, Phase 1 in March 1979 was signed in the spirit of union integration and social partnership, and the preamble contained seven items setting out the objectives of co-operation. In the Phase 2 Agreement in 1980, there were five such items, and from Phase 3 onwards in 1981 there was only one. Simultaneously with this watering down of definitions the agreements themselves became shorter. Whereas Phase 1 had 84 pages, Phase 6 in 1984 had only 24 pages.[51] In the same period, British Shipbuilders became ever keener to emphasise that the Blackpool agreement had never been more than an undertaking to *try* to avoid compulsory redundancies. There had never been, they insisted, an unconditional promise that they would do so.

These changes were not an immediate consequence of the change of government in 1979. Rather, the shift came when the Thatcher government had been in power for four years, and it is interesting to note that this was a time when throughout Europe governments of whatever complexion were taking a tougher line. Indeed, in the autumn of 1984 Britain asked for more subsidies for shipbuilding from the EEC than did either Germany or Denmark. There seemed, moreover, to be limits to how far the government, even with its new and tougher approach, was prepared to go in order to cut capacity. The idea of having no merchant yards at all left was uncomfortable for a Conservative government, something which Conservative back-benchers remarked on in a debate of the House of Commons in November 1984,[52] and developments in Britain can thus not be understood solely in terms of 'Thatcherite politics'.

THE END OF BLACKPOOL

From 1980 onwards, a number of minor cases had gradually whittled away the Blackpool Agreement, beginning in April 1980 with the Robb Caledon proposal. British Shipbuilders reported to Confed that the Dundee company had to close down and that the Blackpool Agreement with its rejection of compulsory redundancies had therefore to be circumvented. Robb Caledon was discussed on many occasions, and the final settlement, on Christmas Eve 1981, involved a combination of voluntary redundancy (where, however, 'the voluntarity behind the notices was doubtful in many cases') and guarantees of new jobs for the remaining people.[53]

Simultaneously, the government initiated talks on privatisation which had been part of the Conservative Party manifesto for the 1979 election. In March 1980, Adam Butler, Minister of State at the Department of Trade and Industry, told Confed that the government intended to begin denationalisation, and this declaration of intent was repeated in the following two years. Confed repeated its objections and reaffirmed its total opposition of each occasion.[54] The privatisation of Scott Lithgow in 1984 was regarded by Confed as the final violation of the Blackpool Agreement. However, there was little they could do, as the shop stewards of the yard had agreed to the step. As the general secretary of Confed, Alex Ferry, stated: 'Then we knew in our hearts that Blackpool was dead.'[55]

Alongside the pressure on Confed from the government and from British Shipbuilders there was increasing internal tension between the localities and the national union leadership, which emerged as early as the spring of 1980, when there was criticism of the Phase 2 Agreement signed in March:

. . . although there had been general acceptance that the best agreement possible under the circumstances had been obtained, there was considerable criticism of the lack of consultation at yard level on the final agreement.[56]

SPLITS BETWEEN YARDS

The decentralisation of responsibility for productivity within British Shipbuilders also meant a challenge from below for Confed. The growth of local productivity agreements weakened the power given to Confed by the Phase 1 Agreement. Indeed, a number of such agreements at Scott Lithgow in the spring of 1982 provoked protests from Confed:

> The shop stewards had reported that things were going quite well at the yard and that recently they had concluded a number of agreements with management on such things as procedure, timekeeping and discipline and they had also concluded a bonus scheme . . . During the dicussion which took place on this report a number of members expressed extreme concern about the general attitude of management and shop stewards at Scott Lithgow.[57]

The Confed leadership was deeply concerned that such local agreements would result in a yard against yard fight for survival, and that there would be a split within Confed. According to Alex Ferry: 'It was an attempt to break through by avoiding national talks.'[58]

PRIVATISATION

The government's proposals on privatisation worked in the same direction. Confed found that its members in the naval yards believed that nationalisation had resulted in contraction and lower wages and that the general commitment found among the workers in the late 1970s was gone. It is true that a poll at the Swan Hunter yard in Newcastle in November 1983 showed that 72 per cent of the employees were against privatisation, but the Confed leadership was well aware of the gap between voting on principles and the practical application of such principles at one's own yard.[59]

Wages were increasingly the subject of criticism at the naval yards. Shipyard workers had traditionally been among the highest paid manual workers. By 1980 they had sunk to 17th place (including overtime; 16th excluding overtime) and in 1983 to 26th (including overtime; 35th excluding overtime).

The process of contraction and centralised wage bargaining in the spirit of Phase 1 and the Blackpool Agreement meant that division between the yards was at first kept under control. But when that spirit evaporated in the mid-1980s, the peacemaking role of Confed became more and more problematic. Tension between the naval and merchant yards came to the fore at a Confed delegates conference in Tynemouth in 1984. Privatisation was the issue in question:[60]

Shop stewards' from Vicars (naval yard):
> 80 people out of 2,500 came to a meeting about privatisation. We have tried to tell people of all the dangers of privatisation but all people are concerned for is a pot of gold . . . [*i.e.* that according to many employees there the naval yards would be able to pay more if privatised].
> I have to tell you that there are many lads who believe that SNC [The Confed Shipbuilding Negotiation Committee] has let them down [i.e. wages would have been higher if they had negotiated themselves at the yard].

Shop stewards from Yarrows (naval yard):
> We are prepared and stand up and fight for the right of every yard — within the British Shipbuilders *or privatised* [my emphasis] — to fight for their jobs.

Sammy Barr, shop steward at Govan Shipbuilders:
> We have to fight against privatisation. At least we keep ourselves intact.

A resolution against privatisation and closures or compulsory redundancy was adopted by acclamation, and the government's policy of privatising naval yards plus Swan Hunter and Cammell Laird was 'totally condemned'. The lack of opposition from British Shipbuilders to such a policy was deplored, and it was argued that a strong and united trade union movement under the leadership of Confed would provide the best basis from which to oppose the government's policies. Confed was called upon by the delegates to carry out an immediate and vigorous campaign among the membership to alert them to the dangers of privatisation, and it was reaffirmed that decisions had to be taken by all unions on a common basis (i.e. within Confed), 'otherwise we will create total division rather than unity'.[61]

In spite of the resolution, however, the debate revealed a gaping division between delegates from naval yards and those from merchant yards. In fact, the warship builders did not want to sign the national agreement on pay. They wanted their own agreement.

THE CAMMELL LAIRD AFFAIR

The Cammell Laird affair began in May 1984, when British Ship-builders presented a statement to the effect that there were practically no orders on the books, and that potential orders had been lost or in some cases delayed. Of the 640 surplus jobs identified in October 1983, only 280 had been cut by volunteers taking redundancy, leaving a balance of 360. Then in early 1984 a new target of 1,000 additional redundancies was announced and by May, of this new total, 850 still remained to be cut. Furthermore, by the autumn of 1984 yet another 450 jobs were at risk.[62]

A range of protest actions began at the yard in June 1984, reaching a climax in October when a rig was occupied. The occupation, which did not have the backing of the total workforce was illegal, and the authorities demanded that it be brought to an end. Several union leaders took part in the occupation, and the conflict sharpened when the last 37 on the rig gave themselves up to the authorities and were imprisoned. By then, however, it was obvious that the workforce of the yard was divided: many had returned to work, and Confed was asked to intervene.

The imprisonment of the union leaders was exceptional, but without total local committment to the action the President of Confed, Jimmy Murray, could or would not engage Confed. Morever, the personal antipathy between Murray and the General Secretary GMBU, Ken Baker, was well known. Murray was Deputy General Secretary in GMBU, a post he had taken up when the Boilermakers were forced by their declining membership to join the General and Municipal Workers Union in 1982. The fusion of a skilled union such as the Boilermakers with the unskilled GMWU had caused much frustration amongst the Boilermakers and much personal rivalry within the new union. Given the personal frictions within the leadership of GMBU, Murray's refusal to engage Confed in the action at Cammell Laird made his position impossible, and in October he resigned as President of Confed.[63] His resignation was a clear hint of union division.

THE GROWING WEAKNESS OF CONFED

Confed's weakness had already been demonstrated in January 1983, when the Phase 5 Agreement was signed after an industry-wide strike threat which Confed called off only 20 hours before the deadline. Although the Confed leadership considered they had a decisive majority for a strike, support was not total. There were varying degrees of enthusiasm in the unions.[64] Staying power would have been doubtful if there had been a lengthy industrial action. British Shipbuilders' view of the outcome was clear: 'We drove the agreement through hard from the centre.'[65] Alex Ferry, while not contradicting this, responded: 'They first offered us £3.50 a week and we finally got £7.'[66]

The conclusion is clear. By 1984, Confed was a weak organisation without much influence on shipbuilding politics. There no longer seemed to be the same need for Confed's participation in the contraction talks, and the emphasis had by then anyway moved from the national to the local level, where yard stood against yard in a fight for survival and better wages. This was a situation more conducive to local co-operation with management than to conflict.

Centralised wage negotiations, however, remained, since this was a crucial part of British Shipbuilders' cash-flow control. The national agreement gave no room for manoeuvre at the local level except in terms of minor improvements to wage agreements. The outcome was frustration at the local level and this frustration rebounded on Confed. For example, when in October 1982 Confed called for a national three-day strike to protest at the plans to close Robb Caledon, the entire workforce of Vicars refused to participate. The naval yards could contemplate coming out for one day, but not three. The whole action therefore collapsed.

Thus the strategy of centralised management control within British Shipbuilders led finally to the displacement of Confed as a bargaining force, its position eroded from above by exclusion from high-level financial discussions and from below by the impotence of unions at the local level and divisions between yards faced with pressure to compete in the concessions they made. Despite their dissatisfaction, shop stewards at the naval yards, for example, could no longer exert pressure on local management for wage rises on account of the control over wages within British Shipbuilders. A senior manager expressed it in an interview with me: 'We control on behalf of Confed.'

In the minimal space for manoeuvre left to Confed, protectionist steps were considered by some of the affiliate unions as a means of saving British shipbuilding. Arguments reminiscent of those used by the French CGT were increasingly heard, for example by the AUEW in their plan of 1984:

> Foreign competition which depends on state aid, and in many cases, cheap and exploited labour, is being allowed to take over. It is widely believed that British shipping and shipbuilding were once great because of 'free trade'. But Britain's maritime industries were at their greatest when government provided support.[67]

A new Navigation Act was proposed:

> Protection for domestic shipping would give a secure base from which companies could operate in international trade. It would also create demand for a large number of additional British ships and provide badly needed jobs for British seafarers.
>
> It makes sound economic sense to tie in a new policy on shipping with a new policy for shipbuilding. If British shipping needs ships it is right that they should be built and repaired in Britain so that the country as a whole can benefit.[68]

Similar arguments were brought forward by the boilermaker and shop steward at the Govan Shipbuilders, Sammy Barr:

> In the period when the tense discussions were taking place in the Boilermakers' Society and the yards about the future of shipbuilding there was a sharp difference of opinion as to whether we should include in our demands that British ships should be built in British yards — That British ships should be built in British yards has been the policy of the Boilermakers now for a number of years and I hope that it will be the policy of the Amalgamation [Confed].[69]

During the short period of time from 1975 to 1984 Confed described a parabolic orbit. From an organisation loosely kept together by

139

national wage negotiations which left much room for local variation, it was transformed by talks within the Labour Party on nationalisation and nationalisation itself into a policy-making and lobbying organisation. The culmination of this process was the Blackpool Agreement. Later, Confed gradually fell victim to Atkinson's strategy of centralised control/decentralised responsibility within British Shipbuilders, to the government's strategy of privatisation, and to the tension between naval and merchant yards. In the end, Confed was undermined both from without and from within.

The increased power of Confed in the 1970s had also been a personal tribute to Alex Ferry, who in 1977 became its General Secretary. Realising the possibilities offered by there being a Labour government, he quickly learnt to operate within the corridors of power and exploit the situation to increase the influence of Confed. He came to Confed from AEUW in Glasgow at the age of 46, having begun his union career as a shop steward for the convenors at the Singer factory on Clydebank and having joined the Labour Party at the age of 16. As General Secretary of Confed he soon won considerable respect both within the union movement and in management circles, and in 1981 stood for the new post of General Secretary of the Labour Party, backed by a number of centre-right union leaders at a time when the major unions made no secret of their dismay at the disarray in the party. He was beaten by a single vote. In 1984 he stood for the post of General Secretary of the TUC but here there were stronger union interests than those Confed could mobilise. If Ferry was in large measure responsible for Confed's growth, he also helped to prevent its total dissolution when the organisation came under pressure in the 1980s. Despite all its difficulties Confed continued to function.

Developments within the modern British shipbuilding industry can therefore be summarised as follows. The move away from a division according to craft with definite demarcation barriers began in the 1960s and was accelerated during and after the work-in on the Clyde in 1971–2, although the barriers were never completely broken down. (In 1984, for instance, there were still some yards where the boilermakers, despite their merger with the General and Municipal Workers two years earlier, tried to negotiate their own agreements).[70] Over the same period, a process of centralisation took place and increased power was given to Confed, which with nationalisation and the general commitment this produced contributed considerably to an 'era of very good industrial relations'. The culmination of this development, favourable to both labour and the industry, can be found in the Phase 1 and the Blackpool Agreements in 1979. From 1980 onwards, a movement of centralised control and decentralised management responsibility within British Shipbuilders gradually introduced a new kind of division between naval and merchant yards. Other factors, such as wage restraint and the proposals for privatisation, worked in the same direction. In this context Confed ceased to be able to act as a power base for Labour. The centre of gravity moved once more to the localities, where the 'era of very good industrial relations' continued, this time in spite of severe restrictions on wages and on the role of shop stewards and although much strain arose at the national level as Confed lost power.

Confed was obliged to call on the services of Labour MPs for lobbying, just as their counterparts have done in other countries in Western Europe. After 1982, however, management and government seemed to have little need for the unions. Their participation, which had been crucial at the beginning of the contraction process, when the potential for protest was far greater, could now be ignored. Lobbying *via* the Labour Party also ceased to exert much influence once it was out of office. More important was the 'interdepartmental' lobbying within the government, where the Ministry for Northern Ireland and the Ministry for Scotland tried to effect decision-making within the Ministry of Industry, thus in its own way reflecting the local divisions discussed above. Details of the forms of local co-operation between management and unions will be discussed in the next section.

LOCAL DEVELOPMENTS

Since most negotiations within British Shipbuilders are centralised, there is little scope for local changes to national agreements. Wages can hardly be increased at all, and the framework for redundancy schemes is centrally determined. The only room for negotiations at the yard level is on the question of which departments should take job cuts and how many should be lost. The driving force in the search for increased productivity has been much more the inter-yard fight for survival than wage incentives, since wages have deteriorated relative to other groups. Instead, it is precisely this intense competition between yards that has made possible the exercise of decentralised management responsibility without wage pressure. While this is true for the merchant yards, at the naval yards the demand for higher wages has produced a sense of frustration at remaining within British Shipbuilders, i.e. yard against yard competition has indeed been reinforced, although here with a different outcome.

The existence of good industrial relations at the yard level — buffered by a sense of animosity towards other yards and within an overall system of centralised control — is in a sense quite straightforward. As shop steward Sam Guilmore at Govan explained:

> The situation now is that neither management nor the unions have any power, which is a condition for disputes. That is the basis of the 'good' industrial relations.[71]

GOVAN SHIPBUILDERS

In 1973 and 1975, the welders at Govan were in dispute and finally conducted a go-slow. There was also a walk-out.[72] The threat of unemployment at that time produced a collective response since the threat was still collectively experienced, i.e. gains for the workforce as a whole were still thought possible. But actions like these were not repeated. By 1976 it had become apparent to the workforce at Govan that the market for ships was extremely weak, and the fear of redundancies altered the whole climate of labour relations as the last orders were nearing completion.[73]

Saving work became an urgent priority for management and men alike resulting in joint approaches to the government to find orders. The Boilermakers voted to introduce flexibility to all sections of the workforce, and lines of demarcation were eliminated. The agreement was estimated to be worth 20 per cent in terms of productivity but, because of the order situation, the workers agreed not to demand extra wages. Moreover, the Boilermakers' officials led the talks with the government, seeking 'spec' orders to avoid mass redundancies. The undertakings of the Govan workers should be related not only to the threat of unemployment but also to the general sense of commitment evoked by the decision to nationalise the industry.

In the late autumn of 1977, negotiations between British Shipbuilders and the Polish government about orders for 22 cargo vessels and two crane ships reached a critical stage. The order would secure work not only on the Clyde but in other hard-pressed areas as well.

However, the whole deal was threatened when 1,700 outfitting workers at Swan Hunter's Tyneside yard refused to end an overtime ban in support of pay parity with the Boilermakers. Confed officials urged the men in vain to give British Shipbuilders the required guarantee of trouble-free production.

The probability was that if the dispute at Swan Hunters could not be resolved than at least some of the orders for the yard would be reallocated to the Clyde. It was, as Woolfson underlines, a potentially embarrassing situation for the Clyde workers, since they had been the recipients of such magnificent economic and moral support during the work-in five years earlier. But the local Glasgow evening newspaper expressed the feelings of many, when it urged the workers through its editorial columns to take full advantage of the situation:

> Now, just because their colleagues in the north-east have made a kamikaze decision, there is no reason why the Clyde shipyard workers should cut off their noses to spite their face. It would be misplaced brotherhood for the Clydeside workers to refuse to build the ships.[74]

Confed's opinion as expressed by its then General Secretary, Jack Service, was that the first priority was to secure the building of the ships in Britain. If the issue was not resolved, it was feared that the whole order might go to Japan. From Swan Hunter, however, an appeal was launched for the Govan workers to 'black' the Tyne orders for four ships offered to them. Workers at Austin and Pickersgill in Sunderland on Wear had refused to accept any reallocated orders, whereas the men at Smiths Dock on Teeside had voted to take two of the ships, some days after a sympathy strike for the outfitting workers at Swan Hunter. For Confed this inter-yard division was extremely difficult. Their confusion was not made easier by British Shipbuilders' readiness to tout orders around the other British yards, demanding detailed concessions on flexibility.

In the event, after some hesitation, the Govan workers agreed to accept the reallocated orders. At a mass meeting of 3,000 people only four voted against. The Govan decision, supported by the Robb Caledon shop stewards in Dundee, effectively undercut the attempt by the convenors at Swan Hunter to use the prospect of the Polish orders as a lever in the negotiations. They could do nothing but charge the Govan workers with betrayal.[75]

The Govan workers subsequently fulfilled their pledge to British

Shipbuilders. Indeed, when some of the foremen and assistant managers took industrial action, the workers decided that they would not be laid-off by the dispute. The ghost of the work-in was revived as the men agreed to 'work-on' without supervision, in order to complete the order on schedule.[76] Later, with the Polish orders running out and the prospects of new orders very poor, 500 men volunteered to work on the Fair Holiday — an inconceivable concession a few years earlier.[77]

However, collective protests, though rare, continued to be made. In the preclude to the Blackpool Agreement, British Shipbuilders announced in August 1979 that there would be 10,000 jobs lost within the industry, 4,000 in Scotland. The announcement was experienced as a collective threat and triggered off a collective response in the form of an immediate walk-out on the Clyde.[78] However, the general absence of new orders removed any possibility of returning to a work-in, and the option of enhanced redundancy payments influenced many. The collectively-experienced threat soon evaporated. Already, in August 1978, the Shipbuilding Redundancy Payment scheme had been introduced, under which the total average payment amounted to £2,500 per employee. Although the payment to those workers nearing retirement age was much less generous, they could hardly expect collective support if they wanted to stay on. Thus they, and other groups of weaker workers, had to face the threat individually, and this was the chief reason why the workforce soon returned after the walk-out.

The Blackpool Agreement implied a joint understanding between Confed and British Shipbuilders for voluntary rather than compulsory redundancies.[79] Govan, with over 700 surplus workers, attempted to 'open the books' to all those employees who wanted to volunteer, but the shop stewards protested. After negotiations it was finally settled that employees over 55 could accept voluntary redundancy. The shop stewards have since then been in favour of early retirement pensions from the age of 60 but have tried to oppose 'the golden handshake'. However, this opposition has been difficult: 'People say no to the handshake at the meeting. Then they go back door to the management and sign their notice.'[80]

Designated a 'core merchant facility', the Govan yard escaped the worst consequences of the contraction, although it has experienced considerable job cuts, from 5,600 in 1977 to 2,200 in 1984. This process has been accompanied by local incentive schemes in a context where orders are few. Faced with this pressure, open demarcation disputes have disappeared, although demarcation still constitutes a large part of the day-to-day affairs of the union ('People don't change their habits overnight or the way they are thinking').[81]

The cut of 3,400 jobs in seven years has occurred without sackings. The size of the reduction was centrally determined, as were the payment schemes, and within this framework local negoations have dealt with the principles of how to select people to be made redundant and — to some extent — the timetable for the implementation of the cuts. Local room for manoeuvre has been small. The unions have repeatedly insisted on selection by age, in addition of course to no forced redundancy. It is this demand for selection by age which has caused most friction between management and shop stewards. Management has argued for a more general selection of 'volunteers' in the slimming down and rationalisation of the labour force. The unions have not wanted to participate in the selection process but, according to the personnel manager Bob McCann there has been a 'silent understanding' when the company made the selection.[82] Their continual insistence on no forced redundancy has paid off. The threat of unemployment has been individually experienced.

JOHN BROWNS

Govan is a short distance down river from the heart of Glasgow, and a bit further down the Clyde is Clydebank. John Browns was established on its north bank in 1851 and became one of the largest and most famous shipbuilding and engineering works in Britain. From 1851 to 1972, 656 vessels were built, an average of one ship every 67 days. Famous ocean-going liners such as the *Lusitania, Queen Mary* and *Queen Elizabeth I* and *II* were built there. John Browns also had comprehensive naval production facilities.

In the 1960s, however, the yard obtained contracts for a new type of vessel, the offshore jack-up drilling rig. Six were completed before the bankruptcy of UCS, but this attempt to exploit the growing North Sea market to diversify production was not enough to save the yard from the problems it shared with the rest of the British shipbuilding in those days. In February 1968 John Browns merged with Charles Connell, Fairfields, Alexander Stephan and Yarrows under a new name, Upper Clyde Shipbuilders.

As we have already seen, Marathon took over John Browns in 1972 after the work-in. Officially, Marathon argued at the time that the main reasons for acquiring the yard were easy and convenient access to the North Sea and the proven capabilities of the Clydebank personnel. The fact that John Browns had already built some rigs was an advantage but could hardly have been a decisive one. If the expanding oil fields in the North Sea were the main source of interest, it is still not clear why the Americans turned to a yard on the wrong coast of Scotland at a spot above the Erskin bridge which made the building of large vessels impossible. Indeed, during the years in Clydebank most of the jack-up rigs they built were brought back to the US and sold to the Caribbean market. It is therefore difficult not to relate their interest in John Browns to the availability of government money.

The labour force had been whittled down to some 750 by the time Marathon finally pulled out in 1980, and the French firm Union Industrielle d'Entreprise (UIE) took over the yard. But in 1976 and 1978 Marathon had threatened to shut down operations when the Labour government intervened after pressure from the shop stewards and the Scottish TUC (see below). The fact that Marathon received 17 rig orders in the year before it withdrew, not one of which came to the Clydebank yard, underlines the suspicion that the multinational had only really intended to stay as long as there was government economic assistance.[83]

Daniel McGarvey's concession on retraining during the union leaders' negotiations with Marathon was much criticised by workers at the yard, especially the welders. Latent demarcation disputes between the Boilermakers and other unions flared up but, despite these initial difficulties, the Marathon agreement was largely adhered to. In May 1974 there was a walk-out resulting in a six-day strike. This was not simply a sectional dispute but had more to do with a change in the company's industrial relations personnel and general dissatisfaction over continuing wage restraint. Apart from this conflict, labour relations were peaceful. As orders dwindled, however, the employers gradually adopted a policy of worksharing, and at one stage of suspension and eventually of voluntary redundancy, which gradually took the labour force down to 750. This process of uncompromising contraction did not encourage aggressive union politics and industrial action. Good behaviour was thought to give one a better chance of keeping one's job. In 1978, as part of the extended haggling over the price of the last rig for the British North Sea Oil Corporation, the workers offered a flexibility deal to the company which is described in detail below. And by the time UIE began to take an interest in the yard, the workers were prepared to concede staggered holidays and the use of outside contractors to boost labour force during busy periods, as well as a higher degree of interchangeability.[84]

As industrial relations became more peaceful, both management and unions turned their attention to the government. The minutes of meetings between management and the shop steward executive committee in 1978–9 illustrate this development well. In May 1978 the managing director, John Craig, told the shop stewards he had been lobbying various government departments. Failure to secure an order would mean that 90 days' notice of redundancies would have to be lodged by the end of July. The stewards warned that such a notice could trigger off unrest which could be difficult to contain.[85]

Typically, not only management but also the shop stewards lobbied the politicians. Their bargaining counter was their power to mobilise the workers. The Labour government had been in office since 1974 and new elections had to come soon. For this reason, the government was keen to avoid industrial unrest. In June 1978 the shop stewards met with Scottish Office ministers and then reported to management:

> The Ministers had emphasised that the Government was prepared to give all reasonable support to Marathon. They appealed to the Stewards to ensure that no precipitate action on the part of the workforce should be allowed to prejudice existing, delicate negotiations.[86]

By August the shop stewards who had been putting pressure on management, were gradually coming to realise that decision-making within Marathon took place in the US. It was the government, therefore, that became the main target of pressure. The meeting held on 18 August is an accurate reflection of the complex interests involved:

> The Stewards expressed disappointment at the news . . . The Stewards were now quite clear that a meeting of stewards to be held next Wednesday would lead to a Mass Meeting on Thursday (24.8.78). The Press and T.V. would be asked to the meeting and statements would be issued. No further delays can be allowed as the Stewards are under considerable pressure to take some action to secure employment. The only alternative to this course of action would be for the Company to guarantee that no suspensions will take place till more work is secured. It is now 17 months since the last order was secured and if necessary a bridging operation will have to be instituted to preserve employment.

Under no circumstances could there be a repetition of the 1976 situation, when some men were suspended for 8 months.

The Shop Stewards maintained that they had been extremely responsible but that circumstances were now against the whole matter remaining confidential. Unfortunately, various Government ministers are on holiday but attempts will be made to contact them over the week-end. The Shop Stewards Executive Committee had received assurances in June that the Government would support Marathon if the situation deteriorated — that is the time for these Ministers to demonstrate their good faith. Mr Craig understood that the Stewards were concerned but doubted whether too much publicity was a good thing. Potential clients might be disuaded from ordering at Clydebank if there was any kind of industrial trouble.[87]

Three days later a meeting was arranged with the shop stewards executive committee, the Managing Director, Craig, and Gregor McKenzie, Minister of State of the Scottish Office. The same arguments were repeated,[88] and the Minister of State stressed the importance of preserving a low profile as far as possible, while the Managing Director still hoped for 'an order from Clarkson [although] he was more hopeful now of orders from NGOC and for the Beatrice field'. Craig now promised that the company would not institute formal redundancy procedures till at least 31 August, in order to allow breathing-space for further negotiations.

The day after the meeting with the minister in New St Andrew's House, management and shop stewards made mutual concessions and agreed that the government had to make the next move:

> There was a general concensus that the meeting the day before with Mr Gregor McKenzie, Scottish Office Minister had gone pretty much as expected. Mr McKenzie had not been in a position to offer any panaceas and further contact would have to be awaited.
> The Stewards for their part agreed to hold off having a mass meeting till next week. This is the longest that a mass meeting could be deferred, given the existing lack of certainty on the question of work-load.
> Mr Craig repeated the assurance he gave to Mr McKenzie that he would hold off giving redundancy notices till 3rd September but he could not postpone the matter further.
> The matter of an article appearing in the *Scotsman* regarding

Marathon's future was discussed and there was a general agreement that this was unhelpful as it would lead other newspapers to make enquiries and publish unhelpful articles.[89]

Local co-operation to pressurise the government gradually developed. Mobilisation of the workers was almost the only weapon available to unions *or* management. On 30 August a joint management-trade union memorandum was handed to McKenzie, and the government was invited to urge BNOC to place an order with Marathon for a rig and to finance an investment programme in the yard to enable to the company to diversify.[90] However, nothing happened. On 11 September the company intimated that 900 employees out of 1,150 would be made redundant,[91] and the unions pledged to fight, not against management but against the government. This is a pattern which was to be repeated in Bremen five years later (pp. 42–4).

Jimmy Reid, one of the leading people in the shop stewards' executive committee, and one of the leaders of the work-in in 1971–2, made it clear who he regarded as to blame. At a press conference he blamed civil servants in the Scottish Office for ignoring proposals from both management and workforce which he claimed would have secured the yard's future, and disclosed the content of the joint memorandum in August. He repeatedly stressed that he was confident Marathon would still win orders if only the government intervened.[92]

Later in the autumn, churchmen helped to increase the pressure on the government. Five clergymen met with Bruce Millan, the Secretary of State for Scotland, who assured them that he and his ministers were actively engaged in trying to resolve the problems of Marathon. The government had already authorised expenditure of £16.5 m in grant aid to build an oil rig for the National Gas and Oil Commission of India, but this initiative was no longer enough.[93] The local people expected more from the government.

Before taking further steps, the government wanted concessions from the workforce, and the shop stewards executive committee signed a document guaranteeing increased productivity on behalf of the whole workforce. The cost reductions this would permit were to be the workers' contribution to bridging the price gap between what the British North Sea Oil Corporation was prepared to pay and the production cost of new rigs. This contribution was calculated at one-third of the gap; the company and the government then undertook to pay one-third each. The agreement was ratified by the entire labour force and accepted unanimously.[94]

The workforce and the government were prepared to keep the yard open and to pay a price for it. The government was prepared to intervene with a new package of support. In the end, however, the American multinational was the strongest party of the three. At a tripartite meeting in London, the company management told Bruce Millan that it was no longer interested in the Clydebank company and that it wanted to withdraw. Marathon, Mr Woodfin told Millan, were 'prepared to settle their debts with the British government on the spot and pull out of Clydebank as soon as the current rig is complete'.[95] He also told the government that as far as the British North Sea Oil Corporation rig was concerned, Marathon had reached its limit at the price quoted and had no intention of reducing it further. Bruce Millan declined Marathon's offer and asked if there was any way which could be found round the problem. After some discussion it was agreed that the workforce would have to share an increased burden, and an attempt would be made to formulate a new productivity agreement.

The rescue talks in the winter of 1979 only resulted in a temporary breathing-space. The multinational had declared its intentions and had the power to fulfil them. Cash flow within the multinational knew no national borders, whereas the government was bound by the limits of the nation state. At the beginning of 1980, Marathon withdrew from Clydebank, leaving Joseph Craig, Managing Director of the yard, in the same situation as his employees. With the help of government money, he then brought in the French UIE as new owner.

During talks with government the mobilisation of the workforce was used as a threat but the threat was never carried out. Instead, the old John Browns is a very good illustration of a rapid contraction which has not threatened overall stability by producing collective reactions. Industrial relations have been peaceful since the work-in, and the workforce has agreed to increase productivity on several occasions since Marathon took over in 1972. Moreover, developments since the beginning of the 1970s have meant that the workforce has had to adjust to new product areas with consequences for the security of employment.

In 1983 the UIE yard went bankrupt, and another French concern, the Amrep group, was brought in to take over. Only a year after that crisis, the yard ran out of orders and when a jack-up rig order was at last placed with the work-hungry yard, in December 1984, it was after the workforce had signed a new no-strike agreement. Shop stewards emphasised the yard's 12-year strike-free record, forgetting the six-day walk-out in 1974. However, even ten years is not bad, and workers were happy to assure clients that they were determined to maintain this approach to industrial relations.

The contraction process at UIE was peaceful. The yard management and the shop stewards co-operated against the threat of unemployment, much as they did at Govan, brought together by the external threat of the declining market. Continuing day-to-day friction clearly illustrates that such co-operation did not happen without an effort. The difference between UIE and Govan was that UIE, as a privately-owned yard, could direct its pressure on the government, whereas for Govan, working within the framework of a nationalised concern, the room for manoeuvre was much smaller. Here the impact of local interests was diluted in the talks of the higher-ranking union officials with government officials.

Apart from the impact of long-term, general contraction, UIE has experienced the problems of a highly fluctuating market for its products. In order to keep up with delivery terms, not less than 1,100 people were hired on a short-term basis in the spring of 1983. The company established its own labour recruitment office and introduced a trading programme. In April the workforce increased to 2,000 people. An agreement was reached between unions and management on the 'concertina method' of recruitment, i.e. hiring labour on short-term contract and then firing them. This labour was used as a kind of cyclical regulator. A shop steward told me: 'We have to accept a permanent core of workers which is fairly good. When the volume of work increases we take on new temporary workers on the same conditions as the permanent workers.'[96]

Here 'same conditions' means the same wage and working conditions, but not the same security of employment as the permanent workers. The many new workers knew from the beginning that they would have to go after a few months and that they could hardly expect backing from the core of permanent workers. The very rapid slimming down from 2,000 to 750 in a short space of time in the autumn of 1983 was therefore quite undramatic, in fact less dramatic than the mass hiring in the spring.[97] The same strategy was envisaged when the yard got the order in December 1984 for a big jack-up rig — the biggest ever built in Britain. Round the core of 530 workers it was planned to create a least a further 500 short-term contract jobs from the spring of 1985. And there were hopes of another major order in 1985 which could provide a further 1,000 temporary jobs.[98]

A problem arose, however, in the autumn of 1983 when the company wanted to reduce the number of permanent workers from 750 to 550. Those full-time union officials present when the management communicated its intentions immediately rejected the proposal, but the shop stewards changed their minds shortly after the meeting. The chairman of their executive committee told me: 'We have always said that we are not for compulsory redundancy. But we had to think of the best for the company.'[99]

Real talks soon started, therefore, on reducing the workforce from 2,000, not to 750, but to 550, and very soon an agreement was signed. A comparable social plan in 1980 had cost the company £650,000; the company was now prepared to pay £1 m. The basis of the package was the government's redundancy payment of £145 per employment year. At UIE nobody had been employed for more than 11 years. In addition the company had to give one week's notice for every year of employment and to achieve the job cuts the corresponding wage was paid with the request to stay at home. As an extra incentive the company paid three weeks' wages, tax free, for every year of employment.

Of those people made redundant, 130 were expected to take the 'golden handshake' or the severance agreement. Forty pipeworkers and 30 other workers were to be made compulsorily redundant. The seven shop stewards in the executive committee put forward the agreement at a joint shop stewards meeting with all the 30 shop stewards, and then at a mass meeting with all employees. There were some protests from those affected but there were no grounds for more spectacular outbursts of collective action or grass-roots mobilisation. The social plan had 'individualised' the threat of unemployment to those people hit and for many of those who voluntarily accepted the golden handshake no threat was experienced at all.

THE UNITED KINGDOM: CONCLUDING REMARKS

The history of British shipbuilding is the story of a long and continuing decline. The union structure (organised according to craft instead of industry), the industry's structure (labour-intensive rather than capital-intensive), and the threat of unemployment aggravated by extreme cyclical fluctuations, have been the motivating force behind the numerous demarcation disputes. In analysing the impact of these conflicts, cause has often been confused with effect. For instance, the disputes were often said to be the cause of the sad performance of British shipbuilding from the 1950s onwards. They probably did intensify the decline of the industry, but essentially they were its effect and symptomatic of the process of decline itself.

Demarcation disputes gradually petered out from the mid-1970s onwards, not because the concern over loss of jobs ceased to be felt but because nationalisation in 1977 and subsequent specialisation within the nationalised concern created a new situation in which new patterns of reaction developed. The changing labour market in the shipbuilding regions also contributed. Competition for skilled labour with the rising new industries in the 1960s had encouraged the institution of personnel policies involving employment guarantees which were taken up by the newly nationalised industry. Then, from around 1980, the increasing tendency towards privatisation under the auspices of the Thatcher government further reinforced the basis of yard-to-yard co-operation in eliminating demarcation, despite the increasing number of redundancies.

Nationalisation was accompanied by the establishment of close contacts between British shipbuilders and the unions. Union leaders were now required to deliver the support of their membership during the contraction process.

Encouraged by the Labour government, British Shipbuilders adopted a style which allowed a strong and very centralised union to sign agreements for all workers within BS. In 1979, a single bargaining agreement — the Blackpool Agreement — replaced the 168 agreements, whereby each yard and each craft had bargaining separately, and a plan to reduce capacity was concluded at the national level with the strengthened Confed. The agreed aim of the 1979 settlement was contraction without compulsory redundancies — one of the clearest examples of concerted action for contraction resulting in a 'social plan' which individualised the threat of unemployment. The similarities with the Swedish case are obvious. The Blackpool Agreement evaporated after a few years when BS argued that compulsory redundancies had now become unavoidable, and when the government increasingly pressed for the privatisation of the 'profitable' naval yards — developments which undermined much of the Confed's authority and momentum. Low wage settlements engineered by the introduction of centralised cash flow control within BS from 1980 onwards also eroded much of the general commitment to fighting for the industry which nationalisation had engendered. These developments were strengthened by the decision of BS management to decentralise responsibility for

153

increased yard productivity.

The outcome was co-operation between management and shop stewards at the local level as individual yards fought for survival. Instead of demarcation disputes there was a tendency towards yard against yard competition and action. Replacing the traditional craft-based division within the workforce a new division was developing. The period when Confed was strong and exerted authority was hardly more than an interlude reflecting the temporary need for the participation of responsible unions in the contraction process.

6

The Netherlands: Tripartite Talks but Divided Interests

Shipbuilding has traditionally played an important role in the commercial life of the Netherlands. At the beginning of the 1970s almost 5 per cent of the labour force employed in industry worked in shipbuilding (excluding employees in subcontracting industries). This share is much higher than in the four countries studied so far. In West Germany, for instance, the figure was less than 1 per cent.

Up until the crisis the larger Dutch yards were concentrated in Rotterdam and Amsterdam. On the Rhine, upstream from Rotterdam, there were a number of medium-sized yards, which the bridges further downstream largely prevented from expanding to produce large ships during the tanker boom. In the north of Holland there are many small yards which are not included in this survey.

By the middle of the 1970s the main yards were Rotterdamse Droogdok Maatschappij (RDM), Verolme Dok-en Scheepsbouw Maatschappij (VDSM), with its main yard in Rozenburg some twelve miles downstream from Rotterdam, Wilton Fijenoord in Schiedam, five miles downstream from the heart of Rotterdam, P Smit in Rotterdam, K M de Schelde in Vlissingen, on the peninsula of Zuid Beveland, some 50 miles south-west of Rotterdam, and Nederlandse Droogdok en Scheepsbouw Maatschappij (NDSM) in Amsterdam. These all belonged to the large RSV group Rijn Schelde Verolme, which also had shipbuilding interests in Brazil and Eire. The Gusto yard in Schiedam and the Amsterdamse Droogdok Maatschappij (ADM), which concentrated on repair work, were also included in the discussions about the contraction of the main yards. Van der Giessen de Noord in Krimpen a/d Ijssel, some 15 miles east of Rotterdam, was an important builder of ships up to 'Panama size' (80,000 dwt).

Some of the yards listed concentrated increasingly on warship production in the 1970s. From around 1970, KM de Schelde (KMS) in Vlissingen built only warships, specialising in frigates. Wilton Fijenoord in Schiedam began by building corvettes for Indonesia and now produce warships almost exclusively. RDM in Rotterdam has specialised in submarines, whereas previously the yard had concentrated on merchant ships and repair work.

In 1975 the main yards employed in all some 13,000 people in *new construction*, with more than 10,000 in the RSV group.[1] By 1984 less than 3,000 of these jobs were left. Therefore the ten years since 1975 have seen the almost total elimination of the Netherlands as a builder of large ships. However, this does not mean that they have lost their role as a shipbuilding nation, since small and medium yards are much more important in the Netherlands than elsewhere in Western Europe. These yards have not been affected to the same extent as the main yards.

In 1975, 50,000 people worked in the whole of Dutch shipbuilding, of which just over a quarter were employed in new construction at the main yards. In 1980 the overall figure was 34,000 and in 1984 it had again fallen to 29,000;[2] whereas the large yards almost totally disappeared, employment in the small and medium yards declined by 25 per cent, from 37,000 to 26,000.[3]

The fate of the main yards was sealed in December 1982 when the flagship of Dutch shipbuilding, RSV, was forced to seek government aid after the failure of a restructuring programme. Government cash to a total of Fl 2.2 bn had flowed into the group from 1977, giving the government a 46 per cent stake. In February 1983 the new coalition government of Christian Democrats and Liberals, elected less than half a year earlier, said no to another Fl 300 m, and more than 6,000 employees were laid off.

The embarrassing question of how so much money had been squandered demanded a political answer. MPs, backed by public opinion, were keen to know exactly what had happened to the Fl 2.2 bn and a parliamentary inquiry was appointed to discover who was responsible.

The RSV inquiry committee finished its work in December 1984. It then published a 6,000 page report in 16 volumes and weighing 13 kilograms. The committee found that many people were to blame but put the main responsibility onto the RSV management and, above all, the liberal politician Gijs van Aardenne, Minister of Economic Affairs from 1972–81 and again from 1982.[4]

RSV was an amalgam of 117 individual companies formed in 1971. The intention was to create a powerful and centrally-planned group which could stand up to Far Eastern competition. However, far from standing up to the competition, the group needed increasing financial support. The break-up of RSV marked the end of the large yards, although some of its companies continued shipbuilding almost as before (notably KM de Schelde and a part of RDM, both of whom were heavily engaged in naval contracts).

The concentration of the larger shipyards and the contraction process is shown by the changes in the employment figures (see Table 6.1).

Table 6.1: Employment in Dutch shipbuilding, 1970–1984
(figures in brackets refer to new construction)

	1970		1975	1980		1984	
RDM	3,700	(1,550)	3,200	(950)	1,600	(700)
VDSM[a]	3,100	(1,450)	1,450	(−)	800	(−)
Wilton Fijenoord	4,400	(1,200)	2,750	(1,000)	800	(2,200)
P Smit	1,050	(500)	300	(50)	200	(50)
K M de Schelde	3,750	(1,350)	3,350	(1,400)	2,600	(900)
NDSM[b]	3,100	(1,900)	400	(−)		(−)
RSV group[c]	20,000	(8,600)	12,000	(4,400)	7,900	(2,900)
Gusto	1,250	(1,250)		(−)		(−)
ADM[d]	1,500	(−)	1,500	(−)	1,000	(−)

Notes: a. After separation from the RSV group in 1983, VDSM continued under the name of Verolme Botlek. From 1980 only repair work. b. From September 1978 reorganised under the name of NSM. c. Ceased as a group in 1983. d. Exclusively repair work.
Source: Compiled by the Ministry of Economics, the Hague.

CEBOSINE AND THE UNIONS

The larger yards in the Dutch shipbuilding industry are represented by CEBOSINE (*Centrale Bond van Scheepsbouwmeesters in Nederland*) in Delft. It is an organisation which has relatively strong administrative resources and is able to act as a spokesman for its member companies in talks with both government bodies and unions and which, in terms of status and influence, could be compared to VDS in West Germany and CSCN in France.

After World War II the unions were split along political and religious lines, the main tendencies of which were Catholic, Protestant and Socialist. Union organisation consisted of tight, clearly-defined vertical segments, but with a degree of overlap at the leadership level and considerable understanding between the leaders of each segment. This yielded a high degree of political stability during the immediate post-war period,[5] but by the end of the 1960s this clear structure began to disintegrate.[6]

In 1975 the Socialist (NVV) and Catholic (NKV) unions formed a federation and in 1979 the final decision was made to form a single organisation, Federatie Nederlandse Vakbeweging (FNV)[7] The member unions on NVV and NKV and later of FNV have had a high degree of autonomy, which is why it took so long to consolidate the new structure at branch level. The metal workers' union Industriebond NVV and NKV formed a federation in 1979 and the final merger into Industriebond FNV occurred in 1981. Up until then they were separately represented in the tripartite talks in shipbuilding, although they co-operated closely.

The Social and Economic Council, Sociaal-Economische Raad (SER), is an institution for tripartite co-operation in economic and social affairs. Fifteen members each are appointed by the employers, the unions and the government. The main task of the council is to make recommendations for economic and social policy. At the beginning of the 1970s union affiliated to NVV and the parties of the Left in parliament began to criticise the council sharply.[8]

The Social Economic Council and other institutional factors contributed to the development of the unions into highly centralised organisations, which were increasingly accused of neglecting the interests of their members.[9] This weakness was underlined when the Works Council Law of 1950 introduced the *ondernemingsraad* at the enterprise level. Initially they were only consultative committees, but following extensions of the law in 1971 and 1979, however, they are now very similar to the German *Betriebsräte*.

Important issues to be discussed in the following section will be the extent to which the general developments here were reflected, in shipbuilding and the influence they had on the contraction process in the industry.

THE ESTABLISHMENT OF A FRAGILE MONOPOLY

As for all other West European shipbuilding countries, the Japanese advance during the 1960s brought difficulties for the Dutch yards. In 1965 the *Commissie Nederlandse Scheepsbouw* was appointed under the chairmanship of M.G. Keyzer, former Undersecretary of State for the Ministry of Communications. The members of the commission were yard owners, shipowners, bankers and civil servants from different ministries. In the steering committee of the commission the socialist metal workers' union had one representative and it was obvious that the whole inquiry was regarded as a matter between the government and the industry; union participation was no more than a token gesture.[10]

The Keyzer commission set to work with urgency. Meetings were held several times a week and a number of reports were published. The final report came in 1966; it considered technical, economic and social questions and weighed 4 kg.[11]

The report was a masterpiece of social and economic architecture, a monument to an epoch when there was a strong belief that society's difficulties could be mastered by rational and determined action. The main conclusion of the report was that Dutch shipbuilding should convert to supertanker construction and accept the Japanese challenge. This conclusion had much in common with the proposals of the Federal German government and the Geddes Report in Britain at that time. It was suggested that the Dutch yards be given financial assistance in the form of low interest loans if they signed an undertaking to convert to tanker yards, with each yard specialising in a certain size of ship. To achieve this end the individual companies would be required to co-operate and finally merge.[12]

But these optimistic plans could not prevent what was to happen and Dutch shipbuilding faced the same uphill struggle as that of the other West European countries. The first serious set-back came at the end of the 1960s in Amsterdam. The NDSM yard there had to build hulls in two parts to be put together after launching. The restricted yard area, which could not be expanded, did not allow for more efficient continuous launching of the hull section by section. The process soon proved to be too expensive and NDSM was run down.

Cornelius Verolme became its temporary saviour. He was the self-made architect of a post-World War II shipbuilding empire. He was born in 1900, son of a farmer and merchant in the province of Zeeland. Having interrupted both his apprenticeship in the metal trade and his studies at an evening technical school, he entered the RDM yard as a draughtsman-designer at the age of 19. By the age of 24 he had risen to a management position and had taken a degree in civil engineering.

Cornelius Verolme started by building his first yard at the same time and in the same place as he built his first ship, letting the building of the one finance the building of the other. The speculative element of this strategy was obvious:

. . . in the beginning our production costs play a very small role indeed! During the first few years we produced as little as possible ourselves, but we did buy as much as possible, so that we needed few hours for actual production and we tried, in conjunction with effective purchasing, to sell our installations as expensively as possible . . . We achieved profits unheard of in the shipbuilding business.

This was during our growth period, to which I want to add, that even later, once we had our own shipyards, the number of man hours required for the construction of our ships was not of prime importance. The profits margins were so high that, despite the fact that our production costs were also probably too high, we made very impressive sums of money. If the course of the cost factors from our beginning until September 1970 were plotted graphically, it would be seen that only in the last period, that is during the last few years, has there been an increasing effort to make production costs as low as possible.[13]

Thus after 20 years Verolme had built up an empire, but it was to prove fragile, and by 1970 Verolme's sphere of influence had shrunk.

In 1967, the year when the Suez Canal was closed, Verolme asked for a government guarantee for the conversion and expansion of his yard in Rozenburg (Botlek) to supertanker construction. Such a conversion would be completely in accordance with the Keyzer report. But a few weeks later, RDM and de Schelde (which in 1966 had merged into a corporation called Rijn-Schelde), together with Wilton Fijenoord, came forward with the same demand. They all wanted to build a dock to repair supertankers on the Maasvlakte.

Verolme's competitors banded together. The mergers took place on a wave of amalgamation that characterised the late 1960s and was based on the generally held belief that size equals strength. Again reference could be made to similar developments in Germany and Great Britian at this time. However, in point of fact, Rijn-Schelde was only a loosely-organised, non-integrated federation of largely independent companies. There was little inclination towards that technical and commerical integration which was the guiding principle of, for example, the British Geddes Report.

To begin with, the government was prepared to respond favourably to Verolme's request, but when Rijn-Schelde and Wilton Fijenoord — united for the occasion into an *ad hoc* group — presented their vaguely defined plan for a competitive dock for the repair of very large tankers, it hesitated. Granting Verolme's request would disadvantage the group and distort competitiveness conditions. The government therefore insisted that Verolme and the other applicants for government money should elaborate a common plan. But this required a degree of co-operation which the fiercely individualistic shipbuilders were completely unable or unwilling to achieve. The matter dragged on for months, despite technical and financial advice favourable to the Verolme plan.[14]

The government was faced with a dilemma: its proposal to bring the yards together to co-operate on a common dock-plan had come to nothing; but turning down Verolme's request, on the grounds that the desired co-operation with the others was lacking, would harm the national interest. On the other hand, granting the request would be considered as giving privilege to Verolme — always a controversial figure and strikingly antagonistic to the establishment — and a setback to this competitors, for financing two dock plans was out of the question. The way out of these difficulties taken by the Minister of Economic Affairs was to give Verolme a Fl 75 m guarantee to finance his new dock if he agreed to take over the ailing NDSM and guarantee employment there. To acquire the NDSM shares and finance the merger, Verolme would get another government guarantee of Fl 30 m. Verolme jumped at the chance, took over NDSM and started the construction of his dock. This was in 1968 and the deal was considered a success.[15] However, it soon became clear that the operation had further weakened Verolme's already tight financial position. The fundamental problems were exacerbated rather than resolved by the merger. Within a year a bill for a series of errors and miscalculations was presented to the government.

The construction costs for the new dock had been substantially underestimated. The problems in constructing the giant oil carriers had not been fully foreseen and caused severe overspending and heavy losses, first at Amsterdam but very soon also at Verolme's own yard in Rozenburg (Botlek) close to Rotterdam. Having no financial reserves to cushion the setbacks, Verolme turned again to the government, asking for more credit. The government agreed but extracted its price.

Verolme obtained a government guarantee for a temporary Fl 25 m credit to tide him over but only after having ceded the legal ownership of his shares, having promised to seek government approval for all new shipbuilding contracts and having agreed to an independent analysis of his company. At first Verolme had fiercely resisted but finally he had to give in, and the government became deeply involved in Verolme's shipbuilding activities. However, the cash-flow situation of the company deteriorated and, at the age of 70, Cornelius Verolme had to step down from control of his empire.

After the intervention in Verolme the government faced a new dilemma. Even the partial nationalisation of Verolme was politically out of the question and, moreover, the government wanted to limit and if possible reduce its financial involvement. Bankrupting Verolme with the consequent loss of jobs in Amsterdam and Rotterdam was equally undesirable.

At this point Rijn-Schelde, who had been watching closely the deterioration of Verolme's cash-flow situation, dropped a hint that it was interested in taking over part of the Verolme company. Consequently, in January 1970, the government set up the Winsemius Commission, consisting of a number of experts from the ministries and from the industry. The unions had one representative, apparently fulfilling the same token role as in the commission of 1965.

The Winsemius Commission took 15 months to complete its task. Initially there was no basis for agreement. Rijn-Schelde was only prepared to take over the profitable sectors of the bankrupt Verolme and at minimum expense, leaving the major share of the financial burden to the government. However, the report of April 1971 proposed the establishment of one strong company formed out of the Rijn-Schelde companies and Verolme.[16] The new Minister of Economic Affairs, Roelof J Nelissen (*katholieke volkspartij*, KVP), adopted the report as his own. The mammoth RSV was created, emcompassing virtually the whole of the Dutch shipbuilding industry involved in large-scale ship construction.

When, nearly 15 years later, there was an inquiry into RSV, criticisms were made of the politics of the government which had assisted Rijn-Schelde in making Verolme merge:

> Cornelius Verolme fought the merger till the very end; he even went to court but lost. For Rijn-Schelde the deal was clearly profitable: it acquired the Verolme organisation and its future profits at a low price, with a clear two-to-one leading position in the new organisation, and it had forced a dangerous competitor into oblivion. All this was done with a good deal of prodding and encouragement from the Minister of Economic Affairs and his department, where distrust and ill-feeling towards Cornelius Verolme were scarcely hidden.[17]

From the outset, RSV faced the same problems as British Ship-builders did later. It started with a legacy of unsolved problems. It was an artificial creation, originating more from the desire of the government to disentangle itself from an embarrassing dilemma than from an objective evaluation of the benefits of two independent companies joining forces. The forced merger inherited a legacy of ill feeling and a strong inclination towards parochialism in the differents parts of the new company: it had no common sense of direction, no common philosophy or strategy. Verolme had been a strongly centralised organisation whereas Rijn-Schelde was a loosely structured group of largely independent companies. The new corporation was a hotchpotch of companies involved in ship-building, ship repair, naval yards, machine and engine works and light mechanical construction which competed hotly with each other and in which there was a great deal of overcapacity, obsoleteness and 'a number of "profit centres" persistently producing losses'.[18]

For the first few years, RSV's problems remained hidden behind the worldwide boom which prevailed up to 1975 but which for RSV reached its peak in 1973. Management made no effort to reduce excess capacity and reallocate personnel, but the high profits the company was earning were not conducive to integration or to the closing down of weak units.[19] In a newspaper interview the presi-dent of the supervisory board of RSV, De Vries, confirmed the fact that the company was not obliged to take its cash flow problems seriously: 'So long as the government did not explicitly tell us that it really was for the very last time, we of course went to them again to ask for subsidies.'[20]

THE START OF TRIPARTITE CO-OPERATION

Up to the mid-1970s there had been a tradition of union participation in shipbuilding policy but not the exercise of any real influence. In practice, shipbuilding politics only involved the government and employers.

By 1975 it was increasingly obvious that the shipbuilding crisis would be long lasting and that more drastic action was required and could be expected. Moreover, in view of the possible consequences of such steps the value of much more active union participation in the restructuring talks increased. As a result, in the Policy Commit-tee for shipbuilding, *Beleidskommissie Scheepsbouw* (BS), appointed in June 1976 by the Minister of Economics, Ruud

163

Lubbers, unions were given a more active role than in earlier inquiries. The setting up of the committee had also been produced by intensive consultations between the government, the employers and the unions concerning its terms of reference. These preliminary talks were reflected in the directives to the *Beleidskommissie*: it was given the responsibility of promoting a sound and self-supporting shipbuilding industry 'maintaining the best opportunity possible for labour.'[21]

The emphasis given to labour's interests was not just an empty gesture. The subsequent work in the committee would demonstrate that greater efforts were being made to get the unions more involved in the talks and decision-making. It is therefore, justifiable to speak of increased union influence from 1976 onwards, as the crisis deepened.

The Beleidskommissie delivered its first report in January 1977, six months after its formation. The report was a 'grand work of social engineering' as was the Keyzer report ten years earlier: the belief in the possibilities of steering the societal process seemed to have been unshakable. The commitee was unanimously of the opinion that a capacity level of 70 per cent of the level at the end of 1975 should be a provisional target. In order to arrive at the planned reduction, five shipbuilding regions were identified and within the regions shipyards were divided into three classes based on the size of the labour force.[22]

One, perhaps unintentional, effect of this 15-fold classification by region and size was that later the protest among the shipyard workers against job cuts was widely scattered. As will be demonstrated, there was never any common resistance. Decisions on the contraction process were taken at the centre as in Sweden but not with anything like the same degree of contact between the leaders and grass-roots of the trade unions.

Armed with the region and size grid and the resultant 15 boxes the commitee elaborated plans for a 70 per cent and 50 per cent reduction with mathematical precision. The committee never envisaged equal cuts for each yard (i.e. the use of the 'cheese-cutter principle'). On the contrary, it was unanimously agreed that there should be investment only in those firms which offered the best prospects, and that a number of yards would have to close. This view was close to that which could be heard in the German IG Metall during that short period of optimism before the full implications of such an approach became apparent: identify the dead wood and prune it out.

At this stage the committee's proposals could be represented as being logically based on hard facts. However, there was more than this to be considered when selecting the yards for development or closure. Before such decisions were made the committee recommended the formation of local groups of yards 'so that the social consequences may be the best in the circumstances'.[23]

Using purely numerical considerations, it was calculated that the required reduction of 30 per cent in capacity could be achieved by cuts of 37.5 per cent for large yards, 22.5 per cent for medium-sized yards and 20 per cent for small yards. These calculations were made by the *Beleidskommissie* and unanimously agreed upon in a spirit of confidence in the possibilities for social and economic engineering. The next step was the execution of these precise plans. This work the committee handed over to 'impartial discussion leaders' for the different groups. Under their supervision a reorganisation plan would be prepared for each yard grouping and submitted to the main committee within six months. The reconciliation of these different proposals was the responsibility of the *Beleidskommissie*.[24]

For practical reasons the 15 boxes were transformed into five groups and group 1 contained the large yards in the RSV group. However, whatever the grouping the effect was the same: different local interests were played off against each other and resistance to plans was diffused. The organisational framework created for the contraction process invited a struggle for survival under the unwritten law that somebody, however unwilling, had to get out of the boat.

In group 1, a reduction in employment from 9,200 to 5,300 in new construction seemed likely. However, neither of the yards selected for survival was profitable and keeping them alive waiting for better times called for the introduction of a special emergency package. The package would enable the yards to accept unprofitable orders and at the same time help them to balance their books. Whatever the price, the yard would be guaranteed government support for 75 per cent of the loss. The *Beleidskommissie* had first proposed 90 per cent, but the union representatives were apprehensive about the scheme because of the lack of any control over the use of the money, and 75 per cent made it easier for them to accept.

Compulsory redundancies would 'be prevented as much as possible by social measures'. When this was not feasible, 'a number of measures, to be defined later', would come into force, 'aiming at mitigating the consequences for the employees'. Large-scale compulsory redundancies would be avoided by spreading the reorganisation programme over a period of time. The planned social measures would include: training schemes for new jobs with the same employer, a reduction in the number of foreign workers 'not originating in the EEC countries' (*sic*), and the application of measures for the reduction of working hours.[25]

It was implicit in the report of January 1977 that all new construction of large tonnage would be stopped. This was a blow to the Verolme yard in Rozenburg. However, such a drastic step was too much for Parliament where all the local interests involved were represented. Instead of a closure, the Second Chamber decided to go on with offshore production in Rozenburg, an attempt which ended some years later in fiasco.[26]

Everybody agreed that shipbuilding capacity had to be pared down: but no one would agree where the paring should take place. When cuts in Rotterdam were blocked. Amsterdam was the logical alternative. The parliamentary debate on the report of the *Beleidskommissie* makes it clear that the basis of common interest in the committee was so fragile as to be almost non-existent. As far as implementing the shipbuilding scheme was concerned, as opposed to drawing it up, the committee had no basis for agreement. The role of social architect is one thing, but giving the necessary leadership to implement the blueprint in a society of conflicting interests when there can be few if any clear winners is quite another. The architects in the *Beleidskommissie* were soon to learn that not always are particular consequences the outcome of a deliberate intention to produce them. Their approach was grounded in the problem-solving techniques of the post-war era of economic growth: when all stood some chance of benefiting. But this was no longer possible in January 1977.

THE CHALLENGE FROM THE REGIONS

It soon was to become clear that union involvement in the steering of the contraction process was problematic. The room for manoeuvre between different local interests was small, and as early as November 1976 the representative of the NVV in the *Beleidskommissie*, Jaap Meynikman, who was influential within the national board of NVV in the sense that he always received full backing there for the steps he took in the *Beleidskommissie*,[27] had to defend his participation in the tripartite talks.

The unions' officials in charge of shipbuilding, together with representatives of the yards, formed a 'report-back' group (*achter-ban*) where Meynikman could get confirmation for the steps he took in the committee. When meeting this group, Meynikman had to assure them that it was a misunderstanding to think that the unions had bound themselves to approve in advance what might be decided in the *Beleidskommissie*: '. . . when the whole plan is ready, then we will test it in relation to our points of departure and decide if we will be able to participate.'[28]

Meynikman assured the group that the employers and government representatives were now convinced that there were two crucial purposes for union participation in the committee: the way subsidies were given (i.e. how to control the use of the money spent), and the social plan for the reduction. However, he was quite aware that the managements at the different yards had to agree with the employees how redundancies or plant closure were to be implemented. The need for such a reduction was not rejected by Meynikman. In the union 'report-back' group it was noted that the government and the employers together had to produce the money required for the retraining of those people made redundant and for any early retirement. At least Fl 60 m had to be put on the table before there could be any talk of a social plan.

In response to questions about the significance of a reduction to 70 per cent, Meynikman was remarkably cautious and only talked about a union readiness to be flexible when the plan was discussed. The chairman of the *achterban* group meeting concluded by thanking the representatives present for their co-operative behaviour throughout the proceedings, in spite of the fact that 'there had been several opportunities for being aggressive towards each other'. Clearly alerted to the potential divisiveness of the proposals, he emphasised the need for a united front in their relationship with the employers and the government.

At another meeting in December 1976 with union representatives in charge of shipbuilding questions, the question was raised whether nationalisation would not be a better solution than subsidies which could not be controlled. It was also emphasised that the prerequisite for participation in a restructuring operation would be a long-term contraction process with no compulsory redundancies.[29]

By the beginning of January 1977 Meynikman clearly realised that there were the conflicting interests in the union movement and among the participants in the *Beleidskommissie*. In the 'behind the scenes' discussions with union representatives he talked about a 'chaotic situation' in the tripartite talks over the plan.[30] His reports were in striking contrast to the impression that rational calculation lay behind the proposals which soon were to be presented to the public.

One week later Meynikman told the 'report-back' group that the unions had blocked the work of the shipbuilding committee for a fortnight during the talks about the social section of the plan.[31] He stressed that the union representatives on the committee were still insisting on no compulsory redundancies. And he tried to appease the group by saying that no decisions had been made on which yards to close. That would first have to be discussed by the discussion leaders of the five groups.

In March 1977 talks on the contraction of capacity in Amsterdam opened. A local movement emerged, with spokesmen for the city, the yards and the unions, which demanded guarantees for the continuance of new construction in Amsterdam. It was by then obvious that the central talks were about to be fragmented into different local protest movements, each with their own campaign goal.[32]

At a heated meeting in April 1977, Meynikman was attacked again.[33] Union participation in the talks on reduction was called into question and the goal of nationalisation of the whole shipbuilding industry as in Sweden and the UK was brought forward. It was the reduction plan in particular which caused uneasiness, but the subsidies were also criticised for not being satisfactorily controlled. A formal proposal was made for the unions to withdraw from the tripartite talks and it was also suggested that the unions should reject any plan resulting from these talks. The voting on the proposals was very close: 20 voted for the proposal to leave the *Beleidskommissie*, 25 voted against, and five abstained.

One of Meynikman's arguments when he defined continued participation was that a complete 'no' to the social plan would mean a social plan without any union influence. He also asked the meeting for the reasons for their sudden change of mind about a reduction of capacity. It was necessary to make decisions as soon as possible, and a go-slow policy could be dangerous: 'In the *Beleidskommissie* we could have an inquiry lasting five years. But then we would have no shipbuilding industry left.[34]

Meynikman thus highlighted the very nub of the whole problem. The unions were participating in what was, in a national context, a losing game without any possibilities of general gains, and the decision that had to be made would necessarily be criticised by those adversely affected. Meynikman's defence for participation in spite of this was quite logical: the alternative would be no influence at all. Integration in the decision-making process meant having some influence, though exactly how much depended on the strength of the unions' power base when compared with that of the government and the employers. It was therefore a matter of power relationships which, of course, could and did shift over time.

For the union representatives participation in the tripartite discussion was always a balancing act. They always risked being regarded as 'manipulated' by the grass-roots and those not sharing their view, and they always risked being accused of 'irresponsibility' by the other parties to the negotiations. Mobilisation of the grass-roots was their main, perhaps only, basis of power in the tripartite talks. Too little mobilisation would mean too little power in the tripartite talks; too much mobilisation risked the possibility of forced withdrawal from the talks, either as a result of reaction by the employers and/or government, or as a result of pressure from the rank and file in the unions. It was always a question of a fine balance between influence and disciplined mobilisation within the context of continuously changing circumstances.

Two major problems faced the unions: the elaboration of the social plan for the contraction of Dutch shipbuilding, and the internal criticism of the plans for yard closures. The social plan provided the way by which the cost of the run-down could be minimised for the unions as collective organisations. The acceptance of compensation for redundancy and early retirement individualised job loss and relieved the unions of making the choice of risking a confrontation from which little or nothing could be gained and in which all union influence could be lost. However, the closure of whole yards was a threat collectively experienced by whole sections of the union. The union leader responded to criticisms of their involvement in yard closures by saying that nothing had been decided and that they would make up their minds later when the whole plan was clear. But in order to exert any influence at all in the *Beleidskommissie*, it is quite obvious that they had to become involved in, and give credibility to, developments there. The alternative would be to leave the talks. Such a consideration adds new significance to the debate about the nature of tripartite *co-operation*:tripartite bargaining is no doubt a better term.

Capacity had to be reduced: everyone agreed on that. If not in Rotterdam, then in Amsterdam. In the spring of 1977 the preliminaries to such a step began. The former Minister of Economics, Roelof J. Nelissen, who had become a member of the supervisory board of the large AMRO Bank after his departure from the government, was commissioned to investigate different possibilities, all of which carried the assumption that Amsterdam would be a centre for repair work in which ADM was generally regarded to be the pivot. One of the problems for Nelissen was that ADM and RSV disagreed on the question of who should own the reconstructed yard. A much greater stumbling-block was that the local metal workers' union refused to consider any proposals which restricted new construction in the city.[35] Support for this position came from an internal and confidential RSV memorandum demonstrating that the productivity of NDSM was higher than at the other new construction yards of the group.[36]

In Amsterdam the Communists tried to articulate the unrest that the uncertainty about the future had created. The unions were accused of disregarding the interests of the workers and demands were made that they should leave the tripartite talks. The NVV-NKV union defended their participation, which, they argued, had not been without benefits for the membership:

> The fact is that Dutch shipbuilding for the last year and a half has been on the brink of an abyss. Japan takes our orders at a price that is almost 50 per cent under our costs. Therefore the *Beleidskommissie Scheepsbouw* has drawn up a plan . . . which the government has adopted. The government declared itself prepared to place Fl 250 m per year for a period of four years at the disposal of the yards in order to cover loss-making orders, and Fl 1 bn in order to restore the yards. This is a decision which is taken in the interest of the employees. Thanks to the billion subsidy, the Netherlands for the time being have been able to take more orders than their foreign competitors. In 1976 there were in all 104,800 grt in new orders at Dutch shipyards. In the first half of 1977 there was already more than double that, 218,500 grt. There are probably more orders in prospect, which will give Dutch shipbuilding time to recover, with the safeguarding of as many jobs as possible.[37]

However, this did little to quell the opposition to the unions' participation in the tripartite talks. Local action groups were formed and in a letter to the unions they rejected the whole contraction plan and demanded that union participation in the *Beleidskommissie* should stop. Instead of a contraction programme the government should force the shipowners to place their orders in the Netherlands, force the yard owners to invest in their yards, and forbid investments and sale of technical know-how abroad. This protectionist message echoed that of the French CGT.[38]

Of course, the suggested alternatives were politically and economically unrealistic, but nevertheless were an important indication of the growing pressure on the union leadership. It is also difficult to know how widespread such views were among shipyard workers; but even if they were not generally held, they did represent a latent threat or even a challenge to the union leaders which they could not ignore. It was vital for the union to bridge the gap between the views of this vocal element and those prevailing in the committee, but this meant giving an impression of reconciling views which were in fact incompatible. One such attempt has been the call for 'Restructuring, yes! Loss of jobs, no!' (and not only in the Netherlands). But the contradiction in this demand results less from defective reasoning than from conflicting social interests.

The discussion amongst the union leaders was more complex. They recognised that the industry had too much capacity, given the international development in shipbuilding, and therefore did not reject the contraction and restructuring out of hand, although the form it should take was disputed. And, moreover, there was a visible and growing division between the union leaders in Rotterdam and Amsterdam. The Amsterdam leaders argued that investment in offshore production in Rotterdam did not have to mean the closure of new construction in Amsterdam.[39]

PROBLEMATIC TRIPARTITE BARGAINING

At the same time as local pressures increased, work in the *Beleidskommissie* left the world of 'rational planning' with imaginary numbers and came down to the reality of the social plans. A special sub-committee for social problems began working in September 1977. At its first working session it was stated that the committee was necessary because of the increasing unrest among the employees.[40]

At the first meeting it was reiterated that the goal remained the safeguarding of as many jobs as possible, although this intention was left sufficiently vague for it to be acceptable to the different interests. When it came to giving it substance, the foreign workers as a group were among the first to be considered.[41] The discussions about the foreign workers, although in this case their numbers were

171

small, are a good illustration of a general pattern in the social plans used in Western Europe to facilitate the contraction of shipbuilding: the interests represented have generally been those of the economically and politically strong rather than reflecting overall solidarity.

The minutes of the sub-committee for social questions clearly demonstrate that it was much more difficult to come to an agreement about concrete measures. Therefore work proceeded much more slowly than it had done in the *Beleidskommissie* where, particularly at the outset, it had been mainly a question of agreeing principles.[42]

In November 1977 NVV and NKV held a joint meeting of top union officials at which they debated their continued participation in the shipbuilding committee. Votes were taken on two proposals to leave the tripartite discussions. These were brought forward by the unions at Gusto in Schiedam and de Schelde in Vlissingen. They were both rejected, by 48 to 13 (with 8 abstentions) and by 54 to 8 (with 7 abstentions), respectively.[43] Although the overwhelming majority was for remaining in the talks, it is worth noting that those in favour of withdrawing and the 'don't knows' had gained ground even in the higher echelons of the metal workers' union.

After the meeting in November votes were taken among the shop stewards at the different yards. The figures from these votes reveal interesting differences between the local and the central level, and locally between Rotterdam and the other yards. The total figure for all the 17 yards involved was 211 for, and 185 against the proposal to leave the tripartite negotiations, with 9 abstentions: a 52 per cent majority for breaking away from the talks in the *Beleidskommissie*. In Amsterdam the figures were 26 for, and 17 against the proposal (with 2 abstentions), i.e. a 59 per cent majority in favour of withdrawal. In striking contrast to this outcome was the result in Rotterdam, where more than 77 per cent of the local officials were *against* the unions abandoning the shipbuilding committee.[44]

In spite of the clear majority among top union officials and in Rotterdam for remaining in the tripartite committee, it is obvious by the end of 1977 that union participation there was hanging by a very slender thread. The resistance was of such a magnitude that it could not be ignored. The division of the yard into separate groups had had a splintering and divisive effect, with the threatened yards opposed to the policy, whilst those with more optimistic expectations were in support; in particular, Amsterdam stood against Rotterdam. Thus the split did not result in paralysis at the yards, but in demands for action and pressure on the leadership.

The direct provocation to increased resistance during the autumn of 1977 was the report of group 1 which was completed in November. Here it was proposed that Amsterdam alone should have repair facilities. It was proposed that ADM and the repairing division of NDSM be reorganised into a new repair yard with a total labour force of 1,850 people. ADM and the state would participate, and management would be carried out by ADM but the new company would be situated at the old NDSM yard.

At a meeting with the *Beleidskommissie* at the end of January 1978, the NVV representative, David Rijkse, who had succeeded Meynikman as the shipbuilding spokesman for the union, stated that no answer from the unions could be given yet concerning the group 1 report. The report was said to contain too many unanswered questions.[45]

Earlier Rijkse had been under pressure from the grass-roots; at the meeting, he came under pressure from the government and industry representatives. Karel Fibbe, who was to take over the chairmanship of the *Beleidskommissie* from J.A. Bakker, and therefore participated in the meeting, argued that it was impossible to escape yard closures and sackings: this should be the basis for any discussion. Any attempt to escape this reality would in the long run prove to be in vain. In an attempt to keep the unions in the committee (the increasing unrest at the yards making their presence there of still greater importance) a small group was formed in order to try to find a new formulation.[46] However, it was soon to become clear that the problem was not a linguistic one. At the meeting with the shipbuilding committee, Rijkse declared that he could not accept the changes the sub-committee had made. In other words, the changes were too small to satisfy him.[47]

At a meeting with the shipbuilding committee three days later, on 20 February, it was stated that the committee was not prepared to wait for the outcome of extensive union consultation. The work of the tripartite committees had come to a standstill as it could no longer serve as a forum for conflicting interests. At the outset a common formula had been agreed — restructuring and contraction with the loss of as few jobs as possible — but this was accepted because it meant different things to different groups. The report of group 1 spelled out the reality which the unions found unacceptable. The unions' last resource was to try to mobilise the political system for a final and decisive parliamentary debate. At the meeting with the *Beleidskommissie*, Rijkse made it quite clear that if the Minister of Economics adopted the plan of group 1 the unions would not be in a position to participate in the execution of the plan.[48]

THE GOVERNMENT AND THE 'NORTH-SOUTH CONCEPT'

One month later, on 21 March, the Liberal (VVD) Minister of Economics, Gijs MV van Aardenne, presented a bill to the second chamber of the General States. He confirmed the power relationships in the *Beleidskommissie* and argued accordingly that two new construction yards in the RSV concern would be one too many. Given this starting point, it was inevitable that the so-called 'north-south concept' ('*Noord-Zuidgedachte*', i.e. Amsterdam–Rotterdam) should be discussed. One yard, either in Rotterdam or in Amsterdam, had to be closed. Faced with this choice, van Aardenne took the view of the majority in the shipbuilding committee, and he proposed that parliament close NDSM.[49]

Here it is of some interest to note that this tough approach of the Dutch government was contemporaneous with Åsling's preparations as Minister of Industry for the closure of Arendal and Öresunds-varvet in Sweden (p. 87). The desire to cut non-profitable capacity drastically was the same in the two governments, and the unions were similarly opposed. The difference was that the Swedish unions were not so divided by local interests.

The shipyard workers in Amsterdam stood against their colleagues in Rotterdam and for both sections of the union it was a matter of the life or death of their own yard. At the central level the unions could do little. The split in the union movement was a logical continuation of the tripartite planning procedures which set region against region and yard against yard. This consequence was, so to speak, in-built from the outset of the Beleidskommissie.

The government's decision to close NDSM meant (according to its own figures) that in all some 3,000 jobs would disappear. A total of 1,000 of them could be retained in the new repair company under ADM. It was judged that of the remaining 2,000 half would disappear by natural wastage, and 1,000 people faced compulsory redundancy.

NVV-NKV did not accept the closure of NDSM but they could not withdraw and stand by and watch the execution of the plan. So, while they rejected the decision they directed their energies towards getting as favourable conditions as possible. Rijkse argued that there were more urgent things to do than to bring things to a standstill with an inflexible 'no'. In a meeting with the senior management of RSV he said: 'It makes little or no sense to pay attention now to the basic premises of the *Beleidskommissie*. We are now aiming at direct talks with RSV and not with the *Beleidskommissie*.'[50]

Rijkse demanded that the closure should be phased over three years, no compulsory redundancies, the discussion of a shorter working day, early retirement and maintenance of new construction in some form in Amsterdam. Of these demands, that for no compulsory redundancies was central. Not unexpectedly, the RSV management would not make such a promise unreservedly, since they were not prepared to meet the costs involved.

In a letter to the Social Minister the unions repeated their claims. The government answered by inviting them to a meeting with the Social Minister and the Minister of Economics. The government declared that its goal was a tripartite agreement but would not accept the unions' demand for no compulsory redundancies: 'as few as possible' was the counter-bid. The Minister of Economics, van Aardenne, answered Rijkse that the closure of NDSM could be reconsidered, although the crucial question was still whether orders could be obtained.[51]

It is obvious that it was in the government's interest to keep the unions involved in the discussions. There was rapidly increasing grass-roots pressure in Amsterdam and it was vital for the government to keep this under control. The unions for their part had obvious reasons for remaining in the talks and so the tripartite talks continued, but were transferred to a new forum.

Even though there was total disagreement on the group 1 plan, Rijkse considered it important not to break away, although there was considerable pressure throughout those days in March 1978 for the union to do so. Rijkse defended his point of view to the four other groups of shipyards in the *Beleidskommissie's* inquiry: 'If we break away from the *Beleidskommissie* there will be no more talk about restructuring, but a final closure, concern by concern.'[52]

For Rijkse the issue remained the same as for the union leadership: compromise and exert some influence, or conflict with the obvious risk of no influence at all. This risk must have been considered the more serious as the union movement was split.[53]

THE OCCUPATION OF THE NSDM YARD

In Amsterdam the action committee intensified its efforts from 20 March onwards. An occupation had already been considered sometime earlier, but now there was a long discussion as to whether or not an occupation should start immediately. Finally it was decided to occupy the yard the next morning.

One of the moving forces in the local branch of NVV was Henk Vos. His personal notes from the preparatory meetings on 18–20 March, and the minutes and memoranda from these meetings, revealed that the plan for the occupation was prepared in detail. Henk Vos, 35 years old, was district officer in Amsterdam of the Industriebond NVV and since 1971 had been in charge of the ship-building, aircraft and car industry. On 20 March he and the unions in Amsterdam learned of the content of van Aardenne's bill to Parliament. In the evening the union leaders decided to hold a meeting of all the employees of NDSM the following day. They realised that they could not rely on support from Rotterdam and that the situation was embarrassing for the union. Vos informed the national board that action had to be taken in Amsterdam and he got the go-ahead.

On the morning of 21 March Henk Vos spoke to the 3,000 employees who had been called together by their union leaders. The rally was much more an organised demonstration than a spontaneous outburst from the grass-roots:

> Our only possibility was to exert political pressure. Mobilisation of the members and maximum publicity were our weapons. How to use the weapons was a question of leadership. Our dilemma was Stikker's north-south concept. He meant that shipbuilding in both the north, i.e. Amsterdam, and the south, i.e. Rotterdam, was impossible. He argued that a choice was necessary. Indirectly and by implication he told the employees in Rotterdam that if they expressed their solidarity with the employees in Amsterdam in a fight for the preservation of the yards in both places their chances of survival would decrease. It was an impossible situation for the union. Stikker was both president of RSV and discussion leader of group 1 which was practically identical with RSV. It meant that he was given government legitimacy and quite another plat-form for action than if he had acted only as a president of the concern. This made our position even more difficult.[54]

Henk Vos and the shop stewards at the yard, Ben van Horsen (NKV) and Klaas Weldman (NVV), elaborated the plan of campaign which left little room for spontaneous outbursts. Even the speech to the management was prepared word for word and put into the text of the 'synopsis' which was then elaborated: 'Seize the management of NDSU and ask them if they will participate loyally. If yes then stay! If no then go!'[55]

The action was much more spectacular as a plan than in its execution. After a week it was no longer possible to maintain the momentum at its original intensity and it began to peter out. The 'occupation' had more the character of a series of token strikes, although there was a massive demonstration in Utrecht on 23 March, attended by workers from other yards. But the ambitious planning in Amsterdam could not conceal that, when it came down to it, the shipyard workers in Amsterdam were alone and could not reckon on support from other yards. The militancy soon subsided, though it did not altogether disappear at NDSM. Politically, the protests in Amsterdam were embarrassing and no politician could afford to neglect them.

Rijkse continued his talks with the management of RSV, at the joint meeting with the Minister of Economics and the Social Minister, discussed above. He argued that the reduction in capacity was too great and unfairly distributed.[56] Not unexpectedly, the RSV directors did not agree. The whole question had long since left the realm of industrial relations and was now a very important political question and awaited a political solution. Until then RSV was not prepared to move.

The parliamentary debate over the final decision took place in September 1978. In Amsterdam the fighting spirit was rekindled and the local branch and the shop stewards drew up plans for a new occupation, if anything as detailed as those in March. They included particulars of communications, guard duty, logistics, staff duty, etc., and a time-table detailing which shop stewards and local branch functionaries were to be commanders-in-chief during the first week. It would be misleading, however, to argue that the protest and the organisation behind it was entirely manipulated from above. There was obvious grass-roots dissatisfaction without which nothing could have been done. The purpose of the occupation was clear:

> . . . the action serves — after the negative decisions by the Minister of Economics and the Social Minister (in March 1978) to exert maximum pressure from the public on the members of the second chamber (of the General States).[57]

The trouble in Amsterdam could not be, therefore, completely neglected by the government, which had an obvious interest in not having the union isolated and paralysed, and so some gesture had to be made. The concession which finally broke the deadlock was to allow new construction to be undertaken in Amsterdam, in a small section of the repair yard with 400 employees. If demand improved, the section would be allowed to expand. On strict economic grounds this step could not be justified, but the argument in its favour could be made in terms of the need to maintain skill and know-how for new construction in Amsterdam. The government promised money for three years.[58]

The immediate effect was that opposition in Amsterdam rapidly disappeared. The money gave new hope to the shipyard workers, or, rather, to 400 of them. That counted for more than the doubts of the more thoughtful.

This final solution left little ground for collective action. It was a typical social plan of the kind so often put into effect in West European shipbuilding countries, a plan that transformed the collective to an individual threat (compare this with the events in Bremen 1982 (p. 47)). In practice, the reorganised NDSM — renamed NSM — with only 450 people left, was doomed as a yard for new construction, an outcome the fight had tried to prevent. The difference between before and after September 1978 was that the social plan quenched the collective protest by directing the threat of unemployment at certain groups, further reducing union opposition made weak by the antagonism between Amsterdam and Rotterdam.

The social plan meant that out of 3,000 employees only 50 were sacked or made redundant: 900 of the age of 57 and over were given early retirement; 950 were transferred to the new repair yard, ADM; 600 were retrained for other jobs; and 450 continued in employment in new construction financed by the government's Fl 40 m concession. The new repair yard of ADM doubled its workforce to 1,850. Three and a half years later, there was no longer any new construction at NSM and the 1,850 workforce had declined to some 1,200.[59]

The protests in Amsterdam in 1978 were the only ones of note throughout the contraction process in Dutch shipbuilding. Thereafter the run-down went through with little dispute. As in Germany after 1983 the potential for protest shrank with the production capacity of the yards.

THE FINAL FALL OF THE GIANT

By 1980 the position of RSV had further deteriorated and its management announced that the group could not survive any further delay in government assistance. Parliament then urged the government to keep the large shipbuilding and offshore sector alive and its workers employed, and to allocate more resources for this purpose. The RSV inquiry committee reviewed the development leading to the 1980 crisis:

> The Minister of Economic Affairs then lost control over the financial consequences of his involvement in the shipbuilding industry: on 1st June 1979 he promised to reimburse RSV for all losses incurred in the large shipbuilding and offshore sections, retrospectively as from 1st January 1979 (despite the fact that he knew that RSV itself had no control over these losses). His commitment was open-ended. Two weeks later the cabinet decided to separate the large shipbuilding and offshore sections from RSV and to reconstitute them in a new 'Rotterdam Offshore and Shipbuilding Combination' (ROS) for which Fl 250 m would be made available — an amount that was insufficient from the outset. More than eight months were spent on efforts to get the ROS started, but in March 1980 the government had to acknowledge defeat: the ROS could cost at least Fl 100 m more. Despite widespread dismay, the Minister then decided to put an end to the building of large ships and construction. He asked RSV to terminate these activities after completion of existing orders . . . for Fl 280 m.[60]

However, RSV, who had been given a promise of unlimited compensation the previous year, refused to do this unless the government would cover a sizeable part of any losses in excess of Fl 280 m. The minister gave in and entered into a secret agreement to that effect. He told Parliament, however, that closing the large shipbuilding and offshore sections would cost him not more than Fl 280 m.[61]

The unlimited undertaking by van Aardenne in June 1979 meant that RSV was relieved of the crippling burden of shipbuilding losses incurred in the past. It could, or so it was thought, concentrate on more promising activities. However, within a year the group was again in deep trouble and despite van Aardenne's previous decision that government financial support to RSV had to come to an end, the Minister of Defence, in 1981–2, took over the responsibility to 'provide RSV with ample cash'.[62] In the autumn of 1982 the Department of Economic Affairs once more considered a cash support for RSV 'on strict conditions', but this time they were overruled by other government departments, particularly Finance, which had been sceptical about the effectiveness of subsidies for years.[63]

RSV had played the game too long and the cycle of financial rescue operations was now broken. After spending more than Fl 2.2 bn in unsecured loans and direct subsidies to RSV, the government considered it was time to withdraw. In this it was backed by public opinion. There was no talk of local protests of the scale of those in Amsterdam in 1978. By a simple court decision in February 1983, RSV became bankrupt.

RSV was dissolved but the main subsidiaries were rescued in what proved a costly operation in two ways. Restructuring involved the laying-off of thousands of workers within the framework of a social plan, total employment falling from 17,000 to 12,000. To finance the surviving sectors of RSV the government relied on naval construction. So in addition to paying for the restructuring process it also made advance payments on naval contracts for a second time (Fl 500 m) and brought forward new contracts for keep the warship yards employed.[64]

FNV LEAVES THE TRIPARTITE TALKS — AND TRIES TO COME BACK

By 1983 FNV had left the tripartite talks. After 1978 the winding-up of the large yards was dictated by market forces, and little was done to prevent it. However, there was increasing criticism within the union, not from the membership, but from the union leaders. In May 1981 FNV disagreed with the government's representatives in the *Beleidskommissie* about the support for social plans in shipbuilding. Supported by the employer representatives, the union wanted the money to continue for this purpose, whereas the government argued that earlier guarantees had already been honoured.[65]

The continuing internal criticism and the lack of alternative proposals made it increasingly difficult for FNV to remain in the shipbuilding committee, merely to preside over the demise of shipbuilding. In 1981 they left the tripartite talks.[66]

There are obvious parallels between FNV's actions and those of IG Metall, which left the tripartite talks in Germany in April 1983 (p. 33). In subsequent events the parallels continued. Neither of them wanted to remain permanently isolated without any possibility of exerting further influence. Both experienced difficulty in re-entering the discussions in a situation where the protest potential amongst shipbuilding workers had largely disappeared, with the consequence that the perceived need for union participation had also decreased.

In February 1984 Rijkse tried to establish a joint front with the industry in order to get the government to spend more. In a letter to CEBOSINE he demanded its support in demands for emergency measures to be taken by the government. However, by then CEBOSINE had taken the same position as the German VDS. In reply to Rijkse, the shipbuilding industry certainly expressed similar apprehensions about the future, but it also argued that the market ultimately had to decide on the future of the industry. CEBOSINE could only promise to 'consider' Rijkse's proposal, while awaiting some move by the government.

Rijkse could do nothing. In April he sent a new letter to CEBOSINE. He was still 'worried about the future', but an additional reason for this was 'a complete lack of initiative from the industry itself'. This the FNV 'interpreted as a complete surrender to those who make decisions', i.e. the government, and Rijkse added that he was 'disappointed in the reaction of CEBOSINE' to his letter in February.[67]

The industry remained indifferent. Rijkse turned to the government. He wanted to participate again in shipbuilding decision-making and made no reservations.[68] However, now the large yards had been liquidated, there was no longer the same need for union participation. The pre-conditions for re-establishing new tripartite discussions such as existed in 1976 were no longer in evidence. The main trial of strength had been over the plan for the yards in group 1. Then there had been an obvious need for union participation to contain worker unrest. The yards from which that protest could be mobilised no longer existed.

THE NETHERLANDS: CONCLUDING REMARKS

The attempts to restore Dutch shipbuilding started with the establishment of a system of tripartite co-operation in which the problems were treated with almost mathematical logic. The yards were divided into 15 boxes, later five groups. The tripartite shipbuilding committee agreed in 1976 that shipbuilding capacity should be reduced to 70 per cent of its 1975 level. Only yards with real prospects of regaining profitability would be supported and closures were considered unavoidable. The unions had just two reservations: the number of sackings had to be 'as small as possible' and it was important to develop controls over the use of the subsidies. The role of the government, employers and unions appeared to be that of providing specialised technical expertise rather than that of representing particular interests.

The division of the yards into different groups meant that all protests against the contraction scheme were kept separate and fragmented. Different localities were played against each other in a fight for survival where everybody knew that somebody had to lose. Eventually the position of the unions in the tripartite talks required their full participation in the contraction process. This policy was increasingly challenged from below, not so much from the grass-roots, which were split between different yards, but from union officials. Increased pressure from these officials on the top leadership resulted in the abandonment of the tripartite talks in 1981.

However, remaining outside the decision-making process on a permanent basis had its own disadvantages, and in 1984 efforts were made by the metal workers' union to re-establish tripartite talks. The proposal was treated indifferently by both the industry and the government and had no success: there was little threat of protest from the shipbuilding workforce and therefore little need for union participation. Developments in the Netherlands resemble those in West Germany, in the sense that the metal workers' union in that country was also pushed from below to abandon the tripartite talks. IG Metall also found it difficult to re-establish the talks, although in Germany the unions could appeal to both the local *and* the federal government. The central decision-making process in the Netherlands was similar to that in Sweden. There, however, the local union officials were much more directly integrated in central decision-making and although tensions between the different districts existed, they proved less divisive than in the Netherlands.

Denmark: Tripartite Talks but Divided Interests

In Denmark shipbuilding is vertically integrated with shipownership to a greater extent than in the other countries surveyed. The main exception is the largest yard, Burmeister & Wain.

In the middle of the 1970s there were six large yards: Burmeister & Wain in Copenhagen, Helsingör Vaerft (Vaerft = shipyard) in Elsinore some 25 miles north of the capital, Nakskov Vaerft in Nakskov on the mainly agricultural Lolland, the southernmost of the Danish islands, Lindö Vaerft in Odense on the island of Fyn, 85 miles west of Copenhagen, and Aalborg Vaerft and Frederikshavn Vaerft on the north-east coast of the Jutland peninsula, some 150 miles north-west of Copenhagen.

From 1971 to 1976 the share of shipbuilding in total industrial employment varied between 5 and 6 per cent. Thus, in terms of jobs, shipbuilding in Denmark was as important as in the Netherlands, and more important than in the other West European countries, where shipbuilding employed only 1–2 per cent of the industrial workforce.[1]

Danish shipyards had a varied and diversified product mix. The only yard which concentrated on tanker construction was Lindö in Odense, owned by the AP Möller group (a conglomerate of interests in a number of industries from oil to shipowning and shipbuilding, and in merchant shipping). The Lindö yard was built outside Odense on a greenfield site in 1959 in response to the increasing demand for larger tankers. AP Möller is much more of a merchant than an industrial concern and the same description would apply to *Östasiatiske Kompagnie* (ÖK) which owns Nakskov Vaerft in Lolland (they decided in 1986 to close down in 1987).

Aalborg, Helsingör (closed down in 1984) and Frederikshavn Vaerft belonged to the Lauritzen concern, a shipowning group, the

Table 7.1: Employment in Danish shipbuilding, 1975–1984

	1975	1980	1984
Burmeister & Wain	3,600	1,600	1,500
Lindö Vaerft (incl. the Odense yard)	5,900	2,600	3,400
Helsingör Vaerft	2,900	1,400	closed
Nakskov Vaerft	2,200	1,100	900
Frederikshavns Vaerft	1,050	900	1,200
Aalborg Vaerft	3,000	3,000	3,000

flagship of which was for many years *Det Forenede Damp-skibsselskab* (DFDS), which concentrated on passenger traffic.

Denmark has few natural resources and has traditionally depended on merchant capitalism rather than production. Consequently, there are very few really large employers. The concentration on trade is reflected in the strong position of the Danish shipowners. This is also explained by the geography of Denmark. Sea transport is important for holding together the peninsula of Jutland, the six major islands and the numerous smaller islands of which this country consists. Therefore there has been a steady domestic demand for different kinds of passenger ships. Government orders for passenger ferries and train ferries for Danish Rail has been important for the yards in Nakskov, Elsinore and Ålborg. The Aalborg Vaerft yard has also attempted to enter the market for the larger and more luxurious passenger cruisers.[2]

As in other West European countries the Danish shipyards have been of major economic importance in the towns and regions where they have been situated. In Nakskov the yard employed half the employed population, in Frederikshavn this proportion was one third, and in Ålborg and Odense 10–15 per cent.[3]

Before the industry's decline after 1975, Danish shipbuilding employed almost as many people as Swedish shipbuilding, despite a much lower level of output reflecting differences in the product mixes. In the middle of the 1960s Danish shipbuilding employed 25,000 people. Of these, 18,000 were employed by the six large yards of which 15,000 blue collar workers accounted for 12 per cent of the workers in the metal work industries. By 1984 employment in the large yards had fallen to 10,500.

In the middle of the 1960s the largest yard was Burmeister & Wain which employed up to 9,000 workers. The second largest was Lindö employing as many as 4,000, and four other yards had between 2,000 and 3,000 employees. By 1975 employment in Burmeister & Wain had fallen but from the mid-1970s shipbuilding began to contract sharply. The employment effect of this rundown on the different yards is shown in Table 7.1.

TRIPARTITE CO-OPERATION, PRODUCTIVITY AND UNION ORGANISATION

In March 1964 a permanent tripartite shipbuilding committee (Handelsministeriets *kontaktudvalg*) was appointed under the auspices of the Ministry of Trade. This included senior civil servants of the ministry, two representatives of the Federation of the Shipbuilding Industry (*Skibsvaerftsforeningen*), and two representatives of the metal workers' union (CO Metal and *Metalarbejderforbundet*) and was established in response to the general problems in Western Europe resulting from Japanese competition. This committee emphasised the need to increase productivity, and recommended talks at the yards between managements and the unions about how to achieve such a goal.[5]

In the Autumn of 1964 *kontaktudvalget* delivered its first report which included a number of proposals to the government and to the yard managements and employees. These included the recommendation that the structure of union organisation should be adapted to the organisation of production.[6]

The organisation of the Danish unions is similar to that in Britain. Industrialisation in Denmark was gradual and industry retained its links with the old crafts. The process was slower and the enterprises smaller than in neighbouring countries. The natural consequence was unionisation by craft rather than industry. A step towards an industrial organisation was taken when the engineering and metal workers' umbrella organisation, *Centralorganisationen af Metalarbejdere* (CO Metal), was established in 1912. By 1980 it had 13 affiliates, ten of which were small traditional old craft unions, each with only a few thousand members. The two largest affiliates together had 180,000 of the 215,000 members. CO Metal had built up its administrative resources and was a centralised organisation rather than a loose confederation. It could participate in the tripartite talks with much greater authority than the Confederation of Engineering and Shipbuilding Unions (Confed) in Britain.

CO Metal acquired its authority from *Metalarbejderforbundet* which with 110,000 members in 1980 was by far the largest affiliate and dominated CO Metal. The power relations within CO Metal was reflected in its representatives to the *kontaktudvalget*. Georg Poulsen was the chairman of *Metalarbejderforbundet*. He was politically the more important and regarded as the 'big brother' of the two representatives, whereas Charles Hansen, the vice chairman of CO Metal, was the shipbuilding expert and the one with the knowledge of detail and technical competence.

However, at the local level much friction remained between different crafts. The rivalry was especially keen between the skilled and the semi- and unskilled workers. Before 1978 only skilled workers' unions were admitted to CO Metal. The joint organisation at shop floor level was the *faellesklubben*, the board of which corresponds to the Shop Stewards executive committee in Britain. The chairman of *faellesklubben* is called *faellestillidsmanden* (*tillidsmand* = shop steward). At the end of the 1970s amalgamations took place within the union organisation. For example, the number of unions affiliated to CO Metal in 1979 at Burmeister & Wain declined from 16 to 9. Demarcation disputes were never as frequent as in Great Britain, but the employers' strike records reveal that they were far from unknown.[7] They caused enough problems to be singled out by the tripartite shipbuilding committee:

> The way in which the workers at the yard are unionised is often quite contrary to the organisation of production. This is a direct invitation to petty squabbles in production planning. Moreover, the frequent division into unions with the attendant system of numerous shop stewards create a large and time-consuming negotiation machinery.[8]

For this reason, the committee unanimously concluded that the shipyard workers should adapt their organisational structure to the structure of the organisation of production, and required the unions to be more flexible and to work actively to break down demarcations between different crafts. This would allow a more flexible use of the workforce and increase productivity. The way the committee with its government-endorsed legitimacy argued is reminiscent of the Geddes committee in Britain which had reported 18 months previously. The advice to the unions in Denmark were even stronger than in Britain. *Kontaktudvalget* authoritatively stated:

> The committee has noted that there still exist demarcation practices everywhere at the yards. Considering the development in

production technology, they are no longer based on facts, and they decrease production and increase costs. With due observance of remaining collective agreements, all obstructing demarcation practices now have to be abolished.[9]

More appropriate wage systems were also demanded, with a readiness to adopt non-traditional solutions. As a compensation for concessions, the unions could reckon upon more information from the managements at the yards.

The committee also discussed the possibility of increasing productivity by means of mergers. But it found that the Danish yards were already highly specialised, so that concentration similar to that proposed by Geddes in Britain offered few advantages. Moreover, the committee, on principle, rejected direct government subsidies as a means of improving competitiveness, but proposed an interest reduction from 6 to 5.5 per cent on ship credit which corresponded to almost 2 per cent of building costs.[10]

In 1967 the Ministry of Finance elaborated favourable tax rules for investment in docks with a capacity of more than 100,000 grt. This coincided with the decision at the Lindö yard to expand its dock capacity to construct ships over 100,000 grt, although it is not clear whether this resulted from the tax concession or improved market prospects. Thus at this time the modernisation plans for increased productivity were the same in Denmark as elsewhere and, as elsewhere, their long-term effect was to increase the difficulties rather than to bring profitability. The difference was that in Denmark only a few yards (in particular Lindö) expanded capacity to produce very large tankers, a development which later proved to be a dead end.

THE DELEGATION OF RESPONSIBILITY

During the boom period of the early 1970s the problems were put on one side rather than forgotten. In its early deliberations the tripartite committee had recognised the need to reduce capacity. The committee argued as early as September 1975 that employment in new construction could not be maintained, even though there was some prospect of new construction activity.[11] Furthermore it saw that if operations were to be slimmed down, negotiations at the yards were important.[12]

There are some interesting differences between this approach and

187

that in the Netherlands. In the Netherlands the institutionalised tripartite talks were handled at top level in an atmosphere of social engineering. In Denmark there was much less detailed central planning and the responsibility for the final decisions was thrust on to the local yards and bipartite talks there, not least as a consequence of the strength of the local branches within CO Metal making detailed central regulation difficult. This downward delegation of responsibility meant a development similar to that in Britain, with yards lining up against yards in a fight for survival. As will be demonstrated below, the pressure from the grass-roots on the participants in the tripartite talks was divided, giving the metal workers' representative room for manoeuvre in the talks. And, as the Danish yards were more widely spaced geographically than those in the Netherlands and Germany, the protests were also more dispersed.

Another difference is that during the contraction process the Danish unions in their economics were much more market orientated, in a way reminiscent of the German IG Metall before 1978. CO Metal has always, on principle, rejected regular government subsidies which it regarded as a necessary evil to offset financial assistance provided by other governments in the OECD. CO Metal has all along accepted reduction in employment and adaptation to the needs of the market. However, there was on occasions a market difference between the profession of belief in market economic principles and the practical needs of the situation. The credit order which was developed (see below pp. 15–16) was keenly watched and government support orders of ships (warships, ferries, patrol boats and so on) were welcomed.[13] 'If other countries press through subsidies we cannot be passive', CO Metal argued. Both as to belief in the principles of market economics and deviation from them, CO Metal acted in concord with the two other parties in the talks. To explain this unanimity in the defence of free trade principles, reference must be made to the role of export industries and trade in the Danish economy.

Even when the contraction process enforced unpopular decisions it was obvious that latent tensions within the tripartite committee were kept under control. The problems were seen as being imposed by external threats and therefore internal co-operation was essential. Internal tensions were, so to speak, suppressed by external threats. This was demonstrated not least in the spring of 1977 when CO Metal called the shop stewards from the yards to a two-day conference on the situation in shipbuilding. Not only the Minister of

Trade, Ivar Nörgaard, but also the director of Skibsvaerftsforen-ingen, Kai Engell-Jensen, were invited to participate.[14] Nor was this the only time they took part — this was the general practice.[15]

AGREEMENT ON REDUNDANCIES

In 1978 the situation deteriorated. In April the Skibsvaerftforen-ingen sent a very gloomy report to the Minister of Labour which concluded that, if nothing were done, employment in new construc-tion would have to be reduced from 11,000 to 7,500 in a year's time, and 3,500 by the autumn of 1979.[16]

In April 1979 the tripartite committee also produced its first comprehensive report since the collapse of the market four or five years earlier. It argued that so far government interventions in Western Europe had generally been designed to attract as many as possible of the available contracts and to maintain as many jobs as possible. Much less had been done to adapt employment and capacity to the new level of demand. But contraction was necessary both in the short and in the long run[17] and only Japan, Sweden, and possibly the Netherlands had begun long-term restructuring[18] (no mention was made of the long contraction and concentration process in France).

The committee considered both the short- and the long-term prospects for Danish shipbuilding and the members unanimously accepted the need for a reduction of capacity. The only question was whether Denmark had any long-term future in shipbuilding. It is clear that the Danish committee were more pessimistic (i.e. realistic) about the future than many of their counterparts in other European countries. The *kontaktudvalget* clearly distinguished both a cyclical and a long-term structural element in the crisis, while most other contemporary reports were based on the expectation that the market would turn in the near future.

In principle, the *kontaktudvalget* agreed unanimously that only those yards which had the best prospects of survival should be preserved, and that no attempt should be made to save all yards, a strategy which would further weaken the competitiveness of the whole industry. But the question of what criteria should be used for selecting the yards was much more contentious. There were several reasons for this. In the first place, the geographical dispersion of the Danish yards made it difficult to contract by merging the yards in the same area, as was possible in Britain, Sweden, Germany, France

189

and the Netherlands. Second, contraction by singling out yards for closure and, for example, denying them credit support or state orders, was not considered politically possible. This had been French policy in the 1960s, and had been met by outbursts of local protest. Furthermore, the committee argued, all the yards had a reasonable degree of specialisation in different types of ships, and none had obsolete equipment. Economically speaking there was little to choose between them.

There was only one principal by which they could be ranked: by the consequences of redundancy for the local labour markets. It was quite clear that a closure of the yards in Nakskov, Frederikshavn and Odense (Lindö) would be much more painful than in Copenhagen, Elsinore or Ålborg. The group of yards from among which closure could be expected was leaked, and Elsinore was singled out as the yard under greatest threat. Georg Poulsen and Charles Hansen, the metal workers' representative in the committee, had acquiesced in the unanimous recommendation of the committee.

The committee considered that a mandatory closure of yards was so difficult that it advised against such a step.[19] The government should only set up the general framework for the shipbuilding industry within which 'natural selection' would operate. The yards, as privately-owned enterprises, would have the final responsibility for their methods of operation and they could continue building ships. Internal criticism within CO Metal was expressed by the shop stewards in Elsinore and Copenhagen. CO Metal was repeatedly forced to give assurances that it did not intend to participate in any closure of a Danish yard. It would no longer openly admit the possibility of a closure of a Danish yard. However, Charles Hansen, the vice chairman of CO Metal, was not unduly worried by the internal criticism:

> The criticism came from one locality at a time and I had the silent support from the others who were not concerned. The protests were dispersed and I could always reckon upon the support of the others.[20]

The fact that the committee avoided selecting any particular yard to be closed did not mean that it lacked a shipbuilding policy, In the April 1979 report it argued that more state orders were needed and had therefore asked a number of government authorities about their requirements for ships. This demand, including ferries for Danish railways (Dcr 600 m) and warships for the navy (Dcr 200 m), amounted to Dcr 1 bn, approximately half of what would be necessary just to maintain employment at the 9,000 level.[21] The fact that state orders fell far short of what was needed to keep the yards going led the yards to propose a continuation of the credit scheme.

The success of the tripartite *kontaktudvalget* and the consensus amongst the employers, union and government about the superiority of a market solution prevented any buck-passing as occurred in Germany. The view that closures was a matter for local decision contrasted with the 'closure from above' policy practiced in Holland, and the geographical dispersion of the shipyards, and the fact that the closure of one yard improved the prospects of the others, prevented the sort of mass local protests which occurred in France. The decision-making at the central level did not involve local decision-makers from the yards not a 'solidaristic contraction' by means of a centrally-decided 'cheese-cutter principle'. The fact that in Denmark yards were played against yards made the internal union strains and the protest level greater than in Sweden. But the protests which did occur did not pose too many difficulties for the leadership of CO Metal. Their participation in the tripartite talks was never challenged. And even if it was difficult to admit openly that a yard had to be closed, CO Metal could continue co-operating within the committee.

YARD CLOSURE AND THE POLITICAL PROCESS

In analysis of the situation and the prospects of the large yards in 1981, CO Metal found that generally the competitive abilities of the Danish yards had improved 'on account of good financing possibilities', i.e. resulting from *hjemmemarkedsordningen*, the credit support scheme.[22] But it underlined the productivity problems of the yards in Elsinore and Nakskov, and also in Ålborg. At the end of 1982 a political process started to close one of the yards; the way had been clear for such a step since 1979.

At a meeting in Elsinore with some 400 shipyard workers in December 1982, Charles Hansen said that CO Metal could envisage a situation in which it was no longer possible to reduce capacity by means of cuts at all yards. The seriousness of the situation was generally recognised, even if at the meeting much of the problem was concealed by the political rhetoric of Ib Stetter (the Minister of Industry of the new centre-right government) and his Social Democratic predecessor Erling Jensen, whose constituency was

191

Elsinore and who, relieved of the responsibility for the closure decision, attacked the government in front of the yard workers. Jensen
argued for one state-ordered ferry to each of Elsinore and Nakskov
'not knowing exactly what such an order would mean for the
economy of the Elsinore yard'.[23]

It was clear that the government had no intention of ordering new
ferries, because the existing ships were not due for replacement for
another five or six years. However, a parliamentary majority voted
for new ferries and all the yards were invited to tender. The tenders
proved difficult to compare. However, it seems to be clear that
Lindö put in the lowest bid, followed by Aalborg, Nakskov and
Helsingör, in that order. Danish Railways (DSB), with responsibility for the ferries, was dissatisfied with Helsingör Vaerft (who
put in the highest bid) after the problems with an earlier ferry
delivered from that yard.

Lindö in Odense made the lowest offer but even if *kontaktudvalget* had supported them the finance committee of *folketinget*
would probably have refused the money because there was no pressing need for the ferries. In the tripartite committee *Skibsvaerftforen-
ingen* argued that the yard with the lowest bid should have the order.
But because it was well aware of the political implications it
suggested that as an 'escape clause' another yard could get the orders
for employment reasons 'if the difference was not too large'.[24] For
the same reasons CO Metal wanted orders for one ferry to go to
Nakskov and one to Elsinore. Although it was criticised by the shop
stewards from Ålborg, that criticism was neutralised by the support
from Nakskov and Elsinore. However, the government could not
spread the orders and if its strategy was to make any sense Nakskov
should build both ships. This time the government got the majority
in the parliament and Nakskov received the orders.[25] The decision
gave political breathing-space to the government. When in 1986 ÖK
(the owner) announced that it wanted to close down its Nakskov yard
the government did not intervene. Neither was it pressurised by CO
Metal or *Skibsvaerftsforeningen* to do so.

When the decision was made, Lauritzen indicated that it wanted
to withdraw from shipbuilding in Elsinore. It was obvious that the
government would do nothing to intervene and save the yard. Some
attempts were made by the employees to take over the yard: they
bought shares and even employed a managing director. But all was
in vain. The government denied the new regime credit guarantees
for the two orders they managed to negotiate.

These events provoked no crisis of legitimacy within CO Metal despite obvious tensions within the union and local criticism. However, this criticism was growing. The responsibility for closure had been taken over by the government, although with the more or less outspoken support of the tripartite committee, which argued that resources were no longer available for continued support of the yards on the same scale as hitherto. The tripartite strategy in *kontaktudvalget* had aimed at general measures like the credit scheme, and when these became insufficient, the tripartite body became a spectator to a process of closure dependent on the financial viability of each yard. Only B & W (which was not a part of a shipowning firm) received government support more directly and for special emergency purposes (see below p. 198).

Georg Poulsen, the chairman of the metal workers' union, in a *kontaktudvalget* meeting argued that it was the political initiative of the unions which had produced the DSB orders for the two ferries. Though it was debateable whether it had been wise to start this particular rescue operation, the problem for Poulsen was that he found it difficult to rebutt the frequent allegations by shop stewards and others that yard closures were part of a long-term strategy planned by the yards and the shipowners. Troels Dilling, the chairman of *Skibsvaerftsforeningen*, assured Poulsen that no such conscious, long-term strategy existed. Poulsen answered that he was 'glad to have gained the assurance of *Vaerftsforeningen* that he could reject these allegations in the future'.[26]

It is obvious that *Skibsvaerftsforeningen* and CO Metal formed a strong coalition within *kontakudvalget* with a mutual interest in maintaining the yards, although both realised that a capacity reduction had to be made. One example of this strength is their success in maintaining the credit scheme, *hjemmemarkedsordningen*, despite increasing criticism (see the next section).

It is debatable who ultimately had the power in the tripartite committee, but what is clear is that it provided a forum where the union and employers could mount joint pressure on the government. The parties tried to find a basis for coincidental interest stronger than their conflicting interests, but for CO Metal it was also a matter of realising that they were participating in a game in which every one had to lose.

The decision-making during the contraction of Danish shipbuilding has no doubt had a co-operative element, more distinct than in other countries studied here, although the Swedish situation seems to be similar. But it would be misleading to regard the decision to close down Helsingör Vaerft as a top-level decision, out of touch with grass-roots. Such a selection has only been made during the European contraction in France, where in July 1960 six yards were selected for closure (p. 56), and this without the consultation of the union. In Denmark, and elsewhere where similar decisions have been made, a bargaining model where the parties tried to find a common interest basis stronger than the conflicting interests seems to fit better. Such a basis and its rise must be seen in context. For CO Metal, for instance, it was a matter of realising that they participated in a 'loss sum-play'.

CREDITS AND LEASING

CO Metal and *Skibsvaerftsforeningen* were unanimous and persistent in their allegation that the Danish yards really did not receive subsidies like their foreign competitors. It is notable that their belief in the market economy was compatible with their claim for the maintenance of the cheap credit scheme, for they did not consider credits to be the direct competition-distorting subsidies they were in other countries. In fact the Danish parliament itself never granted 'cheap' loans: they resulted from a purely administrative decision made by the national bank in concert with the government. It is clear that the recommendations of *kontaktudvalget* resulted in important decisions about large sums of money made available for shipbuilding which were never publicly debated nor submitted for decision by Parliament. By the beginning of the 1980s the ship credit orders were increasingly questioned by both the Right and the Left.

The ship credit orders included loans in accordance with the general OECD rules, i.e. 80 per cent at 8 per cent over 8 years for export orders. These loans were not so fiercely debated, since they were no different from those made in other countries. In 1977 a special home-market order, *hjemmemarkedsordningen*, was introduced to support Danish orders for Danish yards. The home-market order meant loans of 80 per cent at 8 per cent over 14 years, of which 4 were free of interest. In 1982 the duration of credits were cut to 12 years of which 2 were free from repayment.[27]

Technically the OECD and the home-market orders together were called the ship credit orders and were available to shipowners from the ship credit fund. The loan from the fund was paid in bonds with a low nominal interest rate. If the bonds were to be realised on the open market, they had to be sold at a low price so that the yield corresponded to the market interest. Instead the national bank redeemed the bonds at par on the instruction of the government without discussion in parliament. The national bank then sold most of the bonds on the open market at market price, i.e. the loan was refinanced on the open market with the national bank covering the difference between the market and par values.

The central bank's normal surplus of working capital fell correspondingly but this was only indirectly visible in the annual transfer of the surplus to the state budget. The cost from 1974 to 1983 was Dcr 8.5 bn,[28] amounting to Dcr 118,000 per employee in new construction.

In the early 1980s, when this credit system was increasingly criticised, the parties in *kontaktudvalget* were unanimous in their defence of it.[29] The director of the national bank had argued that every Danish shipyard worker was subsidised to the extent of Dcr 120,000. Kai Engell-Jensen, the director of *Skibsvaerftsforeningen*, denied this and asserted that the correct figure was between 10,000 and 30,000, dependent on the interest rate in the market, and CO Metal joined in this defence.[30]

However, the ship credit orders were not enough to keep the Danish yards going. At the beginning of the 1980s the financial leasing system in shipping and shipbuilding developed very rapidly. Under this system ships could be leased for long periods. The leasing company, which owned the ships, quite often consisted of a large number of individuals investing money in individual shares, usually for tax avoidance purposes. By 1983 leasing had reached such proportions within Danish shipbuilding that an expert committee was appointed to investigate. In that year 12 per cent of all new ships in Danish yards were built on leasing contracts. In the first quarter of 1984 the figure was 43 per cent.[31]

It was an example of a tax avoidance breakthrough in a high tax system. High marginal taxes on personal incomes made it desirable to find deductible items so as to reduce the tax burden. By this way the disadvantages of shipbuilding could be turned to private advantage.

For public opinion, however, the system was objectionable. Money put into a notoriously non-profitable industry which had been backed by the taxpayer for so long suddenly, in effect, generated profits which were not ploughed back in productive investment but merely increased the after-tax income of a group of high earners. In the subsequent debate leasing was presented as a way by which the rich bought something but had more money as a consequence.[32]

In the autumn of 1983 the Socialist People's Party on the Left introduced a bill in Parliament to abolish the leasing system. The

Social Democrats felt obliged to support the bill, but only after careful consideration. The chairman of CO Metal, Charles Hansen, met Social Democratic MPs three times before the voting in Parliament, to pressurise them to work for maintenance of the system. The shop stewards at a yard in Frederikshavn wrote to the Minister of Industry expressing apprehension about the bill. They were supported by the yard management, who also wrote.[33]

Such opposition proved in vain, however, and CO Metal, who considered the leasing system vital for the survival of the yards, had to admit openly that it did not support the bill of the Socialist People's Party. The government found it politically necessary to respond and introduced its own bill which was passed by Parliament in December 1983. Certainly the system of *sales and lease back* which some shipowners had practised was not formally prohibited, but it was made so unfavourable that it effectively ceased. The main thing was that the usual leasing system continued to make it profitable — both for owner and leaser — to invest in ships.

The problem which the Minister of Industry and *kontaktudvalget* faced was not only one of public opinion. The system provoked increasing attention within the international organisations of the OECD and the EEC. When the Minister of Industry in Parliament evaluated the economic effects of the ship credit orders and the leasing system after the bill, he found that, for each Dcr 100 m ship financed under the home-market order over twelve years with a market interest at 13 per cent, the subsidy was Dcr 13–14 m. In addition, the leasing arrangement cost the state over Dcr 10 m. If the shipowner that leased the ship was a non-profitable company, the state's loss of income would increase to Dcr 30 m, and the combined subsidy would total Dcr 43–44 out of the 100. Most of the Danish merchant fleet operated under a leasing system in one form or another and two-thirds of the fleet was owned by investment societies belonging to the AP Möller group.[34]

The Minister of Industry concluded that the leasing finance from 1983 had 'strongly contributed to bringing home the orders in question'.[35]

In a memorandum drawn up by the Ministry of Industry in April 1984 it was concluded that the parliamentary decision of December 1983 had not taken away the inducement for using the leasing instrument in shipbuilding. Leasing was a 'selective tax instrument reserved for shipbuilding'.[36]

Before 1984 there had been little interest in combining the leasing system with the home-market credit scheme. Favourable writing off rules and a strong tradition of owning ships for a long time prevented Danish shipowners from using the leasing system to finance their operations. Most of the leasing agreements had been with foreign shipowners so mainly affected exports. But when purchases of leasing shares were accepted as a possible way of financing the building of new ships (although still controversial), this was an inducement for the shipowners to take advantage of the situation. AP Möller introduced the possibility with a contract with the leasing society of Difko for three new product tankers which Difko ordered to be built at the Lindö yard (owned by AP Möller).

The Ministry's memorandum reveals another incentive to use the leasing system, probably more substantial than its use to finance new investment. Earlier, when the Danish market rate of interest had been around 20 per cent, the interest subsidy was over 35 per cent when a 14-year home-market loan at 7.5–8 per cent was acquired. In the 1980s the interest rate fell and the subsidy element on such a loan was reduced to under 20 per cent. The fall of 15 per cent could be compensated for by using the leasing system, which gave a subsidy of around 10 per cent compared with the financial advantage from using the writing-off rules. If the writing-off rules could not be exploited to the full, i.e. if the shipping company had a deficit on its working capital, the subsidy could be as much as 30 per cent.[37] The advantage for Denmark was that other countries, where rates of personal income tax were considerably lower, could not offer financial advantages by introducing leasing, so the use of the system operated to Denmark's advantage.

The question the Ministry asked was whether the combination of home-market orders and the leasing system now provided competitive financing compared with what was available to foreign yards. The answer was not only 'yes', but also that Danish yards now enjoyed extensive advantages, and the Ministry therefore began to consider now to reduce excessive subsidies. In principle there were two possibilities: they could either alter the home-market order or the leasing system.

The core of the leasing system was a transfer of the writing-off of the cost of ships against tax from taxpayers with a low, to taxpayers with a high, marginal rate. Therefore, the lower the marginal taxes of the leaser, the more attractive the system. For a shipowner with a deficit, and therefore without taxable income, leasing as an alternative to buying was more favoured than a highly profitable company.

Another problem was that leasing could produce difficulties within the OECD and the EEC. Norway had already raised the question of including leasing in the rules of the OECD, and the EEC commission had indicated that it wanted to examine the question.[38]

On the other hand, there were also advantages with the leasing system. If the alternative of tightening the condition of home-market credits and keeping leasing arrangements untouched was preferred, the yards could be expected to intensify their efforts to replace the decreased number of orders from Danish owners with export orders.

However, this raised the problem that the support element for leasing-based export orders would be 6–11 per cent higher than that for the home-market orders, an improvement which was unlikely to pass the notice of foreign competitors.

The author of the memorandum tended in his recommendation towards an unchanged home-market order system and a tightening up on leasing, well aware that a different decision would have a differential impact on the yards. A tightening of the home-market order system and unchanged leasing possibilities would be especially advantageous for the export yards, especially Burmeiser & Wain and Aalborg Vaerft, which would be particularly adversely affected by any reduction of the advantages from leasing.[39] In December 1984 the system was changed so that only 55 per cent of the acquisition value of the ship could be leased.

However, in an extreme situation of no orders in 1986, when all the Danish yards faced impending closure, the combined efforts of CO Metal and *Skibsvaerftsforeningen* again pressurised the government to return to the earlier and more generous leasing rules.

It is clearly misleading to claim that Danish shipbuilding was not subsidised. The documents convincingly reveal a subsidy element which is comparable to that in other countries. The fact that this was not submitted to the Danish parliament nor paid through the state budget makes no substantial difference. The other argument, that the scheme was also in operation for orders at yards in other EEC countries, can also be dismissed. Danish shipowners usually ordered at Danish yards.

The joint support by *Skibsvaerftsforeningen* and CO Metal for the ship credit orders and the leasing system is as understandable as is the coincidental interest of industry and unions in obtaining government cash. *Skibsvaerftsforeningen* and CO Metal not only shared a belief in market principles, but also had a common readiness to deviate from those principles in practice. However, in one respect they were more market-oriented than their counterparts in other countries. They were less interested in direct rescue interventions for individual yards and more inclined to working rules which could be generally applied.

BURMEISTER & WAIN: AN OUTMODED LEADER

Burmeister & Wain on Refshaleöen, a stone's throw from the centre of Copenhagen, was erected during the mid-nineteenth century and soon became foremost in Danish shipbuilding. At the beginning of the twentieth century it had achieved world fame and was one of the leading companies in marine engineering. It was by far the largest Danish yard, renowned since the 1920s for its well-organised and militant workforce. Frequent strikes and disputes and a strong Communist faction led the yard to be known as the Red Yard, a reputation which survived into the 1970s long after the militancy hard largely disappeared.[40]

However, since 1959 B & W has lost its leading position, as the Lindö yard has expanded and as B & W problems grew. Lindö came to represent what was best and most modern in shipbuilding techniques: B & W what was old and obsolete.

New investments were made in the mid-1950s and new facilities were ready by 1960, but these did not embody the same technological advance as has occurred at Lindö. There were frequent development problems. Since 1959 the structure of the local labour market had meant a shortage of skilled workers and numerous complaints have been heard of inefficiency in work performance. The years from 1960 to 1966 (with the sole exception of 1964) showed increasing deficits. In April 1967 management and owners asked the government for emergency assistance and an inquiry committee was appointed, consisting of civil servants from the Ministry of Trade.[41]

After one month the inquiry reported that the use of labour and capital over a long period of time with such poor results was not in the best interests of the country. It also raised the question of the closure of the yard. If operations were to continue at all, it was argued, productivity had to increase considerably. In 1965 management had asked the shop stewards about restructuring the union organisation, but got the answer that such a question was an internal union affair. By the time the inquiry had delivered its report in May 1967 the shop stewards were more flexible in their attitude. The inquiry had pointed to the division of the union of the workforce into 16 trade unions, and the consequent frequent demarcation disputes and time-consuming negotiating machinery, as a main reason for low productivity.[42]

The government intervened to rescue the yard, but the problems continued. In 1973, in the middle of the tanker boom, the situation again became acute. Selling the yard to a Japanese consortium was discussed, as was a take-over by the employees, who were offered loans to buy shares in the company. The Lauritzen group also showed interest. There was an extended cash-flow crisis in the winter of 1974, and in the following April the controversial and hitherto unknown 32-year-old, Jan Bonde Nielsen, with no experience in shipbuilding, emerged as the main shareholder of the more or less bankrupt company. He had started his business career in floristry and his acquisition of the shares in the shipbuilding firm had been speculative. He had also married into the Foss family, the majority owner of one of the biggest Danish industry groups, and had thus been appointed a member of boards of different enterprises in Danish commerce and industry.

Bonde Nielsen succeeded in keeping the yard afloat for five years and during this period industrial relations changed radically. Up to 1975 the Communists dominated in the yard unions. From then on the Socialist People's Party (*Socialistisk Folkeparti*, SF), to the left of the Social Democratic Party, took over their role. Four of the five shop stewards in *faellesklubben*, the shop stewards' executive committee, were SF members.

Bonde Nielsen invited the shop stewards to regular talks about the prospects of the yard and they were kept better informed and regularly consulted. The Socialist shop stewards, Bjarne Jensen and Helge Larsen, who negotiated with him over five years, describe him as a modern patriarch:

> Bonde Nielsen was popular among the shipyard workers. He had a patriarchal style. He arrived at the yard at a quarter to seven each morning to have his morning coffee with the shop stewards. He invited shop stewards to a luncheon with red wine and steak whereas he himself sat with a packed lunch and mineral water. He was always around at the yard and talking with people. In this way he built up a personal mystique.[43]

In August 1974 Bonde Nielsen put his Plan 78 before the shop stewards. He wanted to close the repair department and concentrate on series production of bulk carriers. Low productivity, it was argued, resulted from the structure of production, not from the shortcomings of the workforce.[44] However, even if he did not hold his employees responsible for the poor performance of the yard it was soon clear to Bonde Nielsen that he had too many of them. In December 1975 he indicated that he wanted to reduce the workforce by 400 people and some months later this figure had increased to 800–900.[45]

In April 1976 the threat of redundancy was combined with a request for wage restraint. Bonde Nielsen had established a shipping company and suggested it would place an order for five ships with B & W if prices were competitive. If wage costs were too great, however, the order would be placed with another yard.[46]

Erik Hansen, chairman of the shop stewards' executive committee, rejected the proposal for wage restraint but started talks with Bonde Nielsen about the redundancy scheme. The shop stewards demanded Dcr 15 m for redundancy payments. A 'social plan' was elaborated to mitigate the effects of the job loss and finance an early retirement scheme in the form of a bonus by seniority.[47]

Faellesklubben did not participate in selecting workers to be made redundant. Many left voluntarily, but not all. The selection for involuntary redundancy was left to management, who used efficiency as the decisive criterion. In June 1976 all 2,600 employees at the yard received a letter for 919 of them. This was a redundancy notice. Yet again the threat of unemployment was individualised, many of the 919 quit voluntarily and there was no ground for collective action, which was limited to political slogans.

Erik Hansen was accused by some activists of being a puppet and a sycophant of Bonde Nielsen. He defended himself: 'Bonde Nielsen is after all the owner of the enterprise and as a matter of fact he is difficult to circumvent. Moreover, I have nothing against co-operation as long as it can help some colleagues.'[48] He continued: 'They have told me that we should occupy the yard. But what should we do here without orders?'

The political activists tried to mobilise the workforce with little success. One of them gave his views:

. . . we sell our jobs and unemployment increases, we receive a small recompense for losing the working community which is a prerequisite for fending off future attacks from the employers, we allow ourselves to be bought off not to oppose the redundancies, we give up at the very moment when we are strongest, because once we are out of the yard there is little we can do against unemployment.[49]

There was an attempt to use the claim for a 35-hour working week as a lever for mobilisation. The hope was to trigger off massive grass-roots action over the whole labour market. However, the role of spearhead was hardly the proper one for B & W in the prevailing situation. Indeed, in December 1976 the workers stopped working five hours earlier on Fridays, thereby dictating the 35-hour week themselves. Twice the shop stewards tried to call off the action. After four walk-outs it ceased. The workers then took a vote on it. The action had no spin-off effect whatsoever on other sites.

The run-down continued at B & W after 1976 using the tactics developed in that year and with the co-operation of the SF shop stewards.[50] In 1978 redundancy payments were somewhat improved.[51] Those who only had two years to go to pensionable age received almost 100 per cent of their pension. The period of notice of redundancy was longer than the one prescribed by law and Bonde Nielsen also paid for retraining for jobs outside shipbuilding and for relocation outside the Copenhagen area. Despite this not all redundancy was voluntary, and the necessity for this was generally accepted. Everyone recognised there was a risk that the whole yard would close and came to accept that contraction was necessary for survival; some people had to be sacrificed for the common good. The earlier industrial militancy of the workforce had changed and there have been increased pressure on the political system.[52] Since 1975 there has been no major conflict with management. There have been some 15 small, locally confined disputes, mostly over demarcation, and some walk-outs for anti-government rallies, particularly after the Social Democrats had lost power in 1982, but the contraction process itself has produced no disputes.[53]

There was tension between the B & W union and Charles Hansen and George Poulsen, the vice chairman of CO Metal and the chairman of *Metalarbejderforeningen* (the biggest affiliate of CO Metal), respectively, after they signed the statement in *kontaktudvalget* in April 1979 that the B & W yard was less important for employment in Copenhagen than other yards for their locality. But by and large the national union leadership has been respected and on 'union questions' there has been little opposition.[54] Union questions were considered by the SF shop stewards to be 'more important than political questions'. 'Political rhetoric is one thing, the safeguarding of the yard another and more important thing.' The Social Democratic and much more market-oriented leadership of CO Metal has not, apart from in April 1979, provoked open protests from B & W. In 1983 the defence of the leasing system was as strong at B & W as it was amongst the CO Metal leadersihp. Charles Hansen tried to persuade the Social Democratic leadership to adopt a lower profile on the leasing questions whilst Bjarne Jensen of the B & W shop stewards' committee put similar pressure on the SF political leaders who had introduced the anti-leasing bill in Parliament.[55] The union

202

viewpoint was obviously given priority over political preference.

In 1979–80 the government was again involved in B & W operations and had to intervene to save the yard. The popular and controversial Bonde Nielsen was dethroned by the Social Democratic government who took over control and in effect nationalised the yard.[56] The contraction process continued, and the 'social plan' was improved. The improvement of the redundancy scheme was financed by a 10 öre deduction per hour from money available for wage increases and by 11 öre per hour contributed by the company. In the early stage of negotiations this scheme was opposed by the younger workers who did not want to forfeit wage increases to finance redundancy schemes.

This resistance was overcome by the shop stewards and Bjarne Jensen commented:

> Good industrial relations have still continued after Bonde Nielsen. The problems we have had we have had in common with management. Our problem is to get our colleagues to understand what we understand.[57]

NAKSKOV AND HELSINGÖR

The town of Nakskov is situated on the Danish island of Lolland and has just under 20,000 inhabitants. It is an isolated industrial area in completely agrarian surroundings, but in 1980 it was Denmark's most industrialised town, with ships and sugar as its main products. Until 1980 the shipyard was by far the largest employer.[58] Fourteen out of 21 members of the town council were Social Democrats and three belonged to SF.

The shipyard was owned by the large trading company *Östasiatiske Kompagnie* (ÖK). At the end of 1975 they told union leaders that they would order six new ships from Japan unless they agreed to wage restraint to make the yard competitive. If the workers refused there would be dismissals which would threaten the very existence of the yard. The shop stewards had little space for manoeuvring. It made no sense to take up arms against the yard management since the move came from the trading company's management, and it was recognised that the yard management had as little influence with head office as the shop stewards. What can be regarded as a commonly-experienced threat from outside forced yard management and shop stewards into local co-operation.[59]

203

Charles Hansen in CO Metal and Herman Burmeister, chairman of the metal workers' local branch in Nakskov, recognised that it was an emergency situation and participated in the negotiations which ended with an agreement in January 1976. The purpose of the new agreement was expressly said to be to guarantee employment: an outcome which was varyingly described, from 'we met each other half way' to 'capitulation'. The final agreement was very close to the original proposal from the owners: a wage freeze combined with 'measures promoting productivity', including a bonus system. The workers had little choice but to accept the wage freeze, but they tacitly refused to increase productivity. The shop stewards, who had unanimously approved the agreement, met increasingly the silent protest from the members.[60]

The way wages developed after the agreement demonstrates the effects of this. In the summer of 1973 the shipyard workers in Nakskov earned 30–50 öre more per hour than the average in the local branches of CO Metal outside Copenhagen. By 1976 the shipyard workers were earning 62 öre *less* than the local averages and this negative differential grew to 472 öre in 1982.[61]

Fritz Sell, the chairman of the shop stewards executive committee, commented on this development in retrospect: 'We wanted to maintain employment and that has cost us many crowns. West Lolland is isolated and there are no other jobs to get if the yard closes'.[62]

'Having no choice' determined the reaction to subsequent developments. For the wage freeze did not improve the prospects of the yard, and by the beginning of 1984 there were only 500 employees left. This run-down was a repeat of the process of gradual adaptation and successive redundancy schemes which had taken place at Burmeister & Wain. In February 1984 total unemployment in Nakskov was 28 per cent. Fifty per cent (715 out of some 1,400) of the members of the metal workers' local branch were unemployed.[63] By then people were willing to consider alternatives to shipbuilding and to the yard. In point of fact, 'having no choice' probably provoked a more flexible response to the contraction than in many other West European yard sites where the yards did not dominate the local labour market to the same extent. When in 1986 ÖK announced that it was no longer interested in keeping its yard there were no grounds for political intervention to save it. The yard was closed down in 1987.

The contraction process at Helsingör Vaerft in Elsinore was in many respects similar to that in Nakskov and B & W. As in these two yards, there were no real protests. There was a short walk-out in December 1981 when DFDS, the parent shipping company, conducted negotiations in Japan over four ships, at the same time as there was talk about the laying off of several hundred employees in Elsinore.

Helsingör Vaerft was an old and shabby yard in an extremely bad situation, squeezed between Hamlet's castle of Kronborg and the ferry harbour with its busy traffic with Helsingborg on the other side of the Sound. It was hampered from developing by its location, although it had established contacts with shipowners and was successful in 'bespoke' production. But it built very few ships in series with the productivity gains such production involved, and the owners invested little in the yard.

From the 1970s it had gone from crisis to crisis, which often occurred when new orders were being negotiated, so that there was little space for the unions to manoeuvre. The unions gradually realised that the whole existence of the yard was threatened, and therefore had 'no alternative' but to be co-operative. Defeatism amongst the workforce spread along with the reduction in jobs from 3,000 at the beginning of the 1970s to 1,200 in the summer of 1983. By the summer of 1983 the impending closure of the yard was more a fact realised by all than a threat collectively experienced. Those who had been made compulsorily redundant during the contraction process had been as a rule selected, department by department, on efficiency criteria, a process hardly any more conducive to collective action in Elsinore than elsewhere.

There was one attempt by the employees to take over the yard, which for a while gave a certain measure of hope.[64] But in the long run all it probably achieved was to smooth the process of closure.

DENMARK: CONCLUDING REMARKS

Since the 1960s, tripartite talks in shipbuilding have been institutionalised in Denmark. The basis for the talks was an agreement on the need to improve productivity and generally strengthen the role of market forces. This emphasis on the role of market forces by the Danish Social Democrats and the unions can be explained by Denmark's industrial structure: Danish industry consists mainly of small enterprises. There has been no political pressure as in other countries towards supporting or nationalising large individual enterprises.

But even if the top union leadership agreed to the market

economic principles and to the reduction in capacity there were protests from the yard workers. However, as distinct from Sweden, protests from the localities were kept dispersed rather than absorbed into decision-making at the central level. The scattered protests also meant that, unlike the Netherlands, the union leadership was not seriously challenged. There was no serious demand that they leave the tripartite talks. However, it should be stressed that there was also concern at the central union level not to provoke a strong local response, a conclusion supported by the fact that between 1979 and 1984 there were no yard closures in Denmark, although the unions in April 1979 in the tripartite talks had admitted that they could imagine closure of a whole yard.

The contraction processes in the six countries all demonstrate that tripartite bargaining is a better concept than tripartite co-operation. This judgement is certainly true for Denmark, where the unions and the industry exerted common pressure on the political power, although there the line between bargaining and co-operation is sometimes difficult to distinguish, particularly as the employers and unions share a market-oriented ideology. In Denmark tripartism has operated without interruption since the 1960s. And to the extent there have been no mass closures of yards (despite large-scale redundancies), so that a semblance of a shipbuilding workforce continues to exist, the tripartite bargaining has been successful. This helps to explain why, as distinct from Germany, France, Britain and the Netherlands, the unions in Denmark in 1985 were still integrated into the central tripartite talks on shipbuilding.

8

National or International Solidarity?

In Chapter 1 it was argued that the contraction process within the Western European shipbuilding industry was internationally derived but that the framework for the tripartite bargaining was mainly national. Solutions to internationally induced problems were looked for by means of national policies. This chapter considers attempts at international collaboration and evaluates their success.

THE ATTEMPTS TO FORMULATE A COMMON EUROPEAN SHIPBUILDING POLICY

The upsurge in growth credit schemes at the beginning of the 1960s provoked the interest of the EEC. The decade after the Treaty of Rome in 1957 was the major period of attempts by the growing 'eurocracy' to regulate the market economy.

In a question to the Commission in 1964 some members of the European Parliament asked whether the specific problems of shipbuilding did not require a special Community plan. The Commission answered that shipbuilding was in a phase of adaptation and restructuring. The necessity of such a process was realised by the national governments and according to the Commission there were national plans to cope with it. So, even if the protection of shipbuilding in the EEC was said to be in the common interest, the Commission would not elaborate a scheme of its own but would merely help to co-ordinate the national plans.[1] However, in practice the Commission could not do much more than witness the growing national aid arrangements and make statements or confidential proposals to the governments involved.[2]

Certainly, in 1969 the Council at last adopted directives drawn up in 1965 fixing a temporary aid ceiling of 10 per cent on the price, but this was rather a reaction to developments which had already happened than part of a forward-looking strategy. However, in 1969 such an attempt was made, when the Commission elaborated a report simultaneously with the OECD. The EEC report made a projection of market trends, and was very pessimistic for the period up to 1975. But this did not fit in with the general optimism of the Commission, and the prognosis was dismissed as being 'incredible': the report was not released for three years.[3]

In 1972 — in the midst of the tanker boom — the report was finally published despite the fact that 'the authors seriously wondered whether it would not be advisable to abandon' the publication of a document the forecasts of which 'already appeared to be contradicted by the facts'.[4] In the conclusion it was argued that the prevailing favourable situation of the EEC yards should not be allowed to conceal the real problems of the industry.[5] It was further suggested that the recovery could be strengthened by a common policy, and the cornerstone on which the improvement of the EEC yards' position could be built was the setting up of a common level of subsidy within the Community area, with a view to eliminating some of the inter-country anomalies in existing financial support.[6]

In the summer of 1973 the Commission told the Council that it wanted to establish an institutional framework able to deal with the problem of shipbuilding. However, this was totally rejected by the Council. One of the members of the Council stated: 'Why are you dealing with this? The yards have got orders up to the late 1970s.'[7]

The Commission wanted to restructure European shipbuilding gradually so that it could be competitive without subsidies.[8] What such a restructured and profitable industry would look like was not made clear. The Commission suggested that developments in production capacity should be examined at least once a year in consultation with national experts and representatives of industry and the unions. It was even suggested that the Commission should approve all investments over a certain size.[9]

Parts of the shipbuilding industry reacted coldly or negatively to this proposal by the Commission. The general director of the Danish *Skibsvaerftsforeningen*, Kai Engell-Jensen, argued:

We do not understand how the Commission will be able to make the shipbuilding industry of the EEC competitive in a situation of a marked surplus capacity, and when we know from practical experience that the new shipbuilding countries with or without state subsidies will secure their employment, among other things because their yards are a link in their industrialisation policies.[10]

In this Engell-Jensen demonstrated an understanding of the structural element of the crisis and of the threat posed by Japan and, by implication, South Korea and other NICs using shipbuilding for industrial take-off.

The British industry representative John Nicholson was no less critical:

> European integration of this industry which is implicit in these proposals is a vast and questionably advisable undertaking which will only be achieved — if at all — through action by Member States and national industries and is unlikely to be advanced by the Commission's intervention.[11]

Nicholson also criticised the Commission's idea that 'a sound Community shipbuilding industry' was needed to preserve its Independence. This referred to an earlier statement by the Commission that, to ensure the independence of the EEC as a maritime power, it was reasonable and essential to keep shipbuilding production at a level compatible with the EEC's 'economic potential and requirements as regards transport by sea'. Nicholson was glad to hear how the Commission did not seek to influence the decisions made by European shipowners in this field nor favour any attempt to control the volume of European cargo moving in European ships. He argued that the prosperity of European shipping was in no sense dependent on the existence of European shipbuilding.

Beneath the rhetoric of the market economic ideology the message from the Danish and British representatives was clear. Shipbuilding policies and investment control were not matters for the EEC. Co-ordination had to occur at the national level.

The Commission was also criticised by the European Metal Workers' Federation from a different perspective. According to EMF, the investment plans and the control over them only aimed at creating strong European groups, which meant a capitalist response to the power of international capitalism. Capitalism had produced the employment crisis and the proposed remedy was more effective capitalism. EMF rejected that remedy and proposed talks, with all three parties on an equal footing, where the employment question would be treated as part of the same key problem as investment and not as just a consequence of it.[12]

Unions in the Economic and Social Committee of the EEC (ESC), with Georges Creuse from the French CGT heading the signatories, proposed that there should be one public representative on the board of each shipbuilding company in order to control investments and one tripartite control commission at the national level. This proposal was rejected. An amendment proposed by a Dutch union representative, that a common EEC shipbuilding policy was only possible if it intervened in the autonomy of the enterprises, was also rejected.[13]

Although there was a tendency for the employers and unions to form separate groups and vote accordingly in the ESC, a tripartite amendment proposed by the Danish representatives also indicates a division along national lines. The Danes argued that EEC shipbuilding policies should not be expressed in a 'plan' but on a list of fundamental criteria. One of the fundamental principles of Danish economic policy was that the public power should refrain from planning industrial activities, and they did not want any such thing in the European shipbuilding context.[14] Their proposal was approved.[15]

In 1975 H.P. Drewry (Shipping Consultants) Ltd. made a study on behalf of the Commission of the prospects of the industry. In the report it was argued that the three main aims of EEC shipbuilding policy directives, to modernise EEC shipyards by investment, to reduce national subsidies, and to safeguard shipbuilding employment, were incompatible. Safeguarding employment was politically the most sensitive, but it was irreconcilable with the other two. Well aware of the limits of what was politically possible, the report stated that a compromise solution would probably result in the continuance of the *status quo* 'for many years to come'.[10]

In May 1976 the Commission proposed that the Council intervene in order to counter the crisis without waiting until the necessary restructuring measures had borne fruit. The Council should negotiate with the OECD about the EEC share of the reduction.[17] By now Etienne Davignon, the Commissioner for Industry, had to face three main problem areas: textiles and clothing, steel, and shipbuilding. For the first time the Council asked the Commission to formulate an 'overall' industrial policy. The plan for shipbuilding within this framework was ready in November 1977 and the main proposal was that capacity should be reduced from 5 to 2.4 m cgrt to improve the competitiveness of the surviving yards upon which investment should be concentrated.[18]

The idea which the Commission had in mind was to combine

reductions of capacity with financial interventions for restructuring and stabilisation.

It was explicitly stated that employment in EEC shipbuilding had to be cut dramatically, from 165,000 to 90,000. Moreover, of the required 75,000 redundancies only 15,000 could be by natural wastage.[19] Of course, such a step was probably beyond what was politically possible in the time allowed. Therefore the Council responded more diplomatically with the idea that cuts had to be made but that the industry itself had to decide upon their size.[20]

A tripartite meeting in Brussels took place on 2 March 1978. On the previous day, the delegations of the European Metal Workers' Federation (EMF) met to co-ordinate their policies. But the week before this co-ordinating meeting there was a meeting in Copenhagen to co-ordinate the policies of the Nordic federation of shipbuilding unions. They found that a reduction in capacity was necessary and that union shipbuilding policy could not confine itself to saying 'no' to all reductions. The contraction had to occur in planned form, giving the shipyard workers 'acceptable social and economic protection'.[21]

In Brussels one week later they found that only the Nordic and the Dutch federations were interested in a union policy which had as a point of departure the fact that surplus capacity and a structural crisis existed. For example, the British unions considered that British shipbuilding could not be blamed for the prevailing problems. Britain had not participated in building up capacity. Those countries which had done so should also be held responsible for the reduction, whilst the British industry was entitled to substantial investments to put it on a par with its European partners.[22]

The failure to find agreement among the metal workers' unions within EMF saw the start of a fight for survival at the national level as the crisis deepened and the problems become even more complex. Instead of common pressure on the EEC, the alternative was individual national pressure on their own governments. An identification with the problems of one's own country rather than any kind of an international solidarity of interest with shipyard workers in other countries was very clear in the debate at the EMF meeting on 1 March.

The response of the shipbuilders to the size of the cuts proposed by the Commission was as negative as those of the unions. Their EEC Shipbuilders' Linking Committee had already discussed the growing difficulties in 1976. Autonomous European measures had to be considered as emergency measures aimed 'directly or indirectly' at reducing the price difference with Japan to an acceptable level, thus allowing the EEC shipbuilding industry to secure an adequate share of the market. Competitive terms for financing ships built by EEC shipowners at the EEC yards had to be introduced. Investment premiums at a level of 20–25 per cent were considered. A shipbuilding fund should be established in order to enable developing countries to order ships from EEC yards. When shipyards were forced to reduce their new construction activities or close down completely, the social fund and the European Investment Bank should assist with aid for social consequences, retraining, and the stimulation of diversification projects.[23]

At the first tripartite meeting on 2 March 1978, the employers did not exclude the necessity of an adjustment in capacity but they objected to the size the Commission had proposed. The EMF, however, would not even consider a reduction. Everything had to be done in order to prevent such a step, in particular by stimulating demand. During the discussion all parties agreed, however, that any reduction would necessitate retraining and other measures for the people made redundant. The common denominator of the employers and the union representatives was the argument that political steps had to be taken to stimulate demand, both generally and particularly in shipbuilding.[24]

The resistance of the EMF to all employment cuts was soon broken down. Its stance became untenable as the market collapsed and there seemed to be no signs of recovery, especially as a strong group within EMF had previously admitted that surplus capacity existed. Soon the tripartite talks were also dealing with how the job cuts should be handled.[25]

Six months after the Commission's proposal, the situation in the tripartite committee could be described as a broad acceptance of the analysis of the Commission, but a rejection by both employers and unions of consequences of this analysis for the size of the industry.

The EMF representatives stated that they had no means of confirming or questioning the figures quoted by the Commission, but they refused to consider the 2.4 m cgrt, proposed by the Commission for the size of the EEC shipbuilding industry, as a realistic figure.[26]

The employers, whose heavyweights in the tripartite committee were the Dutch Peter Hupkes, the French Dominique de Mas Latrie and the German Fante, nevertheless confirmed the trends outlined by the Commission.[27]

Both the industry and the unions thus required government and

EEC subsidies to keep operations going. They recognised that the prognosis of the Commission was perhaps not incorrect, but they considered that a contraction of the scale proposed was excessive.[28] But everyone knew that only subsidies could keep a higher level of capacity. Thus the framework of a common EEC shipbuilding policy was set. The EEC had to yield to the claims of the industry and the unions, as it had yielded to the farmers' demands when they promoted the Common Agricultural Policy. If the EEC was not prepared to use its money in such a way, the logical response would be fragmentation and increased pressure on governments at the national level. Then different national shipbuilding policies would emerge, the precise details of which would depend on the different proportions of strength between the parties and on other factors in the national milieux. Such a development had already been hinted at in the EMF meeting on 1 March 1978 when the Nordic and Dutch unions stood against the German and British.[29]

The line-up in Brussels seemed to be the same one as at the national levels in most countries: industry and unions against governments, to get them to spend more money.

THE SCRAP-AND-BUILD HOPE

In the autumn of 1978, when the Commission's interventionist proposal had passed through the filter of the Council and with the employers and unions opposed, it was obvious that there was no basis for an EEC shipbuilding policy founded on a drastic reduction of capacity down to 2.4 m cgrt. The alternative policy was to stimulate demand. Therefore the next move of the Commission, at the end of 1978, was to give heed to talks within the International Maritime Industries Forum (IMIF) (a private group of shipowners, shipbuilders, oil companies and bankers which had been in existence since 1976) on a worldwide scrap-and-build scheme. The core and the simple philosophy of this plan was that by destroying shipping capacity there would be an increase in the demand for new ships. It could be regarded as a small-scale application of the experience after World War II: destruction more or less automatically creates a demand which can be stimulated by political decisions. Both shipbuilders and shipowners would benefit from such a programme — simultaneously shipbuilding could be stimulated and the alarming surplus in various categories of shipping could be reduced. By political preventive measures the building up of a new surplus would be avoided. Scrapping and building in the proportion of 2:1 was discussed.

The scheme the IMIF considered involved a 6 m cgrt scrapping each year for the period 1980–2. The undertaking would be 'particularly important from the employment point of view to maintain a nucleus of creative, imaginative and intelligent skilled workers', to enable yard capacity to be expanded when the time for this came. It was these very people who had the least difficulty in finding new employment and they were usually the first to leave.[30]

Talks about this scheme started in the OECD as well in the autumn of 1978.[31] The Japanese unions demonstrated their interest in a letter to IMF, the metal workers' international federation in Geneva,[32] and by the end of 1978 scrap-and-build was seen as something like the salvation of world shipbuilding.

The British unions initiated a scrap-and-build discussion in the EMF in October 1978,[33] with the proposal that the EEC Commission urgently work out a detailed scrap-and-build scheme. It was to be introduced by the Commission for shipowners and shipbuilders in the member states. But Japan and other shipping and shipbuilding countries were to be invited to operate similar schemes, 'with safeguards against low cost competition damaging European shipyards'. The secretariat of EMF elaborated a draft in February 1979.[34]

There were 'some practical difficulties' involved. For instance, there was no use in subsidising the scrapping of ships so old that they were likely to be scrapped anyway. The flags of convenience were not to be allowed an advantage over European owners, and shipbuilding should not be put in a position in which it was unable to compete with the East Asian countries for the new shipbuilding orders. Finally, EMF was not advocating 'unlimited subsidies' in a system where government money ended up in the pockets of the shipowners or got lost in speculation — particularly on ships which would be scrapped in any case. There had to be some kind of guarantee that it would ultimately be used for providing jobs.

In January 1979 the EEC Commission invited representatives of the Shipbuilders' Linking Committee and of the shipowners to a meeting, and a working party on scrap-and-build was established. The unions were not invited to join this new committee, which in effect partially replaced the tripartite committee which had been inactive since the first attempt to establish an EEC shipbuilding policy had failed. The main interest of the new scrap-and-build committee was in technical and financial considerations which were considered to be outside the immediate competence of the unions.

In meetings in January and February 1979 the committee discussed the various aspects of a scrap-and-build scheme. It soon found that it would not be very realistic to think in terms of a worldwide plan.[35]

The financial support to be provided within the scheme should be divided to support scrapping (to compensate for the difference between scrap prices for ships in 'the Far East' and second-hand prices) and financing new construction at favourable terms.

The annual cost of the scheme would be in the region of $150 m to subsidise scrapping and to cover 7 per cent of estimated average new construction prices to act as an incentive for new construction. The total cost of the scheme worked out at $2,429 per worker directly involved in shipbuilding.[36]

Although there remained opposition to the plan within the Commission itself, it was clear that the proposals were welcomed by the two industries concerned.[37] Nor were shipbuilders and the shipowners entirely without success in their talks with the Commission. In May 1979 the total annual costs of the scheme were now estimated at $191 m instead of $150 m, of which $105 m constituted the incentive element.[38] Scrap-and-build support should 'in principle be additional to national support measures', which were mainly designed to offset differences between European prices and the prices of 'external competitors', but which were not able to anticipate or generate additional orders.[39]

Meanwhile, scrap-and-build talks in the OECD about a plan involving Japan had by then got more or less bogged down. If it was difficult to agree upon a common policy within the EEC it was even more difficult within the OECD where, for instance, Japan and Sweden were also members. In any case the OECD was not prepared to take a decision before the EEC did so (or rather was not capable to doing so).[40]

There was a French move in the OECD for an early decision which was supported by the Greek government.[41] The Greeks had a lot of older tonnage and surplus tankers and were perhaps the strongest supporters of the IMIF plan. The talks in Working Party 6, the special shipbuilding committee within the OECD, raised many questions, such as how a scrap-and-build scheme would be financed, and each country was still anxious to find out what the scheme held for it.

The governments became more hesitant when they perceived that the plan would imply new costs outside their immediate control. The

215

idea was that the EEC and the OECD would have a decisive control function, i.e. power would be transferred from the national level to the international arena.[42]

The Danish metal workers were not interested in a Danish economic contribution.[43] The German IG Metall took a similar negative view.[44] This hesitation was based on the fact that the Danish and German merchant fleets were among the most modern ones. The yards in the two countries could hardly hope for many new orders from their own shipowners nor did they have much hope that shipowners from other countries would place their orders with them in the prevailing market situation.

The judgement by the EMF's general secretary, Hubert Thierron, at the beginning of June 1979, was that the EEC shipbuilders were generally very much in favour of a scrap-and-build scheme, but the shipowners were only moderately so. The shipowners' position was rather, scrap now, build later. The governments were undecided. Denmark, Germany and the Netherlands had serious reservations, but the other countries would eventually come round.[45]

From now on there was an obvious tendency within the EMF for the affiliates to begin to support the policies of their own governments.[46] These governments had different interests in a scrap-and-build scheme, and different policies gradually crystallised out. Three months later the unions also began to participate in this process. National identification seemed to be more important than international group solidarity. All the same, in September 1979 the Commission decided on a scrap-and-build scheme to be submitted to the Council and the European Parliament.[47] In October the EMF working group approved the scheme presented by the Commission. However, it had much less of a central place in the strategy of the federation than it had had only six months earlier. Supporting the scheme, but also stressing the other aspects of a Community policy for shipbuilding, became the strategy of the EMF in order to find a common denominator between the interests of different members. The Danish and German federations did not like the scrap-and-build scheme but were hardly prepared to resist it actively.[48] In November 1979 the EMF executive discussed shipbuilding questions, and by then the 'scrap-and-build' scheme had a far less important role than before.[49]

A few days later the Council made an initial examination of the scrap-and-build communication from the Commission. The outcome was rather negative. Germany and Denmark were opposed to the scheme. Great Britain and Italy were very much in favour of it. The other countries were rather hesitant ('yes, but too ambitious'). As to its financing, there was every indication that all the member states would prefer a national solution to a Community one.[50]

In practice the whole plan was now dead. The Commission drew up alternative proposals, but this was more to cover a retreat. The EMF had to revise its support of the scheme. National identification had proved stronger than group identification,[51] and six months later, in April 1980, the main interest of the EMF was in the possibility of opening the Social Fund to the shipbuilding industry and in alternative forms of maritime construction.[52]

The problem which finally undid the scrap-and-build scheme was the fear that the gap between second-hand and scrap prices would be too great. The additional aid which such a scheme would involve raised budget problems which could not be overcome. When the plan was discussed the price on second-hand tonnage rose quickly. It soon became clear that very large sums of money would be required for purchases for scrapping which only governments could provide.[53] No government was prepared in giving up control over such amounts of money to the Commission,[54] particularly those governments with little to gain.

The employers were no more successful in agreeing a common policy. There, too, the separation of national interests developed as the problems with the scrap-and-build programme began to emerge and as it became clear that the advantages would be unevenly distributed. According to the general secretary of the Association of West European Shipbuilders (AWES), Roy Brown, there were 14 shipbuilding countries and 14 shipbuilding policies in Western Europe in 1980. The situation within AWES was almost identical and the only principle to receive unanimous support was 'not to spread the jam too thin', i.e. that contraction should occur by the elimination of nonprofitable companies rather than giving some aid to all yards. The market should decide which companies were profitable.[55] But, of course, agreement on such a principle was much easier in principle and at the European level than in practice at the national level.

The failure of the scrap-and-build plan in 1980 was the second failure of the Commission to implement a common European shipbuilding policy. In 1980 the whole idea had failed. In March 1983 the Commission made a third attempt.[56] The aim of its guidelines for restructuring the shipbuilding industry was to stop EEC shipbuilders from trying to poach contracts away from each other, aided by public money. The proposals were intended as a first step toward a comprehensive EEC maritime policy. It started from the premiss that world shipbuilding capacity was 40 per cent above demand, equivalent to twice the EEC's production capability and almost equal to Japan's. The EEC shipyards were in a perilous position because the highly competitive Japanese yards had successfully reorganised and had turned from producing tankers and bulk carriers to merchant ships, the mainstay of EEC production. The member states said they were reaching the limit of capacity cutbacks which were socially and politically acceptable. Therefore individual yards should focus on modernising their production facilities and methods. The Commission was willing to approve subsidies to enable the yards to become competitive but denounced 'unproductive uses'.

By the end of 1983 there were discussions about how to link cash flow support to investment in new computer, laser welding and other techniques; expand joint research and development programmes; and make favourable credits available for any EEC shipowner to place orders in any EEC yard.[57] These discussions reflected a growing protectionist attitude directed at defending EEC shipbuilding and ensuring a minimum level of output. The target of this strategy was South Korea and other low-price countries.

In November 1983 the EMF supported this approach when its working party on shipbuilding expressly proposed action against Japan, Korea and Taiwan as an important element in a new EEC shipbuilding policy. This element was new, or at least had not been so frankly stated before. The proposal was for urgent EEC action to force Korea (*via* Japan) to increase prices.[58]

However, it must be emphasised that all attempts at united policy at the European level have so far failed. In the end for governments, unions and employers national crisis strategies took precedence over international ones. The same mechanisms which reduced co-operation at the level of the yard when we considered each country's response to the developing shipbuilding crisis, also served to limit collaboration at the national level when joint efforts were made internationally.[59]

THE INTERNATIONAL METAL WORKERS' FEDERATION

The IMF in Geneva is the metal workers' international federation. In 1985, 14 million metal workers in some 165 national affiliate federations in 70 countries constituted the basis of the organisation. Its membership is confined to Western Europe, Northern America and the industrialised parts of Asia and Latin America. There are no members from Eastern Europe or other communist countries. The secretariat in 1985 consisted of a general secretary and the three assistant secretaries from the US, Switzerland, Germany and Japan, a composition which mirrored the geographical distribution of influence within the IMF.[60]

Shipbuilding has played a major role in the policies of the IMF since at least the 1950s when the first shipbuilding conference was held. Such meetings have been held at three or four yearly intervals since 1950, and following the Hamburg conference in 1960, Karl Casserini, the Swiss assistant general secretary, has been responsible for shipbuilding within the IMF. Thus there has been considerable continuity within the organisation in terms of both international contacts and the seniority and technical competence of the officials involved, both essential elements for exerting influence. The interest mix within the IMF is, however, wider even than in the EMF because countries such as Japan and other shipbuilding nations of the Far East are members. Therefore the difficulties on agreeing a common policy which we found in the EMF might be expected to be greater within the IMF.

From the end of the 1960s Karl Casserini and Hans Hagnell (the Swedish metal workers' economist from 1946–71 and Social Democratic MP from 1957–73) tried to develop a more consistent policy. From 1967 Hagnell was chairman of the IMF's shipbuilding committee and he and Casserini emphasised the need to promote productivity increases in co-operation with industry and national governments to form the basis for increasing wages.[61]

Hagnell's and Casserini's approach was to promote highly productive yards which could produce profits and which were prepared to invest and to switch to the production of products other than ships if market prospects changed. Enterprises which were unprofitable in the long term would be closed and their workforces retrained for other employment. To mitigate the upheaval of such transfers, 'social plans' would be developed. The development of this strategy should be seen in its contemporary context of general economic growth. It had obvious points in common with the 'active labour market policy' developed by economists in the Swedish union movement.[62] References were made to the high wages in Sweden, to show that low wage costs were not a decisive advantage. On the contrary, high wages and good working conditions contributed to the high performances of profitable yards and allowed them to compete with state subsidised yards.[63]

At the conference in Genoa in 1964 the IMF required national tripartite committees in the shipbuilding countries to elaborate plans for economic reconstruction of a 'socially progressive shipbuilding industry'.[64] In 1965 a delegation was sent to Japan, to investigate the causes of the 'great competitive capability of the Japanese yards and their rapid and continuous expansion'.[65] The delegation's essential conclusion was that 'the level of the Japanese labour costs could not be the decisive factor', explaining the competitiveness of the Japanese shipbuilding industry. Enterprise structure, the government's shipbuilding policy, production programmes, division of labour, research, training, and the financing and credit systems were much more important.

In 1967 the secretariat argued for international tripartite co-operation.[66] The first phase should involve exchange of information about the development of projects and joint consideration of national structure plans. At the second stage the different shipbuilding policies were to be related to an estimate of market prospects and an international prognosis of the development of demand would then be undertaken. The third phase comprised international tripartite discussions about investment, though the secretariat were very sceptical of achieving any success at this final stage.[67] The problem was that nobody was interested in voluntary restraint. Everybody wanted to exploit their own interests to the full.

The problem of creating a unified front within the IMF was visible at the meeting in Newcastle. Dan McGarvey, president of the British Boilermakers, considered international schemes for reducing capacity or sharing the world market 'impracticable'. Ottorino Marghesan, from Italy, insisted that the solution for Italian shipyards must be found within 'national programming'. The Japanese delegate, Haruso Nishimoto, raised a storm of protest when he declared that 'no subsidies whatsoever' were paid to shipbuilders in Japan. He advocated orders being placed 'in accordance with the principle of free competition', a view hardly compatible with the secretariat's desire for planning. The French FO delegate, Paul Malnoë from St Nazaire, argued that government and industry in France only thought in terms of 'production, competition and profitability, while all too often rising productivity was accompanied by a reduction in the number of jobs'. Hans Hagnell, the president of the conference and the architect of the proposal to an IMF strategy, responded to Malnoë with the example from Sweden where (according to him) the yards received no production subsidies. Hagnell argued that in future Swedish yards would have a smaller labour force, and that in order to become more competitive and to pay higher wages, the industry had to be made more capital intensive.[68] More competitive yards would be to the benefit of the employees.

With such divergent opinions within the IMF, what basis could there be for a united strategy? And a unified international tripartite strategy would hardly be less problematic. In the years of greatest growth nobody was interested in voluntary restraint or the renunciation of self-interest. But the years following the collapse were also a time when everybody looked to their own immediate interests first.

Since the middle of the 1960s the IMF had warned of surplus capacity, but few had listened. In November 1976 and March 1977 the IMF told the OECD that their frequent reports on the situation of shipbuilding since the market collapse one year earlier had been too pessimistic. Although what the IMF had predicted was now a fact, they nevertheless considered they had been too pessimistic. This change in attitude can only be understood in terms of the change in the circumstances from dealing with what is a long-term threat to coming to terms with an immediate crisis. The same change from long-term strategy to short-term reaction was clear also within the German IG Metall at this time, for instance (p. 30). Once shipbuilding had crashed it was a matter of safeguarding as much employment as possible and this need emphasised the importance of the short period. This was seen by the IMF as requiring the distribution of orders to maintain maximum employment, procuring substitute work within heavy engineering industry, environmental protection and off-shore construction, retraining instead of sacking, the reduction of working time, the establishment of a permanent working party within OECD for shipbuilding policies from the point of view of employment, and using the already existing working party for the elaboration of social plans for contraction.[69]

The threat of a growing division between Japan and Western Europe worried the IMF and it tried to do what it could to prevent a further deterioration of the situation. In an address from the secretariat to the Asian shipbuilding seminar held in Tokyo in 1978 this was clearly demonstrated:

. . . no reliable prediction of potential orders is possible. But we can see nothing to make this outlook into the future brighter. All we can do under these circumstances, is to deepen and refine our understanding of the present situation, in order to find out where the roots of the evil lie and clear the ground for positive action.[70]

221

This statement clearly indicated that the IMF had nothing concrete to propose. Instead there were vague generalities. The main task of the IMF was 'to fight the chaotic conditions'. For this international co-operation was 'indispensable'. It had to bring about 'common policies that prevent one country planning measures to the detriment of others', and the OECD would be instrumental in attaining this goal. IMF-affiliates were asked to step up their activities in order to make their employers and their governments comply with the recommendations of the OECD.[71]

NATIONAL OR INTERNATIONAL SOLIDARITY?
CONCLUDING REMARKS

There have been attempts by both the European and the International Metal Workers' Federation to establish a common strategy, but in each case it proved too difficult to ignore national boundaries. The talks within the EMF and the IMF have been little more than a mirror image of the talks within the OECD. The outcome has been a propensity to use the international arena to defend national compromises.

The International Metal Workers' Federation was established more than 100 years ago to further the workers' struggle against capitalists. Workers who at that time lacked power to influence events at the national level looked towards international co-operation and solidarity for assistance. Integration of trade unions at the national level was followed by the effective disintegration of the international organisation as a means of representing collective interests.

The EMF and the IMF have both failed to take any effective action in supporting shipbuilding workers during the contraction of world shipbuilding. Their whole attention has been directed towards the establishment of tripartite bargaining at the international level. The aim has been to lift the national tripartite model up to the international level.[72] But such attempts have failed and events have inevitably brought it back to national level.

Attempts were made within the IMF to produce international schemes with long-term perspectives. But rapidly increasing difficulties in the wake of the market collapse have provoked short-term responses at the national level.[73]

When such organisations as the OECD and the EEC were established after World War II, the intention was to transcend the bounds set by the nation state. It was a logical response to the developments which had led up to the war in which nationalism had played an important role. In Western Europe internationalism was further stimulated by the Cold War. Another external threat, specific to shipbuilding, was the advance of Japan, and this produced temporary co-operation within the EEC (and the EMF). But in the OECD (and the IMF) Japanese competition was an internal problem producing division and ultimately paralysis. By the end of the 1960s, as friction in the world economy reached crisis proportions, there was a movement back to national identification and national solutions to growing problems.

9

The Politics of De-industrialisation

The counter revolutionary effects of the labour movement have
weakened the revolutionary tendencies of capitalism. (Rudolf
Hilferding in Winkler (ed.), p 10)

Chapter 1 posed the main question addressed in this study: what
explains the relatively trouble-free contraction of West European
shipbuilding? It was argued that the evidence of the demise of a
leading industry without major disruption could not in itself be taken
to imply a smoothly functioning social and political process designed
to suppress social discord. A detailed examination of the closure
programmes had to be made to establish how the real possibilities
of industrial, social and political disruption were avoided and what
this told us about advanced, capitalist industrial societies.

COMMON FEATURES

Government subsidies have made it possible to carry through a
gradual but progressive slimming down of West European shipbuilding, and 'social plans' negotiated in tripartite bargains enabled
this contraction to occur without widespread compulsory redundancy. Early retirement and voluntary redundancy individualised the
threat of unemployment and removed the shared experience which
could have formed the basis for collective action and mobilisation by
trade unions.

The social plans have thus caused collectively-experienced
threats of unemployment to evaporate. Such threats have been
transferred to marginal groups within the workforce: the elderly, the
young (denied access to employment) and others who were isolated

and lacked bargaining power, and the basis for collective action was further reduced because the individuals made the choice and were *compensated* by a variety of schemes. When it has been impossible to maintain the norm of no compulsory redundancy, the probability of collective action has been considerably increased. However, compulsory redundancy in itself has not been a sufficient pre-requisite. The threat had still to be collectively experienced. If the individuals or groups to be made redundant could be clearly inden-tified, and hence the threat both personalised and isolated from where effective protest could be maintained, then solidarity and collective action soon disappeared.

It is not surprising that the unions, when under pressure, take care of the interests of their members in the strongest bargaining position. Neither is division and individualisation in times of weakness a new phenomenon. However, there has been one difference when com-pared with, say, inter-war years. The workers' collective spirit and confidence in their ability to influence events seems to have decreased. Solidarity and collective ideals have not disappeared in shipbuilding but their social basis seems to have shrunk to smaller sections of the working class, to be mobilised only when exposed to collectively-experienced threats of unemployment or activated, for instance, to fight for survival of their own working place, often against other yards.

This change is long term and is a change from a belief in their own possibilities and capabilities, that it was in their own power to transform society, that they were responsible for their own future, to a belief in the union more as an intermediary agent for exerting pressure on the politicians in a pluralist system. The collective spirit has not disappeared but it has been transformed from one of 'we do it ourselves' to 'they do it for us'. In some countries and in some branches this change of attitude started as early as at the beginning of the twentieth century; for others it came later. The timing can be explained by a variety of experiences leading to different traditions. The craft workers in Glasgow, for example, who participated in the 'commonsense' liberalism before World War I, had quite different responses from the post-1930 working class on the Clyde.[1] Economic and/or political exclusion from society and the building of an industrial and political movement required and developed different forms of consciousness than that which resulted from integration into society and the acquisition of influence and also of responsibility.

It is important to be clear what is meant by integration. The use

225

of the concept 'integration' is all too often taken to mean successful incorporation, rather than just a temporary phase in a struggle for power involving both conflict and compromise. The contraction process in shipbuilding has been a historical process of action, reaction and interaction, around coincidental rather than common interests.

There has been a widespread belief that the state can mitigate the effects of restructuring which events, particulary in the short period, have done little to dispel. The social plans have allowed local co-operation between unions/shop stewards and managements. Quite often they have campaigned together for government money and the managed economy has been pliant enough to absorb pressure from below: the money spent on shipbuilding is evidence of this. The crucial role of capital to pressure groups in the corridors of political power has created a different situation from that in the 1930s.

The role of the unions was crucial when the social plans were negotiated; they were guaranteeing the social peace. However, the extent of union influence varied between the different countries. It was greatest in Sweden and Denmark and, for a brief time around 1979, in Great Britain. It was least in France. However, having influence does not mean that the unions have in any sense been able to prevent industrial contraction. Often, having influence meant taking responsibility for controversial decisions. The degree of influence is reflected in the terms and conditions for employees affected by the contraction. Few protests indicate a better social plan. Moreover, having influence has its price: with it goes the requirement that the unions ensure that their members accept the scheme.

Real influence also requires power. Almost the only power in the hand of the union leaders was the ability to mobilise the members to exert pressure on the politicians, directly or via public opinion. By ability to mobilise the members I mean the *potential* ability to do so. If the union leaders had the full backing of the shop floor this potential gave them a relative advantage in any negotiations. But the need for this power ran counter to the need for discipline. In the short run, therefore, the union leaders had to try to attempt to find a balance between discipline and mobilisation: between staying in tripartite bargaining and leaving it. An important question in the choice between these options was which one would exert the maximum influence on the shape of the social plan.

The argument that union leaders sought a balance between mobilisation and discipline should not be taken to indicate that the membership were easily manipulated by the union leaders. Neither mobilisation nor discipline is something that can be produced by 'pressing the button'. They are both products of complex inter-actions between the evaluations of the leadership and the degree of discontent among the membership.

The social plans also had their price. In the long run the unions lost influence as the success of the social plans increasingly made it more difficult to mobilise the members. Short-term success in the shaping of the social plans, thereby ensuring no compulsory redund-ancy, has been turned into a long-term problem for the union leader-ship as an effect of these same social plans was to individualise the threats of unemployment. This declining influence of the trade union is best demonstrated by the decreasing need for union participation in the closure programme after 1980, especially in Great Britain, Germany and the Netherlands. In addition, the social plans have exacted a high price in the marginalisation of large groups of young, elderly and otherwise disadvantaged people in an increasingly segmented labour market.

The unions were involved in a decision-making process in which no real gains could be expected and any decision would be criticised. In spite of this, the defence for participation was quite logical: the alternative was to have no influence at all. Integration into the decision-making process meant having some influence, but exactly how much depended on the degree of union power relative to that of the other participants. (See pp. 167–8 for a good example of this provided by the Dutch union representative, Jaap Meynikman.) Influence was therefore a matter of a power relationship which shifted over time, and in which the goal for every participant could at best be only partial success in achieving his objectives.

NATIONAL DIFFERENCES

The preceding analysis has shown important differences between the six countries, in a range from France to Denmark, with the latter country providing the example closest to a traditional model of tripartite co-operation.

In Denmark there have been tripartite talks since the middle of the 1960s, earlier and with greater influence than elsewhere. The basis of this union influence was a pragmatic market economy approach. This basis was a function of the Danish industrial and economic structure with its predominance of small enterprises. This structure produced a kind of 'Schumpeterian' small employer climate and abated the need for government intervention in individual enterprises. The market orientation within Danish social democracy and within the higher echelons of the unions produced a common interest in co-operation. Strains between union leadership and grass-roots have been absorbed by division resulting from a yard-by-yard closure strategy: each protesting in its turn.

Sweden has been rather close to the Danish case. However, the unions did not participate in tripartite talks until the middle of the 1970s. The absorption of the local unions in the national talks was a notable feature in Sweden. Decisions were made at the central level by local decision-makers from the yards, making yard closure difficult. If the yards were played off against each other, corporate decisions among the unions leaders would have been impossible. The 'cheese-cutter principle' of an even reduction of all yards held the strategy together. Therefore Metall left the tripartite talks when the closure of Öresundsvarvet and Arendal was proposed. When the decision to close down Öresundsvarvet had been taken, Metall returned. The Dutch case illustrates the fragility of the integration (as defined above). When the shipyard workers' top leaders lost touch with their members they were forced to leave the tripartite talks. In Britain, the unions were only involved in shipbuilding policies for a short period of time after nationalisation. The union branches were absorbed in the decision-making process at the national level in a way reminiscent of Sweden. Union influence reached its peak when in 1979 a 'no compulsory redundancy' clause was inserted in the Blackpool Agreement. But the Blackpool Agreement was broken after a few years. Compulsory redundancy and the slow growth of wages produced severe strains between the yards. The outcome was co-operation between management and shop stewards at the local yard level in a fight for survival. The period when British shipbuilding unions were strong and exerted influence was very brief and confined to a period when the successful persuance of the closure programme required participation of 'responsible' unions. By the beginning of the 1980s that need had more or less disappeared, just as it had elsewhere (in Germany and the Netherlands, for instance).

In all countries the restructuring of the shipbuilding industry has resulted in increased government intervention, but only in Britain and Sweden has the end result been a completely nationalised industry. In Britain, nationalisation had been part of the Labour Party's programme for socialisation. The Swedish Social Democrats traditionally (with the exception of the years immediately after World War II) concentrated on public consumption and a redistributive welfare policy by means of a distributive incomes policy, rather than on socialisation of the means of production. Capital was given freedom of action within limits set by the Social Democratic government; in fact it was a non-socialist government which finally had to nationalise the bankrupt shipbuilding industry. The German and Danish Social Democratic parties had much more market-oriented programmes than the Swedish Social Democrats or the British Labour Party. Both the rapid reconstruction in Germany after the war and the small enterprise structure of the Danish economy favoured such an approach by their respective movements. In this respect the Dutch Social Democrats were also rather close to their German counterparts. In France, government planning was important, but within a neo-liberal rather than a socialist framework.

The case of Germany reveals considerable pressure group activity in the decision-making process. The leadership at the regional level within IG Metall, where shipbuilding policies were decided, was opposed by the shipyard workers in Bremen and eventually IG Metall was forced to leave the tripartite talks on shipbuilding. In Bremen the chasm between the Social Democratic lord mayor Hans Koschnik and the workers at AG Weser was exposed in the middle of an election campaign in 1983, to the cost of the shipyard workers. Further divisions resulted from the federal structure, which gave the fight for government money a special character in Germany, with endless buck passing between regional and federal centres of decision-making.

In France the contraction policy was bipartite rather than tripartite. The French unions have not been integrated in the process and there have been no co-ordinated protests at the national level. The unions are organisationally weak and, in shipbuilding, less than 20 per cent of the workforce is in membership. Each of the three unions has followed a different strategy, thus reinforcing their weakness. Consequently the need to integrate them in the decision-making process has been small. There has, however, been greater co-ordination of union policies at the local level. There, at least up to the end of the 1970s, the struggle against closure has emerged as a conflict between labour and capital as compared with the other countries (although the Netherlands is a doubtful case), where concentration has been on local labour-capital co-operation to exert pressure on the politicians to obtain more government money. (The Dutch experience is reminiscent of the French one after the unions were forced to leave the tripartite talks.) The state in France has, paradoxically enough, remained much more in the background, playing only a co-ordinating and directing role. However, this does not mean that it kept completely aloof from the social groups which attempted to use it. Even in France the state has been ready to absorb protests when they seemed likely to become too strong.

Two main theories can be distinguished in historical and sociological research. The *integration theory* conceives of society in terms of a functionally-integrated system held in equilibrium by social processes.[2] The *coercion theory* regards society as a structure held together by force and constraint in which struggle between conflicting powers produces the force leading to continuous change. These theories are usually considered alternative explanations and mutually exclusive. But such a conclusion has been challenged by Dahrendorf and his position is supported by the empirical studies reported here.[3] The analysis has shown that consensus and conflict (either latent or manifest) have co-existed side by side. What from one point of view appears as consensual integration can appear as coercion and constraint from another perspective.[4] Theoretically, the two extremes are open conflict on all fronts and total concord in all areas. Between these two extremes there are of course many positions, altering in the historical process, but in reality it seems reasonable to suppose that there is always a certain amount of conflict. Real life is more often a matter of compromise than of consensus.

The state interventions in shipbuilding of the 1970s were not 'system inherent' but depended on the balance of power in tripartite bargaining. The radical eruption of 1968–9 was still fresh in people's minds. The potential for protest was strong, as was the support of public opinion for solidarity with the shipyard workers. However, the outcome was never predestined, but was decided by the degree of coincidental interests and power resources and how they were exploited in the bargaining. The resources available to shipbuilding depended on market forces which in the long term destroyed the power base of the Western European shipbuilding industry. When this was finally realised, at the beginning of the 1980s, and as general rivalry between social groups grew with economic stagnation, the subsidisation of shipbuilding was increasingly called into question and the basis of the tripartite bargaining disappeared.

This chain of events fits with Rolf Torstendahl's observation about the declining basis for what he calls participatory capitalism when economic growth slows. Increasing resources from economic growth allowed popular governments to contain antagonism within the industrial capitalist society. When these prerequisites disappeared participatory capitalism disappeared also.[5]

The empirically-based conclusions of our study are also compatible with Jonathan Zeitlin's theoretical perspective in a recent book.[6] In contrast to theories which reduce the role of the state to passive response to social pressures, or deduce its behaviour from a static functional analysis of social needs, Zeitlin treats state leaders as independent actors with their own goals and priorities constituting parts of historically formed intra-national institutional complexes with widely different structures and capacities. State interest and state structures are developed in the interaction between domestic social conflict and the requirements of international competition. Since few national governments are all-powerful, they have the need to collaborate with a variety of social groups. But the overlap between the state's interest and those of social groups is partial and contingent. Since the state's priorities are fundamentally distinct from those of any of the groups, the potential for conflict is always present. At certain moments, depending on the historical situation, some social interest carry more weight than others, but in the democratic Western European political system few governments will for long be able to ignore completely interests of organised labour.

Theda Skocpol has also thrown doubt upon reductionist state theories, whether liberal or Marxist, in which the state is regarded simply as a political arena in which conflicts over basic social and economic interests are fought out, and in which the start is seen as embodying either consensually-based legitimate authority, or coercive class domination.[7]

> The state's own fundamental interest in maintaining sheer physical order and political peace may lead it — especially in periods of crises — to enforce concessions to subordinate-class demand. These concessions may be at the expense of the interests of the dominant class, but not contrary to the state's own interests in controlling the population and collecting taxes and military recruits.[8]

Skocpol's emphasis on the role of the international context for the state is convincing. Her emphasis on the autonomy of the state is certainly an advance compared with earlier liberal and Marxist models. However, the concept of state autonomy she presents is too simple. She does not discuss the reasons for believing that states and their leaders are autonomous: what the relationship is between group interests and state autonomy or between group leaders and state leaders.

The contraction of the West European shipbuilding industry demonstrates that governments are very sensitive to group interests and have been keen to react to group pressure. But, on the other hand, at other times the state has acted quite independently. Thus the degree of state autonomy in action varies and demonstrates a complex overlapping between dependence and independence of pressure group activities. Moreover, the ways these tendencies operate seem quite independent of the political affiliations of the government. This argument is elaborated in greater detail below when the nature of the 'political market' is discussed. Suffice it here to stress the very great importance of the world market conditions in setting the stage for the relative autonomy of the state in its internal policies.

Jürgen Habermas has show important links between the work of Marxist and non-Marxist scholars and has made impressive efforts with his systems to articulate an undogmatic, evolutionary view. His analysis of contemporary capitalist society diverges considerably from the traditional Marxist analysis. He finds unconvincing the thesis that the state is merely an instrument of capital. The state is of vital importance in guaranteeing compromises, and can mitigate the effects of the capitalist system. Its output consists of administrative resources and measures to govern society. Its input is mass loyalty. Legitimacy (input) is dependent on the motivation of the members. Legitimation problems arise in developed capitalist societies as a result of the fundamental conflict between the social welfare responsibilities and the functional conditions of the capitalist economy. If the state does not succeed in keeping the dysfunctional side-effects of the capitalist economic process within bounds acceptable to the voting public, it will lose its legitimacy. This is marked by increasing conflict over the distribution of income and wealth between wages and profits. The rate of inflation, the financial crisis of the state, and the rate of unemployment each indicate failure in the task of securing stability.[9] The state on the one hand has to raise the required tax from profits, wages and other income and use this to mitigate the adverse effects of growth and, on the other hand, to legitimate the use of it. A failure on one side or other results in crisis.[10]

The problem with Habermas's model is that it is a kind of functional equilibrium model which is dislodged by mutation to another equilibrium. Zeitlin's perspective of a gradual *process* of change (which does not exclude sudden changes) seems more convincing and gains more support from the case of shipbuilding.

This view differs considerably from that of the more or less harmonious integration of the union elites into the decision-making process which we find in many 'corporate state' models of Western society. It is argued here that a more fruitful approach to that of corporate state theory is to focus on the balance of power between interest groups and, in the case of shipbuilding, to emphasise the command over resources to ease temporarily the stress of contraction, rather than taking a vaguely defined common interest as a point of departure. But this is not to argue that all interests are conflictual. The decision about the contraction of the West European shipbuilding industry demonstrates, for instance, that it was easier to hold a common view on the goals than on the means.

My conclusion is close to the view of Andrew Cox who, in a critical article, argues that corporatist theories are in the last analysis reductionist.[11] Their basic premiss is that the modern state allows functional pressure groups not only to influence government policy, but also to become incorporated within the machinery of decision-making as of right. Pressure groups are allowed to shape policy and in return they will put the 'higher interest' of the state before their members' sectional interest. According to Schmitter we have co-operative rather than competitive pressure groups, which have legitimate, hierarchical and institutionalised relationships with government. Pressure group activities based on the defence of sectional interests have been replaced by co-operation with governments, particularly in the economic sphere.[12]

Cox criticises corporatist theories on three points. The argument that the state would secure control by the search for national, rather than sectional, interests has proved wrong. Secondly, the long-term potential for, and the degree of, incorporation of trade unions and industry into government decision-making and policy implementation has been overestimated. Thirdly, far from being a continuing effort by governments to control and direct microeconomic practices, their policies have been *ad hoc*, supportive subventionary and reactive. In corporatist theories the role of the state is monolithic with definite goals and interests. Cox's criticism of this point fits well the evidence of this study.

Marxist corporatist theorists have argued that the state uses trade

233

unions to gain political support from, and to exert control over, their members. Liberal corporatist theorists have argued that these organisations penetrate the state and transform it for their own purposes.[13] The empirical analysis of the present study reveals the narrowness of both views. Organised interests *have* acted as pressure groups to influence political decisions, but not to penetrate the state apparatus nor to take power. There has been a continuous process of response and counter-response between worker organisations and the state, not uni-directional control in either direction.

This fits well within Walter Korpi's model based on a study of Sweden. He has argued that the interaction between labour, capital and the state must be seen as a process of societal bargaining. In this bargaining process outcomes are not predetermined but depend largely on the distribution of power resources between the parties. The relative strength between them can significantly affect the action of the state representatives and thus the pattern of coalition formation in this tripartite bargaining.[14]

The shipbuilding crisis has been related to world economic factors that were difficult to influence, rather than to specific problems of the capitalist system at the local level or national level.[15] There have been doubts about the real possibility of effective action, not only for the unions but also for the state. As this scepticism refers to international factors, the consequence has not been a loss in union or political legitimacy. The problem of legitimacy only arises for a government which fails to persuade that it has done everything in its power to mitigate the effects of the crisis. Prophesies which have been made about a general crisis for the interest representation, as a rule more theoretically than empirically founded, do not find any empirical support in my study.

In retrospect it is clear that industrial policies within the framework of the nation state aimed at fighting internationally-derived developments can only be re-active and retarding.

The Swedish example of an active labour market policy (p. 102), working generally rather than sectorially, could perhaps serve as an example of more active government counter-strategies, though that model has not worked without problems and must be considered as the result of a specific national development which cannot be simply translated to other countries. Thus it can serve not as a general recipe but as an example of how new jobs could be created by means of massive retraining programmes and general investment in knowledge rather than by vain attempts to create a new job corresponding directly to each one which has been lost. Such a strategy could contribute to reducing unemployment and to producing commitment instead of hopelessness.

This is not to say that short-term sectoral interventions to give temporary mitigation have been senseless. Such interventions must be understood as historically-given political responses to economic and social processes.

Closely related to the sectoral problems of intervention in industries is the broader question of the prospects for intervention at the national level with the apparent breakdown in the Keynsian model. What are the options open to the national state exposed to strong international forces? Assar Lindbeck has highlighted the problem:

> Thus at the same time as national governments have raised their ambitions to direct the details of the domestic economies, international forces have made both many targets and several policy instruments less susceptible to domestic national manipulation than formerly. Many new problems can be fruitfully seen in the perspective of these increased domestic policy ambitions in combination with the weakening of the national state relative to the ever stronger international forces. 'People' demand more and more of the national state, at the same time as the national state is losing much of its autonomy because of the internationalisation process.[16]

Skidelsky has argued in a similar way.[17]

Thus regarded, the welfare state is not simply the outcome of pressure on the part of groups of reformers but rather a measure of what powerful opponents of reform either chose to concede to that pressure or what could be conceded given international market forces. The point is not that the welfare measures decided upon were simply the preferred ones of the reformers but that they were also acceptable to their opponents. Welfare is thus not only an alternative to the uncontrolled working of the market but also an alternative to the greater control involved in the demand for socialism.

Such a perspective of social bargaining in a power context provides important insights into the role of the welfare state during the contraction process of the West European shipbuilding industry. It is a perspective which focuses on the link between action and structure. The structure of the state is not impersonal. It is malleable as a result of political actions made by representatives of different social interests in a process of social bargaining. However, as has

235

been argued above, political leaders do not only represent group interests, they have a wider constituency.

My concept of the political market should be seen in this context of social bargaining. *In the political market votes giving political power are bought from voters for welfare and other measures.* As used here the notion of the political market is expressly *not* seen as a functionalist concept presuming an analogy between political parties and politicians on one side and entrepreneurs in a profit-seeking economy on the other. Political parties do not generally formulate which policies they believe will gain the most votes, as entrepreneurs produce whatever products they believe will gain the most profits. Maximisation of votes can never be an unconditional goal. For reasons of credibility among other things, a policital party has to consider the interests of its core supporters, its traditions, ideology, and the need for a degree of continuity in political performance. I have expressly *not* used the concept in the sense of a rational calculation of how to maximise votes, but in the sense of responsiveness to pressures and to changing public opinion in a process of social bargaining. Thus the political market is a place for political strife and social bargaining as much as a place where policy concessions are traded for votes.

The country chapters above demonstrate that the historical process is one of alternatives. The historical explanations which I have used to account for the relatively trouble-free and undramatic contraction process of West European shipbuilding have not explained what 'had to happen' because it was 'given by the system', but what actually happened, ultimately as a result of power relationships. However, ultimately the international market was the factor which in the long run has been decisive for developments in the Western European shipbuilding industries. It set the limits of the managed economies and of the national frameworks of tripartite bargaining.

To counter this would have required a protectionist policy. The problem with this is not that free trade *per se* is more efficient. As Zeitlin convincingly argues, state managers can be seen as natural mercantilists, whatever their economic programme, because they regard wealth as a source of power — of international influence, of government revenues, and of popular legitimacy and support — rather than as an end in itself. Thus regarded, free trade as much as protectionism may be deployed as an instrument of power.[18]

The traditional difficulty with a mercantilist policy is that everybody wants to export but nobody to import. In these circumstances there is a division of interest between the employees in the export industries and those in industries which are looking for protection. The shipyard workers certainly argued for protection. However, their claims were 'diluted' in the unions of which they were only a part, because other members, employed in industries dependent on export, would not support them. In addition, it is not possible to have a partial solution to import penetration; the whole system must be controlled and this requires a total protectionistic policy (e.g. 'no ships built in, say, Korea, will be accepted in European ports'). There was no political support for such a rigid strategy.

The tripartite bargaining within West European shipbuilding demonstrates that industrial democracy is located in the market, not in the workplace.

Chapter 8 clearly demonstrates that there was no international support for equalising differences in wage costs and productivity by means of international action to increase the standard of living of shipyard workers and the strength of the unions in low-price countries. Such differences in fact have been the ultimate basis of mercantilist strategies in these countries.

CONCLUSIONS

I began this study in 1979–80 with the intention of studying the shipbuilding 'crisis'. As a consequence and perhaps without too much reflection I expected great difficulties and social upheavals. But that did not happen. What I observed was a progressive, and relatively peaceful, structural transformation.

In 1986 it is difficult to see any general crisis in the capitalist system. It is more a matter of major restructuring with long-term unemployment as a result. There are many indications to support such a view. In the seven major OECD countries the fraction of wages in national incomes is now lower than before the first oil price rise in 1973. The forecast is that this fraction will decline even further. A large proportion of the unemployed in 1984 had been unemployed for more than 12 months: 63 per cent in Belgium, 44 per cent in the Netherlands, 43 per cent in France, 37 per cent in Britain and 28.5 per cent in West Germany. The introduction of new technology has led to enormous productivity gains, especially in metal manufacturing. A particularly striking facet of this is the introduction of robots, machining centres and completely automated production processes, with obvious implications for employment.

Table 9.1: Average growth rate in the seven major OECD countries, 1975–84

1975	Jan–Jun	−3.2	1979	Jan–Jun	2.9	1982	Jan–Jun	−1.4
	Jul–Dec	5.2		Jul–Dec	3.2		Jul–Dec	0
1976	Jan–Jun	6.6	1980	Jan–Jun	0.5	1983	Jan–Jun	3.0
	Jul–Dec	3.1		Jul–Dec	−0.3		Jul–Jun	5.4
1977	Jan–Jun	5.2	1981	Jan–Jun	3.9	1984	Jan–Jun	5.9
	Jul–Dec	3.8		Jul–Dec	0.4			
1978	Jan–Jun	4.7						
	Jul–Dec	4.7						

Source: ILO, *World Labour Report*, 1984, Table A.1.

This has fallen sharply in mechanical engineering, shipbuilding, steel and automobile manufacturing and many other sectors, a decline exacerbated by the stagnation in demand.

It would be misleading to suggest that the geographical shifts in production, new industry structure, the worldwide operations of large corporations and banks and the rapid advance of new technology have not produced tensions and radical change. But there has been no general crisis: only for certain groups in certain sectors. The exceptional economic progress during the two decades after World War II has certainly slowed down but has remained significant, as the average growth rate in the seven major OECD countries 1975–84 shows (Table 9.1).[19]

We still think of Western Europe as an industrial society. However, in the 1980s in most West European countries only some 30 per cent of the labour force was employed in manufacturing industry,[20] and the increase in the number of white collar grades has meant that only 20 per cent are in the traditionally well-unionised manual worker categories. Thus the centre of the social process is no longer the old industrial working class. This is an essential ingredient of the contraction process in the shipbuilding industry.

What then of the protests which did take place, of the unions' efforts and, on a more general level, the industry's pressure for more government money? Is this to be regarded as a rearguard action with no prospects, reminiscent of the vain fight by the handloom weavers 150 years ago against the new machines? Has it just been a fight to maintain an obsolete structure: Luddite and irrational?

From the shipbuilding workers' as from the weavers' point of view their behaviour can be argued to have been rational. They wanted to keep their jobs and chose a means for achieving that objective. What may appear irrational are often perfectly reasonable attempts to articulate grievances or negotiate with the authorities, particularly when the economic situation offers no alternative prospects. Far from being simply a 'squandering of the taxpayers' money' and a 'maintenance of obsolete structures', they represented the rational expression of the interests of the 'losers' from economic 'progress' aimed at the rest of society — the beneficiaries of that process. This view was well expressed by E.P. Thompson:

> I am seeking to rescue the poor stockinger, the Luddite cropper, the 'obsolete' hand-loom weaver, the 'utopian' artisan, and even the deluded follower of Joanna Southcott, from the enormous condescension of posterity. Their crafts and traditions may have been dying. Their hostility to the new industrialism may have been backward-looking. Their communitarian ideals may have been fantasies . . . Their aspirations were valid in terms of their own experience; and, if they were casualties of history, they remain, condemned in their own lives, as casualties.[21]

Of course, there is an idealising element in Thompson's perspective. Division and sectionalism are ignored and the workers are here regarded as one unified class. The case of shipbuilding in the 1970s and the 1980s reveals a less tidy reality. However, Thompson's strength is in his stress on the importance of the workers' own perspective. Their fight was a conservative fight in Hilferding's sense in the epigraph to this chapter, but it was not a quixotic fight against windmills.

Unions as the organised section of the underclass carry the dual responsibility for the interests of their members and for social progress. Given sectionalism and the new divisions within advanced industrial capitalist societies (e.g. between private and public sector employees, between employed and unemployed) and within the international order, is it possible to maintain that the unions of the advanced industrial countries still represent the interests of the weak and poor? During the contraction process in shipbuilding they have hardly represented the interests of the most disadvantaged. They have been fully implicated in the use of social plans and other strategies designed to concentrate the job loss on marginal groups in the labour market. So regarded, union policies like others should be evaluated in power terms rather than moral ones. But, having said that, the waged workers the unions have supported and represented hardly belong to privileged groups.[22] And, moreover, shipbuilding is only one section of the union movement and one in which the organisation basis was ebbing away. The only possibility for representing the members', or any other, interests depended on the mobilisation of its industrial strength and popular support. When these disappeared the organised shipbuilding workers lost all influence.

This helps explain why the unions have not acted as the engaged and involved forward-looking organisations they once were. Their policies have been defensive of the interests of a declining social group. More than anything else they have required protection by governments. Whether they have been as influential or as strong as they once were, is probably not an important question. It is more a matter of whether they have had the future on their side or not.

Notes

CHAPTER 1

1. All prophecies, founded in theoretical constructs rather than in empirical findings, about the total breakdown of the political and economic system have been confounded. For such theories see, for instance, Bergmann *et al.*, Bierbaum *et al.*, Zeuner and Herkommer *et al.* They all predict the development of class consciousness as a process more or less inherent in the very situation of the working class in a period of capitalist crisis. So regarded they all rest upon statements from an older Marxist tradition (see for instance Goldmann). In this way a crisis in some key branches of the economy seems to have been equated with a crisis in the whole capitalist system.

2. For such an approach see Dahrendorf. See also Rex, pp. 129–40. I have earlier used a corresponding approach in studies of the rise and development of reformist political traditions in some shipbuilding centres in Sweden and Germany (Stråth, 1982, pp. 142–57, and 1984). The concept of integration quite often has overtones of successful incorporation. My perspective is rather that of the temporary compromise between groups in a continuous process of conflict and compromise in the struggle for power. The notion of integration should not disallow the possibility of resolving conflicts without integration.

3. Cf. Anthony D. Smith, p. 12.

4. Reproduced in McCulloch (ed.), pp. 620–1.

5. Röpke, pp. 25–6.

6. Minutes from shipbuilding conferences of the International Metal Workers' Federation in Geneva 1964 and Newcastle 1967. IMF Archives, Geneva. See also Bohlin, p. 39, who supports this view.

7. Almost from the beginning it was economically a fiasco. It was constructed for production in series of tankers up to 200,000 dwt. That was the absolute maximum size the management could imagine when the yard was planned. When it came into use ships of 400,000 dwt. or more were standard. There is however an obvious bias in constructing a long-term trend curve for the development of the production if such a curve is based on dwt or grt. Such a curve mirrors the technological breakthrough but conceals other factors. A concentration on ships more sophisticated than the huge plate hulls of the tankers, for instance, is reflected in such a curve as stagnation or decline. There was no growth in employment corresponding to the rapidly growing tonnage figures. The measure in compensated grt tries to evaluate and include the amount of labour but it is for different reasons a problematic measure.

8. Röpke, p. 128.

9. *Maritime Transport*, 1959–79.

10. For the Japanese development, see Chida, Cornford and Glasgow; Interviews with Mr Isoe Takizawa, Kobe Steel and Mr Kenji Hasegawa, advisor, Kawasaki Heavy Industries, June 1985. For the restructuring of

professional skills see Svensson, p. 305.

11. Stopford and Barton.

12. Kondratieff, pp. 105–15.

13. See for instance Schumpeter, p. 61. See also Rostow who considers the relationship between Kondratieff and Schumpeter in their views on the long wave. Cronin, pp. 38–9, tries to relate social history to long-wave theories. He argues that there exist periodical patterns in industrial conflict and relates this periodicity to economic long-waves theories.

14. Lorenz, 1983, pp. 155–94; Stråth, 1983; Svensson.

15. Stråth, 1982.

16. Stråth, 1984.

17. Stråth, 1982, 1983, 1984.

18. Crouch, pp. 180–2; Villox, pp. 135–8.

19. Zoll et al.

20. *Westinform Shipping Report*, No. 187, August 1961. For the role of the bankers and the combination of bankers' credits and government subsidies during this process, see Glasgow.

21. Hiort-Lorenzen, pp. 11–12.

22. Interview with the chairman of the inquiry committee, Per Nyström, October 1982.

23. Ibid., cf. Schultes, p. 25.

24. Schultes, p. 26.

25. Flieshardt and Sablotny, pp. 95–105.

26. OECD. Recommendation of the Council concerning government assistance to the shipbuilding industry, 30 May 1969. OECD, Paris.

27. Ibid., 16 December 1970.

28. Olsson, pp. 246–50; With Andersen, Stråth, Svensson (eds). See especially the contributions by Herlitz, Ditlev-Simonsen, jnr, Gram and Olsson and the following discussions.

29. Interview with John Ekström, Shipbuilding Division of Ministry of Industry, Sweden — and wp 6, OECD, November 1984.

30. Schulmann et al., p. 178.

31. Interview with A. Pedersen, HDW, Kiel, April 1980.

32. Frisch, p. 373. See also Kuhne, pp. 9–15.

33. Frisch, p. 373.

34. Ljungberg, p. 86.

35. *Geddes Report*, HM Shipbuilding Inquiry Committee, 1965–6.

36. Hamilton, p. 16.

37. See, for instance, reports by the Association of West European Shipbuilders, May, 1982. AWES, Delft and the Shipbuilders' Association of Japan, July 1982. SAJ, Tokyo. Interview with Dr Böhme, Institut für Weltwirtschaft, Kiel, December 1983.

38. International Labour Office. *Yearbook of labour statistics 1983*, pp. 278–82, and references in Table 1.4 above. In 1975 the ratio of employees in shipbuilding to all employees in manufacturing industry varied between 0.5 and 4.3 per cent: W. Germany 0.5, Belgium 0.5, France 1.0 (incl. naval yards), UK 10.0, Sweden 2.1, Denmark 3.2 and the Netherlands 4.3 per cent.

39. Hamilton, pp. 14–15.

40. See for instance Hamilton, Juttemeier, Lammers and Sveriges

Industriförbund . . . 19 November 1980. Federation of Swedish Industries, Stockholm.

41. Hamilton, p. 17.

42. Hardy and Tyrell, pp. 138–43.

43. Skidelsky, 1977, p. 33.

CHAPTER 2

1. For this development see, for instance, Wulf.

2. Schumann *et al.*, p. 178.

3. Flieshardt and Sablotny, pp. 95–105; interviews with Fritz Fischer, works council, Blohm & Voss and A. Pedersen, HDW, Kiel, April 1980.

4. Flieshardt and Sablotny, p. 66; Kappel and Rother, p. 980; the personnel dept., HDW.

5. Interview with Gerd Lilienfeldt, IG Metall, Bezirksleitung, Hamburg, May 1983.

6. Müller-Jentsch and Sperling, pp. 283–5.

7. Esser, p. 192.

8. Election statistics, 1975, 1978, 1981. Works council, HDW Kiel.

9. Müller-Jentsch and Sperling, p. 282.

10. 'IG Metall Vorstand. Überarbeitete Stellungnahme zum Werft-gutachten 1973 unter besonderer Berücksichtigung der 1973 vom VDS der Bundesregierung zugeleiteten Strukturkonzepts', 25 May 1973. IG Metall, Bezirksleitung, Hamburg.

11. Karl H. Pitz, responsible for shipbuilding in the board (*Vorstand*) of IG Metall in *der Gewerkschafter*, No. 9, 1976.

12. Pitz in ibid., No. 1, 1977.

13. Interview with Volkhard Meier, Verband der Deutschen Schiffbau-industrie (VDS), March 1983.

14. IG Metall was certainly not exclusively market oriented: they demanded, as has been emphasised, extensive planning and public financial support for the creation of new jobs in other fields. The key concept of the IG Metall strategy was a *planned* reduction.

15. '7. Nationale Schiffbaukonferenz der IG Metall am 3. März 1978, in Hamburg. Protokoll.' IG Metall, *Bezirksleitung*, Hamburg.

16. 'Bericht über Struktur und Entwicklung des deutschen Seeschiff-baus. 1978', Verband der Deutschen Schiffbauindustrie (VDS), Hamburg.

17. Ibid., p. 1.

18. 'Stellungnahme der IG Metall zum Bericht über Struktur und Entwicklung des deutschen Schiffbaus vorgelegt vom Verband der Deutschen Schiffbauindustrie im September 1978', IG Metall the board (*Vorstand*), October 1978. IG Metall, Bezirksleitung, Hamburg.

19. Ibid., March 1980.

20. Ibid., p. 6.

21. 'Bundesminister für Wirtschaft. Kabinettsvorlage zum Konzept der Bundesregierung für die Schiffbaupolitik und für Maßnahmen zugunsten des Schiffbaus', PM 1 December 1978. Ministry of Economics, Bonn IV B 5 — 2270 03/301; interview with Hans Matthöfer, September 1984.

22. Ibid.; *Bulletin*, 19 January 1979.

23. As the Bremen Social Democrat MP Claus Grobecker in the important budget committee of *Bundestag* picturesquely put it, defending the federal government: 'The Länder governments have in the last weeks and months claimed subsidies . . . for the yards like Tibetan prayer mills.' Claus Grobecker, Pressemitteilung, 11 January 1979. Senator Claus Grobecker's private archives, Bremen; interview with Dr Wolfgang Obernolte, Ministry of Economics, Bonn, August 1984.

24. 'Entschliessung der Konferenz Norddeutschland am 21. April 1983', 'Referat Nationale Schiffbaukonferenz am 21. April 1983 von Bezirksleiter Otto vom Steeg', IG Metall, *Bezirksleitung*, Hamburg.

25. Michael Budczies, president of the Verband der Deutschen Schiffbauindustrie (VDS), in *Kieler Nachrichten*, 22 April 1983.

26. *Handelsblatt*, 29 and 30 November 1983', *die Zeit*, 2 December 1983.

27. Letter from Koschnik to the works councils of AG Weser and Bremer Vulkan, 14 July 1982. IG Metall local branch, Bremen. The figure can only be interpreted as a rough estimate. The letter was written in order to demonstrate how much had been done already for shipbuilding. It was hardly in the interests of Koschnik to lower the figure.

28. Bundestag debate, 12 September 1983. See statements by Grobecker, Gansel, and Klose (SPD), Minister of Economics Lambsdorff and Minister of Finance Stoltenberg. See also *Handelsblatt*, 13 September, 29 and 30 November 1983 and *die Zeit*, 2 December 1983.

29. 'Entschliessung der Konferenz Norddeutschland am 21. April 1983' (speeches by Michael Budczies, VDS and Otto vom Steeg, IG Metall. IG Metall, *Bezirksbeitung*, Hamburg.

30. 'IG Metall. Vorstand. 8. Nationale Schiffbaukonferenz am 17. August 1983', IG Metall, *Bezirksleitung*, Hamburg.

31. 'Ausführungen des Vorsitzers, Dr. Michael Budczies, vor der Pressekonferenz am 31 Mai 1983 anlässlich der Mitgliederversammlung des Verbandes der Deutschen Schiffbauindustrie e.v.', VDS, Hamburg. Of course, the suggestion of such a precise correlation between subsidies and redundancy is a nonsense intended for the political market; the future is never predictable in such an exact mathematical way.

32. The cyclical perspective still predominated in the considerations of the federal government in the autumn of 1978, before the Aid Bill in January 1979. The market was supposed to turn in 1982–3. 'Bundesminister für Wirtschaft. Kabinettsvorlage zum Konzept der Bundesregierung für die Schiffbaupolitik und für Massnahmen zugunsten des Schiffbaus', Ministry of Economics, Bonn, IV B 5-2270 03/301.

33. Letters from IG Metall to the Chancellor Helmut Schmidt, 14 April 1982, and to the Lord Mayor of Bremen Hans Koschnik, 19 April 1982. IG Metall, Bezirksleitung, Hamburg; 'Bundesminister für Wirtschaft. Kabinettsvorlage zum Konzept der Bundesregierung für die Schiffbaupolitik and für Massnahmen zugunsten des Schiffbaus', Ministry of Economics, Bonn, IV B 5 — 2270 03/301; letter from the Social Democratic MP Claus Grobecker to the Minister of Finance Hans Matthöfer, 30 October 1978. Private archives of senator Claus Grobecker, Bremen.

34. Flieshardt and Sablotny, pp. 2–3.

35. *Nordsee-Zeitung*, 29 April 1982.

36. *Weser-Kurier*, 14 June 1982; Cf also *Bremer Nachrichten*, 14 June 1982.

37. 'Gutachten zur Verbesserung der Leistungs — und Wettbewerbsfähigkeit der Werftindustrie im Land Bremen. Juli 1982', IG Metall, local branch, Bremen.

38. 'Gemeinsame Presseerklärung der Betriebsräte AG Weser und Bremer Vulkan AG', 16 July 1982. IG Metall, local branch, Bremen.

39. Letter from Lord Mayor Hans Koschnik to the works councils of AG Weser and Bremer Vulkan, 14 July 1982. IG Metall, local branch, Bremen.

40. Enclosure of 'Gemeinsame Presseerklärung . . .', 16 July 1982. IG Metall, local branch, Bremen.

41. Interview with Heinz Meinking, IG Metall, local branch, Bremen, Hans Ziegenfuss, chairman works council AG Weser, and Karl Schönberger, vice chairman of Bremer Vulkan works council, May 1983.

42. 'AG Weser-Bremer Vulkan: Stellungnahme zum Werftgutachten', IG Metall, local branch, Bremen.

43. Interview with Meinking, Ziegenfuss and Schönberger, May 1983.

44. Letter from the Minister of Economy Lambsdorff to the works councils of AG Weser and Bremer Vulkan, 12 August 1928. IG Metall, local branch, Bremen.

45. 'Stellungnahme der Betriebsräte der AG Weser und Bremer Vulkan AG', 12 November 1982. IG Metall, local branch, Bremen.

46. 'IG Metall. Bezirksleitung Hamburg. Arbeitsplatze sichern. Stellungnahme zum Gutachten für die Werften im Lande Bremen', December 1982. IG Metall, local branch, Bremen.

47. 'IG Metall. Bezirksleitung Hamburg. Erklärung zur Werftsituation im Lande Bremen', 15 February 1983. IG Metall, local branch, Bremen.

48. *Weser-Kurier*, 13 February 1983.

49. *Bremer Nachrichten*, 15 February 1983.

50. 'IG Metall. Bezirksleitung Hamburg. Eriklärung . . .', 15 February 1983. IG Metall, local branch, Bremen.

51. *Bremer Nachrichten*, 17 February 1983.

52. Ibid. and *Weser-Kurier*, 8 February 1983. Interview with Otto Graflambsdorff, Jan. 1985.

53. *Handelsblatt*, 14 February 1983; interview with Dr Wolfgang Obernolte, Ministry of Economics, Bonn, August 1984; Ministry of Economy 'Zur Lage des deutschen Schiffbaus'. Memorandum, March 1983. IG Metall, *Bezirksleitung*, Hamburg.

54. Interview with Günther Erdmann, official in charge of shipbuilding in the government of Schleswig-Holstein, October 1983.

55. 'SPD Hamburg. Ausserordentliche Landesparteitag 21./22.4.1983. Vorlage Nr 46/83', IG Metall, *Bezirksleitung*, Hamburg.

56. *Bremer Nachrichten*, 16 May 1983.

57. 'Bremer Vulkan. Bericht zur gegenwärtigen Lage des Unternehmens', 2 March 1983. IG Metall, local branch, Bremen; *Norddeutsche Zeitung*, 2 March 1983.

58. Interview Meinking, Ziegenfuss, Schönberger, May 1983.

59. *Bremer Nachrichten*, 13, 17 August 1983.

60. *Handelsblatt*, 15 August 1983.

61. Interview with Klaus Grobecker und Heinz Meinking June 1984;

Ziegenfuss, Heseler, Kröger (eds), p. 12. In December 1981 the Senate had intervened in Bremer Vulkan, which faced bankruptcy after miscalculations on a luxury cruiser and as a general contractor for a frigate programme of the federal navy. AG Weser had also made large losses but — as distinguished from Vulkan — up to 1982 they had a so-called profit-and-loss adjustment agreement (*Ergebnisabführungsvertrag*) with the mother company, i.e. Krupp had to guarantee the solidarity of the yard. Thus bankruptcy was impossible as long as the whole concern was not bankrupt. Such an arrangement is tax-efficient when profits are generated, but this is no longer the situation. The repudiation of the agreement in 1982 was a clear signal that Krupp wanted to withdraw from shipbuilding and that they did not intend to put more money into the yard. The steel concern had passed the initiation to the Senate.

Before the repudiation of the agreement Krupp had taken note of the collective agreement and urged stricter conditions of work in order to increase productivity. The works council immediately rejected this. However, IG Metall considered the proposal an attempt to provoke a 'no' from the employees only in order to have an excuse to close down the yard. Under protest both from the works council and internally, IG Metall agreed to the Krupp proposal in an attempt to deflect the provocation. The decision was passed by only a small majority. In opposition to the majority of the union, the chairman of the works council, Hans Ziegenfuss, talked about signing the wage cutting agreement.

The strategy of Krupp had unmistakable features of 'divide and rule'. The split in the labour movement became even clearer when the Social-Democratic government in Bremen had to receive the notice of the profit-and-loss adjustment agreement. Then the anger of the AG Weser workers was turned not only against the majority of IG Metall but also against Mayor Hans Koschnik, for having given money to Bremer Vulkan (December 1981) but hesitating when it came to AG Weser.

62. Interview with Dr Dicter Klink, President of the Parliament (Bürgerschaft). In Bremen, January 1985, and with Lord Mayor Hans Koschnik in Bremen, January 1986.

63. Interview with Koschnik, January 1986.

64. Ziegenfuss, Heseler, Kröger (eds).

65. Letter from Minister President Gerhard Stoltenberg to Lord Mayor Hans Koschnik, 19 August 1981. Private archives of senator Claus Grobecker, Bremen.

66. Letter from MP Claus Grobecker to the Minister of Finance Hans Matthöfer, 30 October 1978. Ibid.

67. Letter from the management to the employees of Bremer Vulkan, 21 September 1982. IG Metall, local branch, Bremen; *Weser-Kurier*, 30 September 1981.

68. *Weser-Kurier*, 23 September 1982.

69. Ibid., 25–26 September 1982.

70. Bremer Vulkan management: 'Hausmitteilung. Interessenausgleich und Sozialplan. Personelle Massnahmen', 27 September 1982. IG Metall, local branch, Bremen.

71. Bremer Vulkan works council: 'Interessenausgleich', Memorandum September 1982. IG Metall, local branch, Bremen.

72. Drewes, Pelsell, Wittemann, p. 8.

73. Monthly statistics 1978–84. Arbeitsamt Schleswig-Holstein, Hamburg and Arbeitsamt Bremen.

74. The unemployment statistics illustrate well the gradual contraction. The figures for Bremen given below are the input figures, i.e. new redundancies and new jobs in shipbuilding, both in absolute terms and as a percentage of the whole labour market.

	Redundancies		Vacancies	
	No.	%	No.	%
1974	547	(1.5)	1,625	(4.0)
1975	859	(2.0)	1,202	(3.1)
1976	1,052	(2.4)	607	(1.6)
1977	1,312	(2.9)	214	(0.6)
1978	854	(2.0)	830	(2.4)
1979	544	(1.4)	258	(0.7)
1980	490	(1.2)	337	(1.2)
1981	604	(1.3)	261	(1.1)
1982	718	(1.5)	95	(0.6)

Monthly sector statistics, Arbeitsamt Bremen. The statistics have been worked up and kindly been put at my disposal by Heiner Heseler, University of Bremen. The German labour market statistics for sectors and different kinds of industries only consider the input month per month. Figures of the actual situation and for output, i.e. how many, have found new jobs each month, are only available at the aggregate federal level. The figures here thus consider the number of newly redundant people for the different years and should not be mistaken for the total level. Nevertheless, the figures are a good illustration of the gradual slowing down process. For a discussion about unemployment in Bremen, see articles by Rainer Dombois and Heiner Heseler, Martin Osterland, B. Roth and U.J. Walther in *Mitteilungsblatt der Zentralen Wissenschaftlichen Einrichtung, Arbeit und Betrieb. 15, Berichte aus dem Projekt Arbeitsmarkt Bremen*, University of Bremen 1986.

Of all employees in the metal industry in 1980, only 1.4 per cent were 60 years old or more. The social plans had been in operation for several years in almost all the metal industry. There were so few elderly employees left in 1980 that a reduced retirement age would have had a minimal effect. 'IG Metall, Vorstand, Tarifpolitische . . .', p. 32. IG Metall, local branch, Bremen.

75. This fits well with the conclusions of Jonathan Zeitlin in a newly published book (edited by himself and Steven Tolliday) about the modern state and the interest organisations. Zeitlin's article will be discussed further in the concluding chapter. Jonathan Zeitlin, 'Shop floor bargaining and the state: a contradictionary relationship', in Zeitlin.

76. Interview with ex-Minister of Finance Hans Matthöfer, September 1984.

77. Interview with the vice chairman of the works council of Bremen Vulkan Karl Schönberger, April 1983.

CHAPTER 3

1. 'La Construction Navale. Chambre Syndicale des Constructeurs de Navires', June 1983, p. 26. CSCN, Paris.

2. 'CFDT. Quel avenir pour l'industrie navale en France?', November 1978, CFDT, Paris; International Metal Workers' Federation Statistics. IMF, Geneva: OECD Statistics. OECD Directorate for Science, Technology and Industry.

3. 'Dubigeon-Normandie. Procès-verbal de la réunion du comité d'Etablissement du 21 janvier 1977', CDMOT, Nantes; Kappel and Rother, pp. 1081, 1083; *Le Monde*, 2 March 1984.

4. Employment Statistics, CSCN, Paris.

5. Personal notes by the CFDT secretary of the Dubigeon works council M. Guiheneuff given at an interview in November 1983; 'L'aggravation de la crise suscite . . .', FO, St Nazaire. The tendency was the same at the other big French yards. Between the autumn of 1975 and the autumn of 1978 the development was as follows:

	Subcontracted			Directly employed		
	From	to				
Chantier de l'Atlantique	789	80	−89.9%	7523	6222	−17.3%
La Ciotat	1116	30	−97.3	6932	5736	−25.9
Dunkirk	96	220	+129.2	3340	3740	+12.0
La Seyne	114	110	−3.5	5876	5340	−9.1
Dubigeon Normandie	699	50	−92.3	3289	2020	−38.6
Total	2814	490	−82.6%	26960	22458	−16.7%

Source: FO La Situation Economique. Memoire 1978 rélatif à la construction navale. FO, St Nazaire.

6. Gallon, p. 320; cf also Candau, pp. 238–40, 273–5.

7. 'La construction naval en France', PM of FO 1964. CDMOT, Nantes, No. FO 245.

8. Garnier, p. 36.

9. *La Livre Blanc*, 1959. A White Book or a White Paper is a report issued by a government to give information.

10. Garnier, pp. 22–6.

11. *Le Contrat Professionnel*, 1968.

12. Lorenz, pp. 152–3.

13. Ibid., pp. 130–3; Chardonnet, pp. 436–44.

14. 'CSCN. La Construction Navale. Juin 1977', CSCN, Paris.

15. Ibid.

16. Ibid., June 1979.

17. Ibid., June 1983, p. 26.

18. 'Réunion tripartite. Déclaration de M. Guy Lengagne', 14 February and 1 March 1983. Ministry of Industry, Paris.

19. *Le Monde*, 2 March, 2 April 1984.

20. Interview with Fabrice Theobald, counsellor to the Secretary of State for Sea, Paris, November 1984; Collation of Aid, Ministry of Industry, Paris.

21. Morvan.

22. Ibid.

23. Works council election statistics, 1980–3, CDMOT, Nantes.

24. Reynaud, p. 256.

25. Ibid., p. 245. The Labour code Cart. L 321–2 rules that in case of redundancy 'qualifications, seniority and family charges' determine the order of lay-offs. There is also an important national agreement, signed by all unions in 1969 (although CFDT and CGT have not signed the modifications in 1973), called *Record National sur la securité d'emploi*, which establishes the general procedure in case of lay-offs. This agreement has been legally extended in 1974 and is generally annexed to the regional collective agreement in the Branche Metallurgie.

27. Reymond, p. 267.

28. 'La construction navale en France', PM of FO 1964, CDMOT, Nantes, No. FO 245.

29. 'CFDT. Quel avenir pour l'industrie navale en France?', November 1978. CFDT, Paris.

30. 'CFDT. Le conseil. Motion adopté les 3–4 Jun 1983'; 'La CFDT et l'avenir de l'industrie navale'. 30 April 1981. CFDT, Paris.

31. 'CFDT. Le point sur la navale'. 30 September 1983. CFDT, Paris.

32. 'CGT. Transports maritimes et chantiers navals: quel avenir pour la France?', 1978. CGT, Paris.

33. 'CGT. Proposition de politique industrielle dans le cadre du IXe Plan', June 1983. CGT, Paris.

34. 'CGT. Pour l'emploi et la relance de la construction navale française', September 1983. CGT, Paris.

35. *L'Humanité*, 8 July 1983.

36. 'FO. Conférence nationale de la construction et réparation navale. La Ciotat 24 et 25 mars 1983', FO, Paris.

37. *Construction Navale Préparation du 7e Plan*, p. 91.

38. 'CFDT. Quel avenir pour l'industrie navale en France?', November 1978. CFDT, Paris.

39. *Construction Navale Préparation du 7e Plan*, pp. 124, 129.

40. 'Déclaration du représentant de la CFDT le 17 decembre 1970' and 'Déclaration commune des représentants de la CGT-FO et de la CGT le 25 janvier 1971', in *Rapports des comités du 6e Plan 1971–1975. Construction Navale*, pp. 154 and 151, respectively.

41. 'La CFDT précise ses positions sur la navale', 2 November 1983. CFDT, Paris.

42. 'CFDT. Le Conseil, Motion adopté les 3–4 juin 1983'; 'La CFDT et l'avenir de l'industrie navale', 30 April 1981. CFDT, Paris.

43. 'FO. Conférence nationale de la construction et réparation navale. La Ciotat 24 et 25 mars 1983', FO, Paris.

44. 'CGT. La situation dans la navale', 20–24 June, 1983.

45. Interviews with Jean-Louis Foucauld, CFDT, Henri Mallet, FO, Yves Gioda, CGT, November 1983.

46. *Libération*, 25 January 1984.

47. 'Réunion tripartite. Texte de la déclaration de M. Guy Lengagne', 14 February 1984; 'Réunion tripartite du 1er Mars 1984. Déclaration de M. Guy Lengagne', Ministry of Industry, Paris; interview with Fabrice

Theobald, Counsellor to the Secretary of State for Sea, Paris, November 1984.

48. Interviews with Jean-Louis Foucauld, CFDT, Henri Mallet, FO, Yves Gioda, CGT, Dominique de Mas Latrie and Jean Pierre Dobler, CSCM, November 1983.

49. 'FO. La construction Navale. Positions et propositions des différentes Organisationes Syndicales. Septembre 1977', and 'FO. Les Commandes touchent le fond. Le 21 octobre 1983', FO, St Nazaire.

50. 'CSCN. La construction navale. Juin 1977', p. 38. CSCN, Paris.

51. 'Déclaration du représentant de la CFDT le 17 décembre 1970' and 'Déclaration commune des représentants de la CGT-FO et de la CGT le 25 janvier 1971', in *Rapports des comités de 6e Plan 1971–1975. Construction Navale*, pp. 154 and 151, respectively.

52. CSCN. *La construction navale*. June 1978, p. 31. CSCN, Paris.

53. Ibid., 1979, p. 22.

54. Ibid., 1983, p. 26.

55. Interviews with Dominique de Mas Latrie and Jean Pierre Dobler, CSCN, November 1983.

56. Interview with J. Meyer, CSCN, October 1981.

57. CSCN. *Le Construction Navale*, June 1984, p. 25. CSCN, Paris.

58. Cohen, 1982, p. 100.

59. Kuisel, p. 246.

60. Ibid., p. 256.

61. Ibid., p. 266. Cf. Cohen, 1969, pp. 220–7, and Carré, Dubois and Malinvaud, p. 601.

62. Crouch, pp. 211–12.

63. Cohen, 1982, p. 102.

64. Ibid., pp. 104–5. One example which is reminiscent of developments in shipbuilding, is the steel concentration scheme in 1978. The steel crisis occurred when the major companies were unable to service the debt accumulated over years of state-guided efforts. Emergency procedures were necessary to prevent immediate bankruptcy. The Barre government rejected any idea of nationalisation. The government solution was rapidly to put together a financial package and reorganise the structure of the steel industry. Similarly, four years later in the shipbuilding industry, the various firms were combined into two separate groups, this time by the Mauroy government. In 1973 most of the obsolete facilities, mainly in Lorraine, were closed and one-third of the workforce, some 50,000 employees, were to be made redundant.

The whole plan was formulated quickly and quietly within the closed community of finance and industry. The last step (the redundancy scheme) could not be carried through, however. A violent confrontation ensued between protesting steel workers, marching on Paris and the police. The government had to retreat and formulate a social plan with a special severance settlement.

65. Barbance.

66. Sicard, p. 32.

67. Fleury passim.

68. Cf. Guin, p. 250.

69. Sicard, pp. 95–6.

70. Interview with P. Malnoë in Sicard, p. 96.

71. Ibid., p. 97.

72. 'Voix ouvrière. Ne pas perdre du temps. Le 13 mars 1964'; 'Exposé de MM Thomas et Piron le 13 mars 1964', CDMOT, Nantes, Mal 16.

73. *Ouest France*, 13 March 1964.

74. 'La construction navale en France', PM of FO 1964, CDMOT, Nantes, No. 245.

75. Ibid., 25 March 1964.

76. *Ouest France*, 11, 15 April 1964.

77. 'CFDT, CGT, CGT-FO. Nous voulons une réponse', 23 June 1964. CDMOT, Nantes, Mal 17.

78. Fancier, p. 78.

79. Interview with Malnoë, June 1984.

80. Interview with Malnoë in Sicard, p. 38.

81. Georges Yvetot, quoted in Guin, p. 394.

82. Dubigeon-Normandie works council election statistics. CDMOT, Nantes.

83. Minutes of the Dubigeon-Normandie works council, 21 January 1977. CDMOT, Nantes.

84. Ibid., 19 April and 6 May 1977.

85. 'Dubigeon-Normandie. CFDT-CGT. Rétablir les faits', CDMOT, Nantes.

86. Ibid.

87. Minutes of the Dubigeon-Normandie works council, 12 July 1977. CDMOT, Nantes.

88. *Ouest France*, 30 September 1977.

89. 'Dubigeon-Normandie. Tract CFDT le 29 octobre 1977'; 'Discours de la CGT à la reprise du travail', CDMOT, Nantes.

90. Minutes of the Dubigeon-Normandie works council, 16 November 1977. CDMOT, Nantes.

91. Interview with M. Guiheneuff, June 1984.

92. Torstendahl.

93. Of course, the stability and real strength of the centralised state is debatable. It is perhaps not a coincidence that this power has been seriously challenged twice since 1950: in 1958 from the right and in 1968 from the left. This is exceptional among the West European democracies. On the other hand, it is typical and relevant, that when it has come to a crisis, this has been met by a powerful and centralised response. Cf. Zysman, pp. 198–9.

94. Ibid.

95. Ibid.

96. The standard work arguing such a viewpoint is Shorter and Tilly.

97. Lorenz, pp. 213–29, has convincingly underlined the crucial role of the shipbuilding up to the 1970s.

98. I am very grateful to Dr Reynold Bourgue, Montreal, for valuable and substantial viewpoints on that question.

CHAPTER 4

1. 'Utredning av Svenska Varvs marknadsförutsättningar, produktions-kapacitet och struktur', Svenska Varv, Gothenburg, the board, 10 February 1978; Ljungberg, pp. 69–70; Ekström, ch. 6.

2. Olsson, pp. 188–96. The origins of specialisation in tanker building go back to the 1920s and 1930s. At that time, Norwegian shipowners were more and more ordering tankers from Swedish yards. Personal bonds were forged with Norwegian shipowners, who even at this early stage realised with possibilities of oil.

3. 'De svenska storvarvens problem. Betänkande avgivet av Varv-skommitten den 2 februari 1970', Mimeo, Verkstadsföreningen, Sthlm F 727–1970.

4. Interview with Nils-Hugo Hallenborg, managing director of Kockums 1968–73, July 1984. Hallenborg was also chairman of the Association of West European Shipbuilders 1971–3; *Lloyds Annual Summary*, 1975.

5. Interview with Hans Laurin, managing director of Götaverken 1971–7, November 1983; Government bill, 1971, No. 117.

6. Interviews with Tony Hagström, Under Secretary of State in the Ministry of Industry 1973–1976, John Ekström, Swedish representative of OECD wp 6 and shipbuilding expert in the Ministry of Industry, and Hans Hagnell, economist in the Swedish Metal Workers' Federation, 1946–71, and MP 1957–73. The parallels to the investment programme of the German state-owned HDW yard at Kiel at the same time are clear.

7. 'Varvindustri', Memorandum by Jan Olsson, 29 October 1974. Metall, Stockholm; 'Varvens andel av industrisysselsättningen i varvs-regionerna år 1974', Metall avd 41, Gothenburg.

8. Employment statistics, Svenska Varv, Gothenburg.

9. Ibid.

10. Government Bill, 1975/76, No. 121.

11. Ibid., 1976/77, No. 139.

12. 'Utdrag ur protokoll vid regeringssammanträde 1976-05-06. Bil 8', Ministry of Industry, Stockholm. Especially concerning the development of the state engagement in Uddevallavarvet, see Nyström, pp. 15–18.

13. Interview with Nils G. Åsling, Minister of Industry 1976–8, 1979–82, February 1984; 'PM rörande innehåll i varvspropositionen år 1978', 12 June 1978. Ministry of Industry, Stockholm.

14. Ibid.

15. Government Bill, 1978/79, No. 49, pp. 8–10.

16. Ibid., 1979/80, No. 165, Parliament's decision (Riksdagens skrivelse) 1979/80, No. 405; ibid., 1980/81, No. 393–394. Åsling's ambition was to wind up the subsidies which had taken gigantic proportions (Sw Cr 12.5 billion during the previous three years and another 6 billion suggested now). The Social Democratic opposition objected and, with the support of two Liberal MPs overthrew the proposal to close Öresunds-varvet.

However, there was a loophole. The bill and Parliament's decision stated that no extra contributions above the 6 billion could be expected. If that amount turned out to be insufficient, Svenska Varv would have to adjust its operations to the prevailing economic realities. It was soon clear that the 6 billion would not be sufficient. In September 1980 Svenska Varv decided to close Öresundsvarvet in order to bring about such an adjustment. The Svenska Varv management achieved what had been impossible for the politicians. Protests were made but resistance to closure was broken. When in June 1981 Parliament debated the shipbuilding crisis and appropriated another 1.7 billion to Svenska Varv, there was no request to overthrow the closure decision.

17. Government Bill, 1982/83, No. 147.

18. 'De svenska storvarvens problem. Betänkande avgivet av varskommitten den 2 februari 1970', Mimeo, Verkstadsföreningen, Stockholm F 727-1970. Interview with Per Nyström, chairman of the committee, October 1982.

19. Memorandum by Metall's economist Allan Larsson, 6 October 1971, Metall, Stockholm; interview with Gunnar Sträng, Minister of Finance 1956-76, January 1985.

20. 'Sammanträde med samrådsgruppen den 21 oktober 1971', 'Varvsindustrins samrådsgrupp' (SIF 14 February 1972), minutes from meetings with the consultation group, 10 April 1972, 5 April 1973, 'Rapport nr 2 över samarbete inom konsortialavtalets ram' (10 April 1972), 'PM arbetet i samrådsgruppen för storvarve' (Jan Olsson, 30 March 1973). Metall, Stockholm.

21. 'Minnesanteckningar från sammanträde för löntagarrepresentanterna i storvarvens samradsgrupp 6.3.1974', Metall, Stockholm.

22. Cf. common study by Metall and the engineering employers' association, Verkstadsföreningen ('Bruttoströmmarna på varvsindustrins arbetsmarknad 1969-1972'), 15 August 1973. Metall, Stockholm.

23. Government Bill, 1975/76, No. 121.

24. Ibid., Cf. 'Om varvssamrådet', Memorandum 6 March 1975. Metall, Stockholm.

25. 'Statsvarvens organisation', Memorandum 22 November 1976. Metall, Stockholm. Cf. also notes 12 and 13 of this chapter and the text they refer to.

26. Letter from Metall, SIF and the supervisors' and foremen's union SALF to the Minister of Industry, 10 March 1977. Metall, Stockholm.

27. 'Minnesanteckningar från överläggningar om varven med industriminister Nils G. Åsling', Stig Malm, 16 May 1977. Metall, Stockholm.

28. 'Minnesanteckningar från mötet med referensgruppen för Svenska Varv AB (Metallgruppen)', Bengt Jakobsson, 23 August 1977. Metall, Stockholm.

29. 'Varv i Kris', the owners' version of the collapse of Eriksberg and the political consequences, written in 1975. Kristian von Sydow's private archive, Gothenburg; interview with von Sydow, May 1984. For an analysis of profitability and finance questions in the Swedish shipbuilding industry 1950-70 see Bohlin. His main conclusion is that the profitability of the yards was closely related to the way they were financed.

30. 'Varv i Kris', p. 10.

31. Interview with Leif Molinder, October 1984.

32. *Arbetet*, 26 November 1974; *Göteborgs-Posten, Svenska Dagbladet*, 31 January 1975; *Metallarbetaren*, 7 March 1975.

33. Interview with Leif Molinder, October 1984.

34. 'Attityder till arbete och företag bland kollektivanställda vid Eriksbergs Mekaniska Verkstads AB', PA-Rådet, February 1970. Svenska Varv, Gothenburg.

35. *Metallarbetaren*, 7 March 1975.

36. Interview with Kristian von Sydow, May 1984.

37. *Göteborgs-Posten, Svenska Dagbladet, Arbetet*, 30 April 1975; 'Varv i kris' (see Note 30), pp. 20–2; Government Bill, 1975, No. 110.

38. Interview with Nils-Hugo Hallenborg, July 1984.

39. Laurin's diary, 24 November 1975. Hans Laurin's private archives, Gothenburg.

40. Ibid., 19 January 1976.

41. 'Eriksbergs ekonomiska krissituation den 9–16 juni 1975'; 'Kommuniké om Götaverkens och Eriksbergs framtida Fartygsproduktion', 9 February 1976. Svenska Varv, Gothenburg.

42. Interview with Inge Karlsson, chairman of the metal workers' union at Götaverken, October 1982.

43. 'Case study in the shipbuilding sector in Sweden', Restricted, 29 April 1980. OECD, Paris, c/wp 6 (80)23.

44. Ibid.

45. Ibid.

46. 'Varv i Kris' (see Note 29), though written in defence of the owners, nevertheless makes a number of valid points.

47. Eriksberg had in fact invested some Sw Cr 450 m during the period 1965–74, for example in a new construction dock and in a gantry crane for supertankers, ready in 1971. Although not as streamlined for tanker construction as the other large Swedish yards, Eriksberg was hardly in such a bad condition as its critics maintained.

48. 'Fackliga referensgruppens yrkanden vid MBL-förhandlingar 1978-02-23', 'De svenska storvarvens problem', Undated PM, key notes by John-Erik Olsson, chairman of the metal workers' union at Kockums. Metall, Stockholm.

49. Minutes from meetings with the reference group, 5 April 1978. Metall, Stockholm.

50. Ibid., 26 April 1978.

51. Ibid., 15 June 1978.

52. 'Estraddebatt i Landskrona 1978-09-09', Svenska Varv, Gothenburg, Bengt Tengroths handlingar Öresundsvarvet AB. Div utredningar 1978–80.

53. 'PM Varvspropositionen', Stig Malm, 26 September 1978. Metall, Stockholm: 'PM ang eventuell varvsproposition', Stig Malm, 31 October 1978. Metall, Stockholm. As to Huss's change of Åsling's bill he reduced employment, 'at least 20 per cent' of the 1977 level before the end of 1980 instead of Åsling's 30 per cent before the end of 1981. For the large yards the figures were: Kockums from 4,500 to 3,300 (Åsling 3,300), Uddevallavarvet from 3,300 to 2,600 (Åsling 2,600), Götaverken (Arendal and Cityvarvet) in Gothenburg from 6,400 to 5,000 (Åsling 4,100), Eriksberg from 1,500 to 0 (Åsling 0), Öresundsvarvet from 3,250 to 2,500 (Åsling 1,450). Åsling in his draft stated that Öresundsvarvet and Arendal 'should be maintained as working sites' but not as shipyards. Huss stated

that production in the long term should be changed at the two yards but dependent on 'the sales development for alternative products' a 'certain' production of ships might be necessary there. (Government Bill, 1978/79, No. 49, pp. 9–10, and draft, 13 September 1978 'Regeringens prop 1978/79 xxx om vissa varvsfrågor', pp. 14–18 [Ministry of Industry, Stockholm], respectively.)

Within the Ministry of Industry at the civil servant level there had earlier in the 1970s been a more realistic/pessimistic view on the prospects of ship-building than obtained at the minister level. Thus, for instance, John Ekström regarded the government Bill of 1974 to be completely coloured by the prevailing crazy optimism within the shipbuilding industry. In 1972 John Ekström had already foretold a slimming down. In the manuscript of his book he suggested the maintenance of one or two new building yards. Before printing he added 'possibly three' as a concession to political pressure. Ekström, 1970, pp. 134–6 and interview with Ekström, November 1984.

54. For a survey of the development of the Swedish industrial relations see Kjellberg, esp pp. 1, 25. 27.

55. *Arbetet* and *Göteborgs-Posten* 9 and 10 November 1977.

56. 'Case study in the shipbuilding sector in Sweden', Restricted. 29 April 1980. OECD, Paris c/wp 6 (80)23; interview with Inge Karlsson, chairman of the metal workers union at Götaverken, October 1982.

57. Ibid.

58. Interview with Inge Karlsson, October 1982.

59. Kockums verkstadsklubb, 28 January 1980. Kockums verkstads-klubb, Malmö.

60. *Nordvästra Skånes Tidningar* and *Dagens Nyheter*, 11 January 1980; 'Redogörelse för sammanträffande med fackliga representanter 1980-01-22', Hans G. Forsberg, 23 January 1980. Svenska Varv, Gothenburg Bengt Tengroths handlingar: Öresundsvarvet AB. div handlingar; Interview with Leif Molinder, October, 1984. For the consequences of the closure see Molinder and Salomonsson and Wikdahl.

61. Stråth, 1982, pp. 274–6.

62. See, for instance, Olström, which is a study of the industrial relations and the work process at Kockums made at the end of the 1960s on the commission of the company and carried through by the federation of the Swedish trade unions, LO.

63. Ibid.; interview with Nils-Hugo Hallenborg, July 1984. Hallenborg was managing director 1968–78.

64. Kockums verkstadsklubb, 3 March 1978. Kockums verkstadsklubb, Malmö; Interview with Nils-Hugo Hallenborg, July 1984.

65. Kockums verkstadsklubb 11 November 1977. Kockums verkstads-klubb, Malmö.

66. Ibid., 17 March 1978.

67. Ibid., 29 March 1978.

68. Interview with John-Erik Olsson, chairman of the metal workers' union at Kockums, February 1984.

69. Ibid.

70. Kockums verkstadsklubb minutes, 24 January 1980. Kockums verstadsklubb, Malmö.

71. Ibid., 9 December 1980, 19 January 1981.

72. Ibid., 12 March, 27 April 1981.

73. Ibid., 4 February 1982. Cf. ibid.; 26 May 1981.

74. Interview with John-Erik Olsson, July 1984.

75. Kockums verkstadsklubb minutes, 28 February, 15 March 1983. Kockums verstadsklubb, Malmö.

76. Ibid., 30, 31 March, 14 April 1983.

77. Ibid., 7 June, 11 July, 16 August, 27 September 1983.

78. Interviews with John-Erik Olsson, February and July 1984.

79. Hamilton; 'Sveriges Industriförbund 19 November 1980', Federation of Swedish Industries, Stockholm.

80. Government Bill, 1982/83, No. 147.

81. Parliament (snabbprotokoll), 1982/83, No. 161, 162.

82. Interview with Leif Blomberg, October 1984.

83. Ibid.

CHAPTER 5

1. Pollard and Robertson, pp. 49–52.

2. Ibid. p. 51.

3. Ibid., pp. 45, 48.

4. Lorenz and Wilkinson, p. 1.

5. *Lloyds Annual Reports*, 1950–80.

6. Lorenz, in a comparative study with a long-term historical perspective, has studied the consequences of different strategies — labour and capital intensity — in Britain and France, respectively. Lorenz, 1983, pp. 155–94. Although lack such a comparative perspective, Pollard and Robertson, Chapters 8–9, have underlined the importance of the more labour-intensive strategy. Indeed, employers seem to have encouraged this development. In British shipbuilding during World War I employers 'stubbornly maintained conservative attitudes and had little faith in proposals to rationalise labour intensive methods of production' (Reid, p. 66). It was frequently managements which put the strongest opposition to dilution, because each firm wanted to retain as much skilled labour as possible.

7. Lorenz and Wilkinson, p. 15.

8. Lorenz, 1983, pp. 197–212, 231–43. See also Eldridge who earlier than most other observers put the demarcation disputes in perspective and as early as in 1968 foretold their gradual petering out. Eldridge, p. 10.

9. Geddes Report, p. 15.

10. Employment statistics. British Shipbuilders, Newcastle.

11. Geddes Report.

12. Ibid., Chapter 21, pp. 89–90.

13. George Brown in House of Commons, 22 December 1965. Quoted in Alexander and Jenkins, p. 14.

14. Alexander and Jenkins, p. 15.

15. Ibid.

16. Ibid., p. 16.

17. Ibid., p. 209.

18. Ibid., pp. 210–11.

19. See, for instance, Paulden and Hawkins, chs. 8–10.

20. Alexander and Jenkins, p. 210.

21. HMSO, Cmnd 4756, pp. 88–9.

22. Ibid., pp. 36–8.

23. Ibid., pp. 141–3, 171–2. Cf. also the Donovan Report and Batstone, pp. 2–9.

24. HMSO, Cmnd 4756, p. 139.

25. The strategy of the committee suggests two contradictory tendencies within the local shop stewards' committees. On the one hand, by attempting to avoid inter-union conflict they give the local workforce greater independence of union officers. On the other hand, however, they also act in the management's interests, by seeking to curb unofficial strikes and other spontaneous action by the workforce.

26. The most comprehensive and complete account is Woolfson. For a more popular view see, for instance, Buchan; Crouch, p. 64. Thompson and Hart give a Communist interpretation of the work-in; Buchan the 'official' Labour Party history; McGill, the industrial correspondent of the *Daily Express*, a right-wing interpretation; and Johns a Trotskyist one (his book was published by the Socialist Labour League, a Trotskyist organisation).

27. For a critical scrutiny of the historiography of the work-in, see Harvie, pp. 158–9.

28. Woolfson, p. 347.

29. Interviews with Jimmy Airlie, AUEW, London, December 1984, and Bob McCann, Govan Shipbuilders, Glasgow, October 1984.

30. Hill Samuel Report, p. 15.

31. Booz, Allen & Hamilton Report, p. 87.

32. Cf. Woolfson, p. 392.

33. Interviews with Jimmy Airlie, AUEW, London, December 1984, Bob McCann, Govan Shipbuilders, Glasgow, October 1984, and Tony Benn, Shadow Cabinet Minister for Industry in 1972, February 1985.

34. The account is based on interviews with Tony Benn, Shadow Cabinet Minister for Industry in 1972, and Jimmy Airlie, one of the two leading members of the shop stewards' committee during the work-in.

35. Benn, p. 65–6.

36. Confed Shipyard Negotiating Committee (SNC). Minutes 16 October, 11 December 1974. Confed, London.

37. Ibid., 9 April 1975.

38. *Hansard Report*, 31 July 1974, col. 808–814; Interview with Tony Benn, February 1985.

39. Jimmy Airlie in *Glasgow Herald*, 9 March 1976.

40. *Glasgow Herald*, 21 December 1976.

41. Ibid., 10 December 1976.

42. Interview with Alex Ferry, Confed, London, November 1984.

43. 'British Shipbuilders National Agreements with Confederation of Shipbuilding and Engineering Unions. 1st July 1977–5th March 1979' ('Phase 1 Agreement'), Confed, London, and British Shipbuilders, Newcastle.

44. Ibid. The value added model was completely dependent on the market and on the cash flow ('what does it cost to produce?' 'how much can

we sell it for?'); the manpower performance model was dependent on the possibilities of improving the workload flow. The workers who earlier relied primarily on shop-floor bargaining to win acceptable terms (Hyman, p. 44) now had to rely entirely on the national agreement, previously of only minimal significance. This development meant the strengthening of the national level within the trade union movement in the short term and a corresponding weakening of the shop stewards' powers. However, in the long term it was difficult to national union officials to control the shop stewards as discontent with decreasing real wages grew.

45. Wage Statistics. British Shipbuilders, Newcastle.

46. 'The Blackpool Agreement, September 1979', Confed, London, and British Shipbuilders, Newcastle.

47. Interview with Dr Martin Stopford, Director of Business Development, British Shipbuilders, Newcastle, December 1984.

48. Ibid.

49. Interview with Sydney Treadgold and Euan Cameron, Shipbuilding Policy Division, Ministry of Trade and Industry, London, December 1984.

50. Maurice Phelps in interview in *Newcastle Journal*, 29 November 1984.

51. Interview with Alex Ferry, Confed, London, December 1984. Cf. 'Brief 1. Corporate performance and government support', Memorandum, Ministry of Trade and Industry SBPL, 22 November 1984. Ministry of Trade and Industry, London; Cf. Norman Lamont, Minister of State in the Department of Trade and Industry in the House of Commons, 27 November 1984. *Hansard*, 27 November 1984, col. 839; Phase 1–5 agreements 1979–83. British Shipbuilders, Newcastle, and Confed, London.

52. See for instance *Hansard*, 27 November 1984, col. 844 (Neville Trotter, Tynemouth), 849 (Piers Merchant, Newcastle upon Tyne) and 856 (Christopher Chope, Southampton). However, cf. Labour's Industry spokesman, John Smith, in the *Guardian*, 19 May 1986, who argued that none of the remaining five yards offering work beyond Easter 1987 had any new orders, and criticised the Under Secretary for Industry, John Butcher, for having stated that he wants to see an end to the 'nonsense of world-wide subsidies'.

53. Interview with Alex Ferry, Confed, London, November 1984.

54. Confed, NSC, Minutes 2 April 1980.

55. Interview Alex Ferry, Confed, London, November 1984.

56. Ibid.

57. Ibid.

58. Ibid.

59. Ibid.

60. Notes from Confed delegate conference, Park Hotel, Tynemouth, 12 December 1984.

61. Ibid.

62. Confed., SNC minutes, 17 October 1984. I should like to thank Dr Joseph Melling, University of Liverpool, for his penetrating discussion with me on the Cammell Laird affair.

63. Confed., SNC minutes, 17 October 1984.

64. Interview with Alex Ferry, Confed, London, December 1984.

65. Interview with Peter Thompson, British Shipbuilders, London,

November 1984.

66. Interview with Alex Ferry, Confed, London, December 1984.

67. 'AUEW-TASS: Shipping and Shipbuilding. Partners in Crisis. A Blueprint for Survival', March 1984, p. 1. AUEW, London.

68. Ibid., p. 2.

69. Sammy Barr in an article in *Shipbuilding News*, September 1984.

70. Interview with John Moist, research officers of GMB, Glasgow, October 1984.

71. Interview with Sammy Guilmore, chairman of the shop steward committee, Govan Shipbuilders, Glasgow, October 1984. Cf. 'Govan Shipbuilders. Productivity Agreement — 1984', Govan Shipbuilders, Glasgow.

72. Woolfson, p. 400.

73. Ibid., pp. 400–8. The discussion about the Polish order here follows mainly Woolfson.

74. *Evening Times*, 30 November 1977. Quoted in Woolfson, p. 402.

75. Woolfson, p. 403.

76. Ibid., p. 405.

77. Ibid., p. 406.

78. *Glasgow Herald*, 18 August 1979.

79. 'Blackpool Agreement'; 'Benefits payable under the Shipbuilding Redundancy Payments Scheme, November 1982', British Shipbuilders, Newcastle.

80. Interview with Sammy Guilmore, chairman of the shop stewards committee, Govan Shipbuilders, Glasgow, October 1984.

81. Interview with Bob McCann, personnel manager, Govan Shipbuilders, Glasgow, October 1984.

82. Ibid.

83. Cf. pp. 127–8 above and Note 34 of this chapter.

84. Minutes from a meeting between management and the shop stewards executive committee at UIE, 14 May 1978. UIE, Clydebank.

85. Ibid.

86. Ibid., 23 June 1978.

87. Ibid., 18 August 1978.

88. Ibid., 21 August 1978.

89. Ibid., 22 August 1978.

90. Ibid., 30 August 1978.

91. Ibid., 11 September 1978.

92. *Evening Times*, 14 September 1978.

93. *Glasgow Herald*, 28 November 1978.

94. 'BNOC order'. Agreement 9th February 1979. UIE, Clydebank.

95. Minutes from a meeting between management and the shop stewards' executive committee at UIE, 23 February 1979, UIE, Clydebank.

96. Interview with Jimmy Hamilton, chairman, AUEW, David Dew, CMB, and Martin McGrath, UCAT, shop stewards' executive committee, UIE, Clydebank, October 1984.

97. Ibid., and Alastair McCallum, personnel manager UIE, Clydebank, October 1984.

98. Interview with Alastair McCallum, December 1984; *Glasgow Herald*, 13 December 1984.

99. Jimmy Hamilton in interview October 1984.

CHAPTER 6

1. Kappel and Detlef, pp. 1221-3; 'Voorstel RSV betrefende grote scheepsbouw en off-shore in te brengen bij de beleidskommissie scheepsbouw', 1 June 1977. BS, the Hague.

2. Ibid. If not only new construction is considered the large and very large yards had a greater share: 65 per cent expressed as a percentage of the turnover and manpower, as compared to 25 per cent for the medium-sized yards, and 10 per cent for the small yards. 'Beleidskommissie Scheepsbouw. Beleidsplan voor de herstrukturering van de Nederlandse scheepsniuwbouw. Delft Januari 1977', BS, the Hague.

3. *CEBOSINE biennial report 1981–1982*, Delft, 1983, p. 36.

4. RSV Report.

5. Cf. Lepszy, who speaks about a *Versäulung* ('pillarisation') of Dutch society.

6. Cf. Meggeneder, who speaks of an *Entsäulung*, as distinguished from the earlier predominating *Versäulung*.

7. The old names, however, were used in parallel for some years. The Protestant union Christelijk National Vakverband (CNV) remained outside the merge. In 1979 they definitely left the merger talks which had been going on since 1969. In reality they had not participated in the talks since the beginning of the 1970s.

Thus the Christian union movement chose a different way from the Christian political parties, which in 1977 established an election alliance which later on resulted in a formal merger between the Catholic people's party and the two Protestant centre parties.

8. Meggeneder, p. 115.

9. However, the Socialist metal workers' union had paid attention in 1963 to the need for keeping in touch with the shop floor. At that time they introduced the *bedrijvenwerker* which were built on the shop floor organisation, the enterprise group. Ibid., p. 119.

10. 'Organisatie Schema Commissie Nederlandse Scheepsbouw 1965', Ministry of Economics, the Hague.

11. Interview with G. de Ruiter, Ministry of Economics, the Hague, May 1984.

12. Centrum voor de bestudering van de Sociale Problematiek in de Scheepsbouw, Rapport Sociale Problematiek Scheepsbouw, the Hague, 1968. The interest subsidy was of the difference between the market interest and 5.75 per cent, although at most 2 per cent.

13. Verolme, pp. 49, 56.

14. Ibid., p. 475.

15. Ibid., p. 499.

16. 'Rapport bevattende de grondslagen voor de waarde bepaling als bedoeld in punt 9 van het op 29 Januari 1970 gesloten convenant tussen: de staat de Nederlanden, het Rijn-Schelde concern, het Verolme concern. 19 April 1971', Ministry of Economics, the Hague.

17. RSV Report.

18. Ibid., p. 502.

19. Ibid., p. 502.

20. *Neue Zürcher Zeitung*, 27 October 1984.

21. 'Beleidskommissie Scheepsbouw. Het beleidsplan voor de herstrukturering van de Nederlandse scheepsniuwbouw. Delft, Januari 1977', BS, the Hague.

22. Ibid.

23. Ibid., pp. 7–10.

24. Ibid., pp. 13–23.

25. Ibid., pp. 26–7, 36.

26. RSV Report, p. 504.

27. Interview with Henk Vos, December 1984.

28. 'Kort verslag van de vergadering Achterban Beleidskomissie Scheepsbouw', 16 November 1976. FNV, Amsterdam.

29. 'Bijenkomst met de bestuurders betrokken bij de scheepsbouw', 15 December 1976. FNV, Amsterdam.

30. 'Kort verslag de vergadering met distriktsbestuurders, betrokken bij de scheepsbouw', 5 January 1977. FNV, Amsterdam.

31. 'Verslag van de vergadering Achterban Scheepsbouw', 12 January 1977. FNV, Amsterdam.

32. 'Samenvatting en conclusies gesprek van Burgemeester Samkalden enWethouder van der Eyden met de heren Sluis, Fluit en Koudstaal resp. van NDSM en IHC Verschure', 10 February 1977. FNV, Amsterdam.

33. 'Verslag van de achterbanvergadering industriebond NVV', 5 April 1977. FNV, Amsterdam.

34. Ibid., p. 8.

35. Handwritten memorandum by Henk Vos, FNV, Amsterdam ('gesprek Nelissen 8.8.1977'); 'Amsterdams Werftbericht Augustus 1977 No. 1', FNV, Amsterdam.

36. 'RSV. Strikt vertrouwelijk. Resultate Scheepsnieuwbouw 1971 tot en met 1975. I van Rijn 23 December 1975'. The study concerned productivity in the new construction of tankers and it could be argued that the number one spot for NDSM was of little value when it was a matter of breaking away from that kind of production.

37. 'NVV-NKV. Amsterdams Werftbericht. 6. September 1977', FNV, Amsterdam. For the Communist criticism see 'De Schroef. Uitgaven CPN-Distrikt Amsterdam AFD NDSM. 6.9.77'. FNV, Amsterdam.

38. 'Aan de Industriebonden NVV-NKV-CNV en de Unie-BHLP, de regering en de fractie-voorzitters in Tweede Kamer', FNV, Amsterdam. See also a leaflet by the action committee at NDSM, 'Verklaring comit'e tot behoud van de volledige werkgelegenheid bij de NDSM', FNV, Amsterdam.

39. 'Bijlage Weekrapport. H. Vos, lopende over de week van 4 t/m 10 September 1977', FNV, Amsterdam.

40. Minutes from Centrale Begeleidingskommissie Sociale Problematiek (CBK), 12 September 1977. BS, the Hague.

41. Ibid., p. 7.

42. See, for instance, minutes from meetings 14 November and 12 December 1977. BS, the Hague.

43. 'Verslag van de gezamenlijke vergadering industriebonden NVV en NKV landelijke achterban Beleidskommissie Scheepsbouw d.d. 3 November 1977 te zeist', FNV, Amsterdam.

44. 'Aan de leden van de Achterban beleidskommissie scheepsbouw

t. k. a. de betrokken districten', 3 February 1978. FNV, Amsterdam.

45. Minutes from the Beleidskommissie Scheepsbouw meeting No. 44, 23 January 1978. BS, the Hague. Letter from NVV and NKV to the Beleidskommissie, 5 January 1978. FNV, Amsterdam.

46. Minutes from the Beleidskommissie Scheepsbouw meeting No. 44, 23 January 1978. BS, the Hague.

47. Ibid., No. 45, 6 February 1978.

48. 'Bijlage Weekrapport. H. Vos, lopende over de week van 12–18 febuari 1978', FNV, Amsterdam. Minutes from the Beleidskommissie Scheepsbouw meeting No. 46, 20 February 1978. BS, the Hague.

49. 'Ministerie van Economische Zaken. Brief 21 maart 1978. 278/V/268', Ministry of Economics, the Hague.

50. 'Verslag gesprek Raad van Bestur RSV — de Industriebonden NVV-NKV alsmede de Industriebond CNV en de Unie BLHP. 28 maart 1978', FNV, Amsterdam.

51. 'Verslag van de op 4 april 1978 op het Ministerie van Sociale Zaken gehouden bespreking over de sociale aspecten van de problematiek in de scheepsbouw en zware metaal', FNV, Amsterdam.

52. 'Verslag vergadering Actie-Comit'e op 30 maart 1978', FNV, Amsterdam.

53. 'D. Rijkse aan de leden van de Achterban Beleidskommissie Scheepsbouw. 24 april 1978', NSV, Amsterdam; 'Kort verslag van en bijenkomst met kaderleden in de scheepsbouw op 17 april in Restaurant Engels te Rotterdam'; 'Verslag van en vergadering met bestuurders scheepsbouw te Rotterdam op 11 april 1978', FNV, Amsterdam.

54. Interview with Henk Vos, December 1984.

55. 'Verslag vergadering Actie-comit'e 18 maart, 20 maart, 21 maart 1978'; 'Aandacht punten Bedrijfsbezetting NDSM', FNV, Amsterdam. Some 50 pages of handwritten notes in Henk Vos's personal files.

56. Letter from A. Stikker and B. Botman, RSV to the Ministry of Economics, 6 June 1978. FNV, Amsterdam.

57. 'Note voor het hoofdbestuur'; 'Notitie inzake actiepunten Amsterdamse scheepsbouw d.d. 18 september 1978', FNV, Amsterdam.

58. Letter from the Minister of Economics to the president of the second chamber of the General States, 27 September 1978. Ministry of Economics, the Hague.

59. Interview with Henk Vos, March 1982.

60. RSV Report, pp. 505–6.

61. Ibid., p. 506.

62. Ibid., p. 507.

63. Ibid., p. 510.

64. Ibid.

65. 'Beleidskommissie Scheepsbouw. Voorstel tot het Verfolg-Beleidsplan voor de herstrukturering van de Nederlandse Scheepsnieuwbouw in de jaren tachtig. Mei/juli 1981', p. 16. BS, the Hague.

66. Notes on FNV exit BS, 1981.

67. Letters from FNV to CEBOSINE, 17 February and 24 April 1984 and from CEBOSINE to FNV, 30 March 1984. FNV, Amsterdam.

68. Ibid., from D. Rijkse, FNV to the Minister of Economics, 24 April 1984. FNV, Amsterdam.

CHAPTER 7

1. 'Handelsministeriets kontaktudvalg. Dansk Vaerftsindustri. Redegörelse april 1979', pp. 18–19. CO Metal, Copenhagen.

2. Interviews with Charles Hansen, vice chairman of CO Metal, April 1981, H.J. Simonsen and Preben Nörby, chairman of CO Metal's local branch in Ålborg and chairman of the shop stewards' executive committee at Ålborg Vaerft, respectively, March 1981. *Aktuelt*, 20 January 1979. On at least two occasions Ålborg Vaerft has lost orders on passenger cruisers to Swedish yards, which has provoked hard feelings and accusations that Swedish competitors have exploited government subsidies which have distorted competition.

3. 'Handelsministeriets kontaktudvalg. Dansk Vaerftsindustri. Redegörelse april 1979', bil G., CO Metal, Copenhagen.

4. Employment Statistics. Ministry of Industry, Copenhagen, Jernets Arbejdsgiverforening, Copenhagen, Dansk Skibsvaerftsforening, Copenhagen. Interviews with personnel managers Oluf Pedersen, Frederikshavns Vaerft and B. Jensen, Ålborg Vaerft, naval architect Jens E. Kudsk Jensen, Lindö Vaerft and production manager Frits Richter, Alborgs Vaerft, December 1980.

5. 'Handelsministeriets kontaktudvalg. Pa ret köl. Samvirke om dansk skibsbygning. December 1967', CO Metal, Copenhagen.

6. Ibid., p. 7. There was a similar government attempt at about the same time to decide how unions ought to be organised in Britain. Both Denmark and Britain had unions organised according to craft or trade instead of industry. Cf. Chapter 5, p. 120.

7. 'Oversigt over ulovlige arbejdsnedlaeggelser 1975–1980', Jernets Arbejdsgiverforening, Copenhagen.

8. 'Handelsministeriets kontaktudvalg. Pa et köl. Samvirke om dansk skibsbygning. December 1967', p. 7. CO Metal, Copenhagen. See above, Note 6.

9. Ibid.

10. Ibid., pp. 10, 13.

11. Minutes Handelsministeriets kontaktudvalg, 30 September 1975. CO Metal, Copenhagen.

12. Ibid., p. 12.

13. Ibid., p. 13.

14. *Metal*, No. 5, 1977.

15. *Finans Tidende*, No. 2, October 1977.

16. Minutes Handelsministeriet kontaktudvalg, 5 May 1978. CO Metal, Copenhagen.

17. 'Handelsministeriet kontaktudvalg. Dansk Vaerftindustri. Redegörelse april 1979', p. 9. CO Metal, Copenhagen.

18. Ibid., p. 11.

19. Ibid., p. 44.

20. Interview with Charles Hansen, February 1984.

21. 'Handelsministeriet kontaktudvalg. Dansk Vaerftindustri. Redegörelse april 1979', p. 48. CO Metal, Copenhagen. (See also Chapter 2, Note 31).

22. 'Analyse af de store danske vaerfters situation og muligheder nu og

i fremtiden. CO Metal 1981', CO Metal, Copenhagen.

23. Interview with the former Minister of Industry Erling Jensen March, 1985 (the quotation) and with Charles Hansen, February 1984.

24. Minutes kontaktudvalget, 31 May 1983. CO Metal, Copenhagen.

25. Interview with Charles Hansen, February 1984.

26. Minutes kontaktudvalget, 31 May 1983. CO Metal, Copenhagen.

27. 'Kontaktudvalget. Skibskreditordningerne i samfundsmaessig belysning', October 1983, p. 7. CO Metal, Copenhagen.

28. Ibid., pp. 9–10. It has been argued that the figure is both too high and irrelevant, because if the national bank had not bought the bonds the shipowners would have chosen a cheaper method of financing by turning to the international capital market. The cost would thus have averaged two per cent less, according to the calculations of the Ministry of Industry. However, this reservation does not change the principle of the system.

29. Ibid., p. 34.

30. 'CO Metal. Den aktuelle situation for vaerftindustrien. 7 April 1983', CO Metal, Copenhagen.

31. Government Bill No. L. 87 1983. 'Bemaerkinger til lovforslaget', p. 4.

32. A leasing interest society bought a ship. Interested members of the society were invited to buy Dcr 100,000 shares. The ship could be written off by 30 per cent a year (25 per cent in the year it was acquired). In respect to tax, each individual shareholder was regarded as the owner and could consequently enjoy this 'writing-off right'. The Dcr 100,000 share was financed by a Dcr 35,000 cash payment and a Dcr 65,000 annuity loan at 15 per cent. Not only the write-offs but also the interest on the loan was tax-deductible. With a marginal tax rate of 70 per cent the net effect after five years was Dcr 7,000 to the benefit of each shareholder.

These deductions meant more for the high-income earner than did their incomes from ship transport. Therefore the leasing price could be set low and the system could be exploired to the benefit of both leaser and owner. In the example given by the parliamentary committee the leaser paid an annuity over five years at an average rate of 8 per cent (Dcr 25,046 a year).

The leasing system could be combined with ship credit orders. It went with over-financing which enhanced the profits of the owners, although it did not automatically imply the presence of subsidies. The largest Danish shipping company, AP Möller, sold ships to leasing societies and leased them back again. More important for the shipbuilders, however, was that money increasingly was withdrawn from taxation and invested in the building of new ships. Dentists, for instance, suddenly became important as shipowners, and regular shipowning companies ceased to own their own ships. Dentists and other high-income earners became so important for new building activities at the Danish yards that the metal workers' unions emphatically defended the right of dentists to order ships.

The conclusion of the parliamentary committee was that shares in leasing societies could yield more than investments in bonds because a number of tax rules which could be favourably combined. Capital of 3.5 bn was generally leased throughout 1982. The state's income loss (i.e. the subsidy element) was, when the investor has been in the highest income class, 10–15 per cent of the initial purchase value. Of course, the leasing system could be combined with ship credit orders. As has been said, over-financing was both possible and usual.

33. Interview with Charles Hansen, February 1984.

34. 'Industriministeriet. Notat verdrörende de seneste års udvikling i reglerne vedrörende leasing samt leasings betydning for danske vaerfters nybygningsaktivitet. 22 marts 1984', p. 7. CO Metal, Copenhagen.

35. Ibid., p. 8.

36. 'Industriministeriet. Notat om virkningerne af en aendring af hjemmemarkedsordningen. 18 april 1984', p. 12. CO Metal, Copenhagen.

37. Ibid., pp. 13–14.

38. Ibid., p. 16.

39. Ibid., p. 17.

40. 'Oversigt over ulovlige arbejdsnedlaeaggelser 1975–1980', Jernets Arbejdsgiverforening, Copenhagen.

41. Report by the B & W inquiry committee, 27 May 1967. Erhvervsarkivet, Århus.

42. Minutes of the board of B & W, 14 June 1967. Erhvervsarkivet, Århus.

43. Interview with shop stewards Bjarne Jensen and Helfe Larsen, Faellesklubben B & W, February 1984.

44. *Öen 2*. Faellesklubben B & W, p. 4. Faellesklubben B & W, Copenhagen.

45. Minutes B & W Faellesklub, 4 December 1975. Faellesklubben B & W, Copenhagen.

46. Ibid., 9 April 1976.

47. 'Aftraedelselön 1978–1979', Faellesklubben B & W, Copenhagen.

48. *Information*, 19 June 1976.

49. *Minavisen*, 3 April 1976.

50. Interview with shop stewards Bjarne Jensen and Helge Larsen, Faellesklubben B & W, February 1984.

51. 'Aftraedelselön 1978–1979', Faellesklubben B & W, Copenhagen.

52. Cf. article in *Information*, 2 May 1979.

53. 'Oversigt over ulovlige arbejdsnedlaeggelser 1975–1980', Jernets Arbejdsgiverforening, Copehnagen.

54. Interview with shop stewards Bjarne Jensen and Helge Larsen, Faellesklubben B & W, February 1984.

55. Ibid.

56. The Export Credit Council could give credits only on economic criteria. However, the Minister of Industry had legal powers to intervene and order the Export Credit Council to give credits for employment reasons as well. In the summer of 1980 B & W employees exerted political pressure in the form of rallies and lobbying. This made the Social Democratic Minister of Industry, Erling Jensen, intervene and order the Export Credit Council to give the credits.

57. Interview with shop stewards Bjarne Jensen and Helge Larsen, Faellesklubben B & W, February 1984.

58. Dalum Christensen *et al*.

59. Interview with Fritz Sell, chairman of the shop stewards' executive committee at Nakskov Vaerft, October 1981.

60. Ibid., and with Herman Burmeister and Valter Andersen, chairman

and vice chairman, respectively, of the metal workers' local branch in Nakskov, October 1981, and with Charles Hansen, CO Metal, Copenhagen, April 1981.

61. Wage statistics of the metal workers' local branch in Nakskov, CO Metal, Nakskov.

62. Interview with Fritz Sell, chairman of the shop stewards' executive committee at Nakskov Vaerft, October 1981.

63. *Metal*, No. 3, 1984.

64. Interview with ex-Minister of Industry, Erling Jensen, March 1985.

CHAPTER 8

1. *Journal Officiel des Communautés Européennes*, 9 March 1964, pp. 673.

2. Ibid., p. 2152.

3. 'First EEC Council Directive on Aid to Shipbuilding. 28 July 1969', EEC, Brussels. Interview with Laurus de Jonge, in charge of shipbuilding in the EEC Commission general directorate III, September 1981.

4. 'Commission of the EEC. Report on the Long and Medium Term Development of the Shipbuilding Market', GD III c. EEC, Brussels.

5. Ibid., p. 155.

6. 'Commission of EEC. Memorandum of working group No. 1 — "Market Survey" — regarding the revision of the forecasts produced in 1969', GD III c. EEC, Brussels, 1972.

7. 'Proposals to the Council on the Shipbuilding Industry, 8 November 1973', COM (73) 1788 finalm EEC, Brussels; interview with Laurus de Jonge, September 1981.

8. *Journal Officiel des Communautś Européennes*, No. C 114/23, 27 December 1973.

9. 'Proposals to the Council on the Shipbuilding Industry, 8 November 1973'm COM (73) 1788 final, EEC, Brussels.

10. 'Skibsvaerftsforeningen. Generelle bemaerkninger til forslaget fra EF-Kommissionen til Rådet om Skibsbygingsindustrien. L5, Januar 1974', GD III c. EEC, Brussels.

11. 'Statement by John Nicholson. The Shipbuilding Study Group Meeting, 9 January 1974', Economic and Social Committee (ESC). EEC, Brussels.

12. 'Sitzung des EMB-Exekutivausschusses. Brüssel, 12./13.9.1973', EMF, Brussels.

13. 'Comité Economique et Social, 119ème session plenière des 27 et 28 mars 1974: Amendement proposé par M Fijn van Draat, *ibid* par MM Heniker-Heaton, de Ferranti, Nicholson et Clark; Avis de la section de l'industrie, du commerce de l'artisanat et des services le 12 mars 1974', ESC. EEC, Brussels; *Journal Officiel des Communautés Européennes*, 16 August 1974, No. C 97/45.

14. 'Comité Economique et Social', 119ème session plenière des 27 et 28 mars 1974. Amendement proposé par MM Carstens, Byskov et Römer. ESC. EEC, Brussels.

15. Ibid. 'Compte rendu des délibérations. Séance du 27 mars 1974'.

16. 'The role of the EEC in world shipbuilding. Problems and prospects', November 1975. GD III c. EEC, Brussels.

17. 'Communication de la Commission au Conseil concernant la construction navale. 2ème. 26 Mai 1976', COM (76) 224 final GD III c. EEC, Brussels.

18. 'Communication de la Commission au Conseil 6 décembre 1977. Assainissement du secteur de la construction navale dans la communauté', GD III c. EEC, Brussels.

19. Ibid., p. 11 The EEC Commission only includes new building of merchant tonnage.

20. The Council's Resolution, 19 September 1978 (C 229). GD III c. EEC, Brussels.

21. 'Rapport. Möte i varvsgruppen, Köpenhamn 22.2.1978', Metall, Stockholm.

22. 'Möte i EMF:s varvsgrupp och trepartsmöte i EG:s varvsgrupp — Bryssel 1.3.–2.3.1978', Metall, Stockholm.

23. 'EEC Shipbuilders' Linking Committee. Ideas for autonomous measures . . . Paris, December 3, 1976', ESC. EEC, Brussels.

24. 'Bericht der Dreier-Arbeitsgruppe im engeren Rahmen', IIIc2/1004/78-0. GD III c. EEC, Brussels.

25. 'Bericht über die Sitzung der dreigliedrigen Arbeitsgruppe 'Schiffbau' vom 12 Mai 1978 im engeren Rahme', V/610/78-DE. EMF, Brussels.

26. 'Select tripartite meeting on shipbuilding 13th April, 1978', EMF, Brussels.

27. Ibid.

28. Ibid. Indeed, in May 1978 EMF was almost more prepared to reduce and contract than were the industry representatives — especially if the contraction were to be accompanied by special redundancy and retraining packages. The Nordic-Dutch approach had by then been accepted in principle, as the policy of the EMF, though the scale of the reduction was by no means settled.

29. Ibid., 12 May 1978.

30. 'IMIF. The World Surplus of Shipping and Shipbuilding Capacity', 20 December 1978. GD III c. EEC, Brussels.

31. 'OECD. Maritime Transport Committee. Working Party No. 6 of the Council of Shipbuilding. Proposals by the IMIF concerning subsidised scrapping and scrap and build scheme. Restricted 18th January 1979', DAF/MTC/79.3 C/wp 6 (79) 3. OECD, Paris.

32. Letter from Taka Yashi Doi, president of Zosen Juki Roren, to Karl Casserini, assistant general secretary and in charge of shipbuilding within IMF, 26 December 1978. IMF, Geneva.

33. 'EMF. Concise minutes of the shipbuilding committee meeting 31 October 1978', EMF, Brussels.

34. 'EMF. Scrap and Build Policy. Draft 11 February 1979', EMF, Brussels.

35. 'EEC. Working party on scrap and build. Report on state of discussions. 28 February 1979. Confidential draft', EMF, Brussels.

36. Ibid.

37. Ibid. Cf. Financial Times, 28 March 1979.

38. 'Outline of a Scrap and Build Programme. 30th May 1979', GD IIIc. 2 doc 313 4 07 79. ESC. EEC, Brussels.

39. Ibid.

40. *Financial Times*, 8 March 1979; *Daily Telegraph*, 9 March 1979.

41. 'OECD. Working party No. 6, 7–8 March 1979. Minutes', OECD, Paris.

42. Ibid.

43. Letter from Steffen Möller to the secretariat of the Nordic Metal Workers' Federation, 14 May 1979. Metall, Stockholm.

44. Ibid.

45. EMF shipbuilding working group, 5 June 1979. Condensed minutes. EMF, Brussels.

46. Ibid.

47. 'Communication from the Commission to the Council on a scheme to promote the scrapping and building of ocean going ships', 25 September 1979. GD IIIc. COM (79) 446 final. EEC, Brussels.

48. EMF shipbuilding working group, 3–4 October 1979. Condensed minutes. EMF, Brussels.

49. 'EMF statement on the shipbuilding and ship repairing industry in Europe 15th November 1979', EMF, Brussels.

50. Letter from the EMF secretariat to the affiliates, 14 December 1979. EMF, Brussels.

51. Ibid.

52. EMF shipbuilding working group, 29–30 April 1980. Condensed minutes. EMF, Brussels.

53. Interview with Hubert Thierron, general secretary EMF, May 1981.

54. Ibid., and Laurus de Jonge, September 1981; 'Report on the State of the Shipbuilding Industry in the Community', 14 September 1981. GD IIIc. COM (81) 432 final. EEC, Brussels.

55. Interview with Roy Brown, former general secretary AWES, April 1983.

56. 'Policy guidelines for restructuring the shipbuilding industry', GD IIIc. 24 March 1983. COM (83) 65 final. EEC, Brussels. Cf. *Wall Street Journal*, 31 March 1983.

57. *Financial Times*, 20 December 1983.

58. EMF shipbuilding working group, 11 November 1983. Condensed minutes. EMF, Brussels.

59. Cf. Osterheld.

60. Information given by economist Anne-Marie Mureau, IMF, Geneva.

61. Interview with Hans Hagnell, November 1982.

62. See, for instance, Edgren, Faxén and Odhner and Meidner and Niklasson. (Cf. above Ch. 4, pp. 101–4.)

63. 'Minutes of the IMF shipbuilding conference 24–26 March 1960 in Hamburg', pp. 49–50. IMF, Geneva.

64. Ibid., 1–3 April 1964, in Genua, pp. 64–5.

65. '21. International Metal Workers' Congress 1968/Secretariat's report p. 105', IMF, Geneva.

66. Minutes of the sixth IMF shipbuilding conference, 21–25 May 1967, in Newcastle. IMF, Geneva.

67. 'IMB. Die sozialen Probleme der Strukturveränderungen im

Schiffbau. Schiffbaukonferene in Newcastle 22–25 Mai 1967', IMF, Geneva.

68. 'World Shipbuilding Conference of IMF in Newcastle, Great Britain', pp. 4–5. IMF, Geneva.

69. Report from meeting between OECD working party 6, and the Trade Union Advisory Committee to OECD in Paris, 22 March 1977. IMF, Geneva. 'Rapport varvsmöte IMF/OECD. 21–22/3 1979', Metall, Stockholm.

70. '2nd IMF Asian Shipbuilding Seminar May 3–June 1 1978. Tokyo/Japan. Agenda item 1: present situation of the world shipbuilding industry with special reference to Asia, by Werner Thönnessen, assistant general secretary', IMF, Geneva.

71. 'Declaration of the 2nd IMF Asian Shipbuilding Seminar Tokyo, May 30–June 1, 1978', IMF, Geneva.

72. 'IMF statement to the meeting of the shipbuilding group with working party No. 6 on shipbuilding of the OECD Council', 10–11 July 1978. IMF, Geneva.

73. 'Address by Karl Casserini at IMF shipbuilding meeting, 26 September 1980', IMF, Geneva.

CHAPTER 9

1. See for instance Weitzman.

2. See for instance Mancur Olson, Jr, p. 111.

3. Cf. Dahrendorf, p. 159.

4. Ibid, p. 163.

5. Torstendahl. The strains in participatory capitalism occurred somewhat later in shipbuilding than in Torstendahl's general scheme (the beginning of the 1970s). The development from participatory to corporatist capitalism with 'iron triangles' of tripartite co-operation which Torstendahl finds from his general perspective is more difficult to find within shipbuilding, however. There, the unions' influence dwindled away in countries like Britain, West Germany and the Netherlands. In France it was always small. The deviation from Torstendahl's pattern is possibly due to the fact that West European shipbuilding was a rapidly declining industry with no power resources. Torstendahl also expressly underlines, (p. 158) that he has not been able to include world division of labour in his model. That division of labour was decisive for the development of the shipbuilding industry.

6. Zeitlin, pp. 29, 36–7.

7. Skocpol, pp. 24–33.

8. Ibid., p. 30.

9. Habermas, 1979. See also Habermas, 1973, pp. 12–18.

10. Habermas, 1973, pp. 88–9. Badie and Birnbaum, pp. 66–7, argue that Habermas's emphasis on the legislative system and parliament as an extension of public opinion means that the state tends to be conceived in a system functionalist way, reducing politics to an equilibrium pressure on the centre and responses to it.

11. Cox.

12. Schmitter, pp. 93–4.

13. For a critical view on Marxist corporatist theories from a Marxist point of departure, see Jessop.

14. Korpi, pp. 208–11. Although he uses the concept of corporatism, Torstendahl in reality seems close to Korpi's view. His corporatist society is a mediating organisation between state and individuals and as distinguished from Schmitter he is especially interested in the forms of decision-making within that organisation. Instead of development of bureaucracy corporatism has for Torstendahl meant that opening up of negotiations. Bureaucracy guards what it has but does not expand. Rather it is transformed to meet new needs and claims.

15. Cf. Einemann, pp. 206–7.

16. Lindbeck, p. 36.

17. Skidelsky, p. 67.

18. Zeitlin, pp. 33, 34.

19. OECD. Economic Outlook. For a more general survey of the restructuring and its implications see, for instance, the OECD publication in 1978 *Face aux futurs Pour une maîtrise du vraiesemblable et une question de l'imprévisible*, esp. pp. 123–45, 175–209, and the International Labour Organisation's *World Labour Report*, 1984, esp. ch 7., with an extensive bibliography and statistical annexe. See also numerous publications within the EEC FAST Programme. For an attempt to put the development into a long-term historical perspective see Attali, esp. pp. 49, 56, 92, 175–89. Cf. also Glasgow.

20. International Labour Organisation, *World Labour Report*, 1984, table A 1.

21. E.P. Thompson, pp. 12–13.

22. Cf. Kocka, 1981.

References

ARCHIVES

Germany

IG Metall, Bremen. Minutes, memoranda, annual reports, statements, correspondence.
IG Metall, Hamburg (Bezirksleitung). Minutes, memoranda, statements, correspondence.
Betriebsrat HDW, Kiel. Election statistics, 'social plans'.
Verband der Deutschen Schiffbauindustrie, Hamburg. Employment statistics, subsidy inquiries.
Senator Claus Grobecker's private archive, Bremen. Correspondence, memoranda.
Ministry of Economics, Bonn. Memoranda.

France

Confédération Française Démocratique du Travail (CFDT), Paris. Minutes, memoranda, correspondence, statements.
Confédération Générale du Travail (CGT), Paris. Minutes, memoranda, correspondence, statements.
Force Ouvrière (FO), Paris. Minutes, memoranda, correspondence, statements.
Force Ouvrière (FO), St Nazaire. Memoranda, statements.
Centre de Documentation du Mouvement Ouvrier et du Travail (CDMOT), Nantes. Minutes, memoranda, reports, etc., on shipbuilding of ACN and Chantiers Dubigeon Normandie.
Chambre Syndicale des Constructeurs de Navires (CSCN), Paris. Annual reports, employment statistics, statements.
Ministry of Industry, Paris. Memoranda, statements.

Sweden

Svenska Metallindustriarbetareförbundet, Stockholm. Minutes, analyses, drafts, notes, statements, reports, correspondence.
Svenska Varv AB, Gothenburg. Minutes, analyses, drafts, notes, statements, reports, correspondence.
Verkstadsföreningen, Stockholm. Reports.
Kockums verkstadsklubb, Malmö. Minutes, notes, statements, 'social plans'.

271

City archives, Gothenburg. Eriksberg files.

Hans Laurin's private archives, Gothenburg. Diary, correspondence, memoranda.

Kristian von Sydow's private archives, Gothenburg. Correspondence, memoranda.

Great Britain

Ministry of Trade and Industry, London. Memoranda, statistics, reports.

Confederation of Shipbuilding and Engineering Workers' Union (Confed), London. Reports, minutes, drafts, collective negotiations and agreements materials.

General, Municipal and Boilermakers' Union (GMBWU), Glasgow. Minutes, memoranda, statements.

British Shipbuilders, Newcastle. Employment statistics, annual reports, collective agreements, wage statistics, 'social plans'.

Govan Shipbuilders, Glasgow. Employment statistics, yard agreements, 'social plans'.

UIE, Glasgow. Minutes from negotiations, 'social plans', yard agreements, employment statistics.

Scott Lithgow, Greenock. Yard agreements.

Harland & Wolff, Belfast. Employment statistics, yard agreements.

The Netherlands

Ministry of Economics, the Hague. Reports from government committees, statistics.

Beleidskommissie Scheepsbouw, Delft/the Hague. Minutes, drafts, analyses, memoranda, reports.

CEBOSINE, Delft. Biannual reports, statistics.

FNV, Amsterdam. Minutes, memoranda, statements, action plans.

Denmark

Ministry of Industry, Copenhagen. Employment statistics, reports.

CO Metal, Copenhagen. Minutes, reports, memoranda, statements, statistics.

Nakskov metal workers, local branch, Nakskov. Wage statistics.

Faellesklubben, B&W, Copenhagen. Minutes, 'social plans', agreements.

Erhvervsarkivet, Århus. Report from the B&W inquiry 1967, minutes of the B&W board 1965–70.

Dansk Skibsverftsforening, Copenhagen. Employment statistics, annual reports.

Jernets Arbejdsgiverforening, Copenhagen. Employment and strike statistics.

International organisations

OECD, Paris. Reports, statistics, memoranda, drafts.
EEC, Brussels. GD III:c: reports, statistics, statements, memoranda, drafts. Economic and Social Committee: Minutes and statements.
International Metal Workers' Federation (IMF), Geneva. Minutes, drafts, memoranda, statements, conference reports, statistics.
European Metal Workers' Federation (EMF), Brussels. Minutes, drafts, statements, conference reports, statistics.
Association of West European Shipbuilders (AEWES), London/Delft. Statistics, statements, reports.

INTERVIEWS

(The titles indicate in what capacity these people were interviewed, not necessarily their actual positions at the time of the interview.)

Germany

Günther Clüver, yard manager HDW, Hamburg. April 1980.
Günther Erdmann, Ministerialrat *Land* government Schleswig-Holstein, Kiel. Oct. 1983.
Fritz Fischer, works council Blohm & Voss, Hamburg, April 1980.
Klaus Grobecker, Senator for Labour, MP, Bremen, April, June 1984.
Herbert Kienke, works council AG Weser, Bremen, April 1980, Oct. 1981.
Dieter Kirchhof, works council Bremer Vulkan, Bremen, April 1980.
Dr Dieter Klink, President of the *Land* Parliament, Bremen, Jan. 1985.
Hans Koschnik, Lord Mayor of Bremen, Jan. 1986.
Count Otto Lambsdorff, Minister of Economics, Jan. 1985.
Gerd Lilienfeldt, IG Metall (Bezirksleitung), Hamburg, May 1983.
Horst Lorenzen, works council HDW, Kiel, Jan. 1984.
Hans Matthöfer, Minister of Finance, Sept. 1984.
Volkhard Meier, Verband der Deutschen Schiffbauindustrie, Hamburg, March 1983.
Heinz Meinking, IG Metall, Bremen, April 1980, Oct. 1981, Feb., April, May 1983, April 1984, Jan. 1985.
Dr Wolfgang Obernolte, Shipbuilding Division, Ministry of Economics, Bonn, Aug. 1984.
A. Pedersen, production manager HDW, Kiel, April 1980.
Alfred Prezewovsky, IG Metall, Kiel, Jan., June 1983.
Michael Rocka, Secretary of the SPD *Landestag* faction, Kiel, Aug. 1983.
Karl Schönberger, works council Bremer Vulkan, Bremen, April 1980, Oct. 1981, April, May 1983.
Dieter Sick, SPD, Hamburg, Aug. 1983.
Werner Trost, works council AG Weser, Bremen, April 1980.
Hans Ziegenfuss, chairman works council AG Weser, Bremen, Oct. 1981, May 1983.

273

France

Michel Banchais, production and marketing manager Dubigeon-Normandie, Nantes, Oct. 1981.
Jean-Pierre Dobler, CSCN, Paris, Nov. 1983.
Jean-Pierre Foucauld, CFDT, Paris, Nov. 1983.
J. Gerardin, deputy general secretary, Syndicat Patronal des Industries Metallurgiques et Navales, Nantes, Oct. 1981.
Yves Giodas, shipbuilding officer CFDT, Paris, Nov. 1983.
Marcel Guiheneuff, CFDT Dubigeon-Normandie, Nantes, Nov. 1983, June 1984.
Henri Mallet, shipbuilding officer FO, Paris, Nov. 1983.
Paul Malnoë, FO, Saint Nazaire, June 1984.
Dominique de Mas Latrie, director CSCN, Paris, Nov. 1983.
J. Meyer, CSCN, Paris, Oct. 1981.
Fabrice Theobald, counsellor to the Secretary of State for Sea, Paris, Nov. 1984.
Eric Thuillez, Shipbuilding Division, Ministry for Sea, Paris, Nov. 1983.

Sweden

Nils G. Åsling, Ministry of Industry, Feb. 1984.
Gunnar Axestam, personnel director Öresundsvarvet, Landskrona, Nov. 1980.
Leif Blomberg, chairman of the Swedish metal workers' federation (Metall), Stockholm, Feb. 1984.
Hans-Owe Carlquist, personnel manager Kockums, Malmö, Nov. 1980.
John Ekström, shipbuilding consultant in the Ministry of Industry, Stockholm, and OECD, Paris, Nov. 1984.
Leif Göransson, metal workers' union Kockums, Malmö, July 1984.
Hans Hagnell, MP 1957–73, economist Metall 1946–71, and chairman of IMF's shipbuilding committee 1964–73, Nov. 1982.
Tony Hagström, Undersecretary of State in the Ministry of Industry, Nov. 1984.
Nils-Hugo Hallenborg, managing director Kockums, Malmö, July 1984.
Erik Huss, Minister of Industry, Nov. 1984.
Bengt Jakobsson, international secretary Metall, Feb., Dec. 1979, Jan. 1980.
Inge Karlsson, chairman of the metal workers' union Götaverken, Gothenburg, Oct. 1981.
Hans Laurin, managing director Götaverken, Gothenburg, Nov. 1983.
Inger Lindquist, MP, Gothenburg, May 1984.
Åke Lundquist, metal workers' union Kockums, Malmö, Dec. 1982.
Stig Malm, chairman of the Swedish Trade Union Federation (LO) and up to 1982 in charge of shipbuilding in Metall, Nov. 1984.
Leif Molinder, personnel manager Svenska Varv, Gothenburg, Oct. 1984.
Åke Nordlander, managing director Verkstadsföreningen, Stockholm, Feb. 1984.

Per Nyström, chairman government committee on shipbuilding 1967–70 and Governor of Gothenburg, Oct. 1982.

John-Erik Olsson, chairman of the metal workers' union Kockums, Malmö, June 1980, Aug. 1981, Dec. 1982, Feb., July 1984.

Reinhold Stolt, chairman of the metal workers' union Eriksberg, Gothenburg, Dec. 1981.

Gunnar Sträng, Minister of Finance, Jan. 1985.

Nore Sundberg, Shipbuilding Division, Ministry of Industry, April 1984.

Kristian von Sydow, managing director Broströms Shipping Company, Gothenburg, May 1984.

Bengt Tengroth, personnel director Svenska Varv, Gothenburg, April, Oct. 1981.

Olle Westin, Shipbuilding Division, Ministry of Industry, Nov. 1984.

Sture Wilhelmsson, information department, Kockums, Malmö, Nov. 1980.

Great Britain

Jimmy Airlie, AUEW, London, Dec. 1984.

David Armstrong, personnel manager British Shipbuilders, Newcastle, Dec. 1984.

Richard Barton, manager in international liaison British Shipbuilders, Newcastle, Dec. 1984.

Anthony Benn, Minister of Industry, MP, Feb. 1985.

Tom Burlison, regional officer GMWU, Newcastle, Sept. 1980.

Euan Cameron, Shipbuilding Policy Division, Department of Trade and Industry, Dec. 1984.

David Dew, GMBU shop steward UIE, Clydebank, Oct. 1984.

Bob Dickae, store manager UIE, Clydebank, Oct. 1984.

T.D. Douglas, regional official GMWU, Belfast, Sept. 1980.

Archie Feirley, shipbuilding officer GMBU, Glasgow, Oct., Nov. 1984.

Alex Ferry, general secretary Confed, London, Sept. 1980, Oct., Nov., Dec. 1984.

Sam Fitzimmons, GMWU, Belfast, Sept. 1980.

Sam Guilmore, chairman shop stewards committee Govan Shipbuilders, Glasgow, Oct. 1984.

Jimmy Hamilton, AUEW shop steward UIE, Clydebank, Oct. 1984.

Erik Hellström, production manager Harland and Wolff, Belfast, Nov. 1984.

Grey Holden, production manager UIE, Clydebank, Oct. 1984.

Harry Hood, special projects manager, Scottish Development Agency, Glasgow, Oct. 1984.

Alastair McCallum, personnel manager UIE, Clydebank, Oct., Dec. 1984.

Robert McCann, personnel director Govan Shipbuilders, Glasgow, Oct., Dec. 1984.

Nichol McCloy, personnel manager Scott Lithgow, Greenock, Nov. 1984.

Martin McGrath, UCAT shop steward UIE, Clydebank, Oct. 1984.

Bruce Millan, Minister of State for Scotland 1974–6, 1976–9, MP since

1959, Nov. 1984.

Jimmy Milne, Chairman Scottish TUC, British delegate EEC Economic and Social Committee, Brussels, Sept. 1981, Oct. 1984.

John Moist, research officer GMBU, Glasgow, Oct., Nov. 1984.

Jimmy Morell, chairman GMBU, Glasgow, Sept. 1980, Oct. 1984.

John Parker, chairman and chief executive Harland and Wolff, Belfast, Nov. 1984.

Bill Porter, regional shipbuilding officer GMWU, Newcastle, Sept. 1980.

Dr Martin Stopford, director of business development, British Shipbuilders, Newcastle, Dec. 1984.

Peter Thompson, board of British Shipbuilders, London, Nov. 1984.

Sydney Treadgold, Shipbuilding Policy Division, Department of Trade and Industry, Dec. 1984.

David Wilson, GMWU, Belfast, Sept. 1980.

The Netherlands

Arie van der Hek, MP and chairman of the budget committee of the General Staaten, May 1984.

Jan de Jong, production manager van de Giessen de Noord, Krimpen, March 1982.

G. de Ruiter, Shipbuilding Division, Ministry of Economics, the Hague, May, Sept. 1984, Jan. 1985.

A. Timmer, personnel manager van de Giessen de Noord, Krimpen, March 1982.

Henk Vos, regional shipbuilding aircraft and automobile officer Industriebond FNV Amsterdam, MP since 1983, April 1980, March 1982, Oct. 1983, May, Sept., Dec. 1984, Jan. 1985.

G. de Vries Lentsch, CEBOSINE, Delft, May 1984.

Denmark

Herman Burmeister, chairman metal workers' union, Nakskov, 1979.

Kai Engell-Jensen, managing director Skibsvaerftsforeningen, Copenhagen, Dec. 1980.

Jakob Fuchs, Shipbuilding Division, Ministry of Industry, Dec. 1982, Feb. 1984.

Charles Hansen, vice chairman of CO Metal, April 1981, Feb. 1984.

Jens E. Kusk Jensen, marketing manager Lindö Vaerft, Odense, Dec. 1980.

B. Jensen, personnel director Aalborg Vaerft, Dec. 1980.

Bjarne Jensen, shop steward B&W, Copenhagen, Feb. 1984.

Erling Jensen, Minister of Industry, MP, March 1985.

Helge Larsen, shop steward B&W, Copenhagen, Feb. 1984.

Bengt Nielsen, shop steward B&W, Copenhagen, Nov. 1980.

Preben Nörby, chairman shop stewards' committee Aalborg Vaerft, March 1981.

Oluf Pedersen, personnel director Frederikshavns Vaerft, Dec. 1980.
Frits Richter, technical director Aalborg Vaerft, Dec. 1980.
H. Sejer-Nielsen, personnel director B&W, Copenhagen, Nov. 1980.
Fritz Sell, chairman shop stewards' committee Nakskov Vaerft, Oct. 1979.
H.J. Simonsen, chairman metal workers' union Ålborg, March 1981.
Ib Stetter, Minister of Industry, March 1985.

Italy

Dr Guido Assereto, marketing director Italcantieri, Trieste, May 1982.
Giuliano Cominardi, director Italcantieri, Trieste, May 1982.
Dr Roberto Pennarola, Fincantieri, Rome, May 1982.
Dr Erasmo Riccobono, Fincantieri, Rome, May 1982.
Dr Antonio Zappi, director and general manager Italcantieri, Trieste, May 1982.

Belgium

Vic Nelen, managing director Boelwerf, Antwerp, March 1982.
Gerrit Rombauts, PMB Antwerp, March 1982.

Eire

Stephen Tracey, Irish Transport and General Workers' Union, Dublin, Sept. 1981.

Finland

Göran Damström, manager technical information Wärtsilä, Helsinki, Dec. 1980.
Tapio Forsgren, managing director Association of Finnish Shipbuilders, Helsinki, Dec. 1980.
Tankmar Horn, chairman Wärtsilä, Helsinki, Dec. 1980.
Esko Honkavaara, Finnish metal workers' federation, Helsinki, Dec. 1980.
Mauri Kavonius, Finnish metal workers' federation, Helsinki, Dec. 1980.
Ari Valjakka, personnel director Wärtsilä, Helsinki, Dec. 1980.

International organisations

OECD, Paris

Jacques Delelienne, directorate for science, technology and industry. Oct. 1981, Nov. 1983.
John Ekström, working party No. 6 of the Council, Nov. 1984.

EEC, Brussels

Romelo Arena, Italian employer delegate Economic and Social Committee, Sept. 1981.
H. Friedrichs, German labour delegate Economic and Social Committee, Sept. 1981.
Laurus de Jonge, GD III:c., Sept. 1981.
Jimmy Milne, British labour delegate Economic and Social Committee, Sept. 1981.
Steffen Skovmand, Economic and Social Committee, May 1981.

ILO, Geneva

Karl Ebel, metal working division, Oct. 1982.

UNCTAD, Geneva

Raymond Glasgow, Shipping Division, May, Oct. 1982, Aug., Dec. 1983.

IMF, Geneva

Karl Casserini, assistant general secretary, May, Oct. 1982.
Marcello Malentacchi, head of health and safety department, Oct. 1982.
Anne-Marie Mureau, economist, May, Oct. 1982, Aug., Nov., Dec. 1983.

EMF, Brussels

Hubert Thierron, general secretary, May 1981.

AWES, London/Delft

Roy Brown, general secretary, April 1983.
G. de Vries Lentsch, May 1984. See under the Netherlands.

OFFICIAL PUBLICATIONS

Germany

Arbeitsamt Bremen, Schleswig-Holstein, Hamburg: Monthly statistics 1978–84.
Bundestag: Verhandlungen des Deutschen Bundestages. 10 Wahlperiode 1983–7. Bd 295; Bulletin, Presse und Informationsamt der Bundesregierung, 19 Jan. 1979.

France

La Documentation Française: Preparation du 7e Plan. Rapport du groupe sectoriel d'analyse et de prévision. Construction Navale. Paris 1976; Rapports des comités du 6e Plan 1971–75. Construction Navale, Paris 1971.
Le Livre Blanc, 1959.
Le Contrat Professionel, 1968.

Sweden

Riksdagen: Government's bill No 82 1970, No 117 1971, No 110 1975, No 121 1975/76, No 139 1976/77, No 49 1978/79, No 165 1979/80, No 147 1982/83: Parliament's decisions No 405 1979/80, No 147 1982/83; Parliament's Industry Committee (*Näringsutskottet*) No 55 1982/83 and Labour Market Committee No 26 1982/83.
Ministry of Industry: De svenska storvarvens problem. Betänkande avgivet av varvskommittén den 2 februari 1970.
Statistical Central Board: Statistiska Meddelanden, 1976: 6.
Länsarbetsnämnden i Malmöhus län: Rapport från avveckling av Öresundsvarvet, Feb. 1984.

Great Britain

House of Commons: Bill 195 22 June 1971; *Hansard* Report, 31 July 1974, March, November 1984.
HMSO Cmnd 2937 1966, 3623 1968, 4756 1971, 4918 1972, 4942 1972. For the titles see under *Literature* below.

Denmark

Folketinget: Government Bill No L 87, 1983.

The Netherlands

Ministry of Economics: Centrum voor de bestudering van de Sociale Problematiek in de Scheepsbouw. Rapport Sociale Problematiek Scheepsbouw, 1968.

OECD

The Council: Recommendation concerning government assistance to the shipbuilding industry, 30 May 1969, 16 Dec. 1970.

EEC

The Fast Programme. List of Publications. Brussels, 1 Oct. 1986.
OECD Maritime Transport, 1971, 1979.
OECD Economic Outlook, Dec. 1984.
OECD. Face aux futurs: Pour une maîtrise du vraisemblable et une gestion de l'imprévisible.

International Labour Organisation

Yearbook of Labour Statistics 1983.

'Semi-official' publications

Lloyds Annual Summary, 1950–82.

NEWSPAPERS AND PERIODICALS

Aktuelt (Denmark), 20 Jan. 1979.
Arbetet (Sweden), 1 July 1975, 12 Nov. 1977.
Berlingske Tidende (Denmark), 26 Aug. 1981.
Bohuslänningen (Sweden), 4 June 1983.
Bremer Morgenpost, 10 June 1980.
Bremer Nachrichten, 12 June 1980, 14 June 1982, 15, 17, 18 Feb. 1983, 13, 17 Aug. 1983.
Dagens Nyheter (Sweden), 3 May 1975, 11 Jan. 1980.
Evening Times (Glasgow), 14 Sept. 1978.
Financial Times, 20 Dec. 1983, 22 Sept. 1984.
Finanstidende (Denmark), No. 2, Oct. 1977.
der Gewerkschafter, No. 9, 1976, No. 1, 1977.
Glasgow Herald, 9 March, 27 Nov., 10, 21, 24 Dec. 1976, 18 Aug. 1977, 28 Nov. 1978, 13 Dec. 1984.
Göteborgs-Posten (Sweden), 6 Dec. 1974, 2 May 1975, 12 Nov. 1977.
The Guardian, 19 May 1986.
Hamburger Abendblatt, 27 March 1983.
Handelsblatt, 14 Feb., 15 Aug., 13 Sept., 29, 30 Nov. 1983.
L'Humanité, 8 July 1983.
Information (Denmark), 7 Jan. 1977, 2 May 1979.

Jahrbuch des Schiffahrtswesens, 1968.
Jyllands-Posten (Denmark), 15 Oct. 1977.
Kieler Nachrichten, 29 March, 22 April, 14 Sept. 1983.
Kockums-Nytt (Sweden), 1978–84.
Libération, 25 Jan. 1984.
Maritime Transport, 1959–79.
Metal (Denmark), No. 3, 1984.
Metallarbetaren (Sweden), 7 March 1974, 1 Feb. 1980, Nos. 14, 16, 1983.
Minavisen (Denmark), 3 April 1976.
Le Monde 26 Jan., 2 March, 7 Aug., 6 Nov. 1984.
Neue Zürcher Zeitung, 27 Oct. 1984.
Newcastle Journal, 29 Nov. 1984.
die *Nordsee-Zeitung*, 29 April 1982, 2 March 1983.
Nordvästra Skånes Tidningar (Sweden), 11 Jan. 1980.
Ouest France 13, 25 March, 4–5, 11, 15 April, 3 July 1964, 9 April, 21 May 1965, 8 Feb. 1974, 30 Sept., 3, 4 Oct. 1977.
Shipbuilding News, Sept. 1984.
Veckans Affärer (Sweden), 11 May 1983.
Vecko-Journalen (Sweden), No. 16, 1975.
Wall Street Journal, 31 March 1983.
Welt der Arbeit, 3 July 1980.
die *Weser-Kurier*, 12 June, 3 Oct. 1980, 30 Sept. 1981, 14 June, 23, 25–6 Sept. 1982, 18 Feb. 1983.
Westinform Shipping Report, Aug. 1961.
die *Zeit*, 2 Dec. 1983, 27 Jan. 1984.

LITERATURE

Philip Abrams, *Historical sociology*, Cornell UP, Ithaca, New York, 1982.
AG. Weser. Gesschäftsbericht 1975. Bremen, 1976.
K.J.W. Alexander and C.L. Jenkins, *Fairfields. A study of industrial change*, Penguin, London, 1970.
Peter Alhanko and Carl G. Holm, *Statligt stöd till industrin*, Industrins Utredningsinstitut, Stockholm, Nov. 1980.
Carl-Johan Asplund and Erik Hafström, *The Landskrona finance project. An example of a practical transformation strategy in Sweden*, OECD, Paris, June 1983.
Jacques Attali, *La figure de Fraser*, Fayard, Paris, 1984.
Bertrand Badie and Pierre Birnbaum, *Sociologie de l'état*, Grasset, Paris, 1982.
Jean Baechler, 'La caverne d'Ali Baba', in *CADMOS* (Cahiers trimestriels de l'Institut Universitaire d'Etudes Européennes), Geneva, 1982, spring-summer edition.
M. Barbance, *Saint Nazaire: Le Port, La Ville, Le Travail*, thesis, Rennes, 1948.
Eric Batstone, *Working order. Workplace industrial relations over two decades*, Basil Blackwell, Oxford, 1984.
Anthony Benn, *Arguments for Socialism*, Penguin, London, 1980.

Joachim Bergmann, Otto Jacobi and Walter Müller-Jentsch, *Gewerkschaften in der Bundesrepublik*, Frankfurt/Köln, 1975.

Christiane Bierbaum, Joachim Bischoff, Sebastian Herkommer and Karlheinz Maldaner, 'Bewusstseinsformen des Alltagslebens', in *Beiträge zum wissenschaftlichen Sozialismus*, 3, 1977, Hamburg-Berlin, 1977.

Jan Bohlin, *Lönsamhet och finansiering i svensk varvsindustri 1950–1976*, Mimeo, University of Gothenburg, 1986.

Booz, Allen and Hamilton Report. See under HMSO.

Samuel Brittan, 'The economic contradictions of democracy', in *British Journal of Political Science*, V, 1975.

Alasdair Buchan, *The right to work. The study of the Upper Clyde confrontation*, Alder and Boyars, London, 1972.

Peter Burke, *Sociology and history*, Allen and Unwin, London, 1980.

Pierre Candau, *Structures oligopolitiques et marché du travail. La réparation navale marseillaise*, Université d'Aix-Marseille, 1961.

Jean-Jacques Carré, Paul Dubois and Edmond Malinvaud, *La Croissance Franåaise*, Seuil, Paris, 1973.

C.S. Checkland, *The Upas Tree. Glasgow 1875–1975 . . . and after*, Glasgow, 1981.

Tomohei Chida, 'The development of Japan's post-war shipping policy', in *Journal of Transport History*, March 1984.

Susanne Dalum Christensen *et al.*, *Nakskov et udkantscentre*, Specialopgave i samfundsfag, Roskilde Universitetscenter, Denmark, 1980.

Stephen S. Cohen, 'France: industrial policy in the entrepreneurial state', in *Journal of Contemporary Business*, 11, 1982.

—— *Modern capitalist planning: the French model*, Harvard University Press, Cambridge, Mass., 1969.

Andrew J. Cornford and Raymond Glasgow, 'The process of structural change in the world economy: some aspects of the rise of the shipbuilding industry in the developing countries', in *Trade & Development. An UNCTAD Review*, No. 5, 1984.

Andrew Cox, 'Corporatism as reductionism: the analytic limits of the corporatist thesis, in *Government and opposition*, 16, 1, 1978.

James E. Cronin, *Industrial conflict in modern Britain*, London, Croom Helm, 1979.

Colin Crouch, 'The state, capital and liberal democracy', in Colin Crouch (ed.), *State and economy in contemporary capitalism*, London, Croom Helm, 1979.

Ralf Dahrendorf, *Class and class conflict in industrial society*, Routledge and Kegan Paul, London, 1959.

Donovan Report. See under HMSO.

C. Drewes, W. Pelsell and K.P. Wittemann, *Vorstudie Arbeitskräfte-Pool. Endbericht zur sozialwissenschaftlichen Begleitforschung*, Soziologisches Forschungsinstitut, Göttingen, July 1982.

Gösta Edgren, Karl-Olof Faxén and Clas-Erik Odhner, *Lönebildning och samhällsekonomi*, Stockholm, 1970.

Edgar Einemann, *Industriearbeiter in der Wirtschaftskrise*, thesis, Bremen, 1982.

John Ekström, *Varvsindustrins problem. Efterfrågan-konkurrens-framtidsutsikter*, Stockholm, 1970.

———— 'Sector policy: the case of Swedish shipbuilding', in: *Reexaminining European manpower politics*, a Special Report for the International Commission for Manpower Policy, No. 10, 1976.

J.E.T. Eldridge, *The Demarcation Disputes in the British Shipbuilding Industry: a Study in the Sociology of Conflict*, Paper for the International Industrial Relations Association's First World Congress, 4–8 Sept. 1967 in Geneva. International Labour Organisation, Geneva, call no 5691.

———— *Industrial disputes*, Routledge and Kegan Paul, London, 1968.

Jon Elster, *Sour grapes. Studies in subversion of rationality*, Cambridge University Press, 1983.

Josef Esser, *Gewerkschaften in der Krise*, Suhrkamp, Frankfurt/M, 1982.

Nicolas Fancier, *Les Ouvriers de Saint Nazaire*, Paris, 1976.

Daniel Fleury, *Les ouvriers de la Brière*, thesis, Nantes, 1980.

Peter Flieshardt and Reinhardt Sablotny, *Schliessung oder Fusion — gibt es bald nur noch einige einzige Grosswerfte?*, University of Bremen, 1980.

Dieter Frisch, 'La construction navale. Parent pauvre du dévelopment économique?', in *Reflets et Perspectives de la vie économique*, No. 5, 1963.

Duncan Gallie, *Social inequality and class radicalism in France and Britain*, Cambridge University Press, 1983.

Max Gallo, *La troisième alliance. Pour une nouvelle individualisme*, Fayard, Paris, 1984.

Elie Gallon, *Protection et déprotection des travailleurs dans la construction et la réparation navale de l'aire toulonnaise*. Thesis, Université d'Aix-Marseille II, 1979.

Jacques Garnier, *Construction et réparation navales en Provence/Alpes/Côte d'Azur*, Université d'Aix-Marseille II, Institut régional du travail, 1977.

Geddes Report. See under HMSO.

Raymond Glasgow, 'Shipping', in Attine *et al.*, *International Transactions in Services and Economic Development. Trade & Development. An UNCTAD Review.*

A. Glyn and B. Sutcliffe, *British capitalism, workers and profits squeeze*, Penguin, London, 1972.

L. Goldmann, *The hidden god*, Routledge and Kegan Paul, London, 1964.

Yannick Guin, *Le Mouvement Ouvrier Nantais*, Maspero, Paris, 1976.

Jürgen Habermas, 'Stichworte zu einer Theorie der Sozialisation', in Jürgen Habermas, *Kultur und Kritik*, Suhrkamp, Frankfurt/M, 1973.

———— *Legitimationsprobleme im Spätkapitalismus*, Suhrkamp, Frankfurt/M, 1973.

———— *Communication and the evolution of society*, Beacon Press, Boston, 1979.

Carl Hamilton, *Public subsidies to industry. The case of Sweden and its shipbuilding industry*, Institute for International Economic Studies, University of Stockholm, Seminar Paper No. 174, 1981.

A.C. Hardy and Edward Tyrell, *Shipbuilding. Background to a great industry*. Pitman, London, 1964

Christopher Harvie, *No gods and precious few heroes. Scotland 1914–1980*, Penguin, London, 1980.

Sebastian Herkommer *et al.*, *Gesellschaftsbewusstsein und Gewerkschaften*, Hamburg, 1979.

Frank Herron, *Labour market in crisis. Redundancy at Upper Clyde*

Shipbuilders, Macmillan, London, 1975.

Hill Samuel Report. See under HMSO.

T. Hiort-Lorenzen, *Skibsvaerftsstötte. Vurdering af omfanget af den offentlige stötte til vaerftsindustrien i Vesteuropa, Nordamerika og Japan og synspunkter vedrörende stöttens årsager og virkninger*, Copenhagen, 1971.

HMSO, Shipbuilding Inquiry Committee 1965–66 (Geddes Report), Cmnd. 2937, 1966.

———— Royal Commission on Trade Unions and Employers' Association (Donovan Report), Cmnd. 3623, 1968.

———— Shipbuilding and Shiprepairing, August 1971, Report No. 22, Cmnd. 4756, 1971.

———— Shipbuilding on the Upper Clyde, (Hill Samuel Report), Cmnd. 4918, 1972.

———— British Shipbuilding 1972 (Booz, Allen and Hamilton Report), Cmnd. 4942, 1972.

Brian W. Hogwood, *Government and shipbuilding, the politics of industrial change*, Fontana/Collins, Glasgow, 1979.

Richard Hyman, *Strikes*, Fontana/Collins, Glasgow, 1978.

Bob Jessop, *The capitalist state*, Martin Robertson, Oxford, 1982.

Stephen Johns, *Reformism on the Clyde*, Socialist Labour League, London, 1972.

Lars Jonung, *Prisregleringen*, SNS, Stockholm, 1984.

Karl Heinz Jüttemeier and Konrad Lammers, *Subventionen in der Bundesrepublik Deutschland. Kieler Diskussionsbeiträge No. 63/64*, Institut für Weltwirtschaft, Kiel, 1979.

Robert Kappel, 'Zur Krise und zur Perspektive des Schiffbaus in der Bundesrepublik', in: *Gewerkschaftliche Monatsheft*, Oct. 1983.

Robert Kappel and Detlef Rother, *Wandlungsprozesse in der Schiffahrt und im Schiffbau Westeuropas*, Bremen, 1982.

Anders Kjellberg, 'The Development of the Swedish Trade Union System — Historical Section', Preliminary version 1968. DUES Project (The Development of Unions in Western European Societies after the Second World War), University of Mannheim.

Jürgen Kocka, 'Organisierter Kapitalismus oder Staatsmonopolischer Kapitalismus', in Heinrich August Winkler (ed.), *Organisierter Kapitalismus. Voraussetzungen und Anfänge*, Göttingen, 1974.

———— 'Theorien in der Sozial- und Gesellschaftsgeschichte. Vorschläge zur historischen Schichtungsanalyse' in: *Geschichte und Gesellschaft* No. 1, 1975.

———— 'Kontroversen über Max Weber', in *Neue Politische Litteratur*, Vol. 1, 1976.

———— 'Gewerkschaftliche Interessenvertretung und gesellschaftliche Fortschritt', in *Gewerkschaftliche Monatsheft*, No. 6, 1981.

———— 'Max Weber et la Methodologie de l'Histoire. Einleitung', in *Comité Internationale des Sciences Historiques. XVIe Congrès International des Sciences Historiques*, Stuttgart, 25 Aug.–1 Sept. 1985, Rapports 1.

Walter Korpi, *The democratic class struggle*, Routledge and Kegan Paul, London, 1983.

N.D. Kondratieff, 'The long waves in economic life', in *Review of*

Economic statistics, XVII, 1935.

Karl Kühne, 'Shipbuilding and subsidies. Pros and cons', in: *Intereconomics*, No. 6, 1966.

Richard F. Kuisel, *Capitalism and state in modern France*, Cambridge University Press, 1981.

Georges Lefranc, *Visages du mouvement ouvrier français*, PUF, Paris, 1982.

Assar Lindbeck, *The national state in an international world economy*, Institute for International Economic Studies, University of Stockholm Seminar Papers 26, Stockholm, 1973.

Jonas Ljungberg, *Varvskris — och sedan?* Meddelanden från Ekonomisk-historiska institutionen Lunds universitet, No. 35, 1985.

Edward H. Lorenz, *The Labour Process and Industrial Relations in the British and French Shipbuilding Industries from 1880 to 1970*, diss., University of Cambridge, 1983.

Edward H. Lorenz and Frank Wilkinson, 'The Shipbuilding industry, 1880–1965', in B. Elbaum and W. Lazonick (eds), *The decline of the British economy*, Clarendon Press, Oxford, 1986.

J.R. McCullock (ed.), *Early English tracts on commerce*, Cambridge University Press, 1954.

Jack McGill, *Crisis on the Clyde*, Davis Poynter, London, 1972.

Jim McGoldrick, 'Industrial relations and the division of labour in the shipbuilding industry', in *British Journal of Industrial Relations*, Vol. XXI, No. 2, 1983.

Oskar Meggeneder, 'Die niederländischen Gewerkschaften in der Krise', in *Zeitschrift des Wirtschafts- und Sozialwissenschaftlichen Instituts des deutschen Gewerkschaftsbundes*, No. 2, 1984.

Rudolf Meidner and Harald Niklasson, *Arbetsmarknad och arbetsmarknadspolitik*, Lund, 1970.

Mitteilungsblatt der Zentralen Wissenschaftlichen Einrichtung Arbeit und Betrieb, 15, 16, University of Bremen, 1986.

Leif Molinder, *The restructuring of the Swedish shipbuilding industry*, Svenska Varv, Gothenburg, July 1984.

Yves Morvan, 'La politique industrielle française depuis la Libération: quarante années d'interventions et d'ambiguïtés', in *Revue d'économie industrielle*, No. 1, 1983.

Walter Müller-Jentsch and Hans-Joachim Sperling, 'Economic development, labour conflicts and the industrial relations system in West Germany', in Colin Crouch and Alessandro Pizzorno (eds), *The resurgence of class conflict in Western Europe since 1968*, Vol. 1, Macmillan, London, 1978.

Per Nyström, *Thordénstiftelsen. Historik*, Uddevalla, 1984.

Werner Oesterheld, 'Schiffbau: Europäische Gewerkschaftspolitik in einer Krisenbransche', in *Information über Multinationale Konzerne*, No. 2, 1983.

Claus Offe, *Strukturprobleme des kapitalistischen Staates*, Frankfurt, 1972.

Mancur Olson Jr, *The logic of collective action. Public goods and the theory of groups*, Harvard University Press, Cambridge, Mass., 1965.

Kent Olsson, *Från Pansarbåtsvarv till Tankfartygsvarv*, Svenska Varv, Göteborg, 1983.

Sydney Paulden and Bill Hawkins, *Whatever happened at Fairfields?*, Gower Press, London, 1969.

Sidney Pollard and Paul Robertson, *The British shipbuilding industry, 1870–1914*, Harvard University Press, Cambridge, Mass., 1979.

Alastair Reid, 'Dilution, trade unionism and the state in Britain during the First World War', in Steven Tolliday and Jonathan Zeitlin (eds), *Shop floor bargaining and the state. Historical and comparative perspectives*, Cambridge University Press, 1985.

J. Rex, *Key problems in sociological theory*, Routledge and Kegan Paul, London, 1961.

Jean-Daniel Reynaud, *Les Syndicats en France*, Seuil, Paris, 1975.

B.C. Roberts, 'The role of the state and public policy in industrial relations', in G. Spitaels (ed.), *La Crise des Relations Industrielles en Europe*, Brughes, 1971.

G. Roberts, *Demarcation rules in shipbuilding*, Dept of Applied Economics, University of Cambridge. Occasional Paper, No. 14, 1967.

Inge Röpke, *Den internationale krise i skibsfart og vaerftsindustrie i 1970'erne*, Institute for Economy, University of Copenhagen, April 1981.

W.W. Rostow, 'Kondratieff, Schumpeter, and Kuznets: trend periods revisited', in *Journal of Economic History*, No. XXXV, 1975, pp. 719–53.

Karin Salomonsson and Magnus Wikdahl, *Varvet som var. Rapport från dokumentationsprojektet*, Landskrona, 1984.

Kamata Satoshi, *Japon: l'envers du miracle*, Maspero, Paris, 1982.

P.C. Schmitter, 'Still the century of corporatism?', in F.B. Pike and T. Stritch (eds), *The new corporatism: socio-political structures in the Iberian world*, University of Notre Dame Press, London, 1974.

Michael Schuhmann *et al.*, *Rationalisierung, Krise und Arbeiter*, Bremen, 1981.

J.A. Schumpeter, *Capitalism, socialism and democracy*, 5th ed, Allen and Unwin, London, 1976.

E. Shorter and C. Tilly, *Strikes in France 1830–1968*, Cambridge University Press, 1974.

Daniel Sicard, *La Crise de l'Emploi dans la 'Métallurgie de Saint-Nazaire en 1964*, University of Nantes, 1978.

Robert Skidelsky, *The end of the Keynesian era: essays on the disintegration of the Keynesian political economy*, Holmes and Meier, New York, 1977.

—— 'The decline of Keynesian politics', in Colin Crouch (ed.), *State and economy in contemporary capitalism*, London, Croom Helm, 1979.

Theda Skocpol, *State and social revolutions*, Cambridge University Press, 1979.

Anthony Smith, *The concept of social change. A critique of the functionalist theory of social change*, Routledge and Kegan Paul, London, 1973.

Joan M. Smith, *Commonsense thought and working class consciousness: some aspects of the Glasgow and Liverpool Labour Movements in the early years of the twentieth century*, diss., University of Edinburgh, 1980.

Mondher Sphar, *Karl Marx. psychanalyse et idéaux indo-germaniques*, thesis, Paris, Sorbonne, 1983.

Martin Stopford and J. R. Barton, 'Economic problems of shipbuilding and the state', in *Marit. Pol. MGMT 13*, 1986.

Bo Stråth, 'Die Arbeiterbewegung in Kiel und Bremen. Bedingungen für das

Entstehen von verschiedenen politischen Traditionen' in R. Paetau, H. Rüdel and P. Wulf (eds), *Solidarität Freiheit und Demokratie in Schleswig-Holstein im 19 und 20. Jahrhundert*, Wachholtz, Neumünster, 1987.

—— *Nordic industry and Nordic economic cooperation*, diss., Amqvist & Wiksell International, Stockholm, 1978.

—— *Varvsarbetare i två varvsstäder*, Svenska Varv, Göteborg, 1982, English summary.

—— 'The illusory Nordic alternative to Europe', in *Cooperation and Conflict*, XV, 1980.

—— 'West European shipbuilding trade unionism', in Fred M. Walker and Anthony Slaven (eds), *European shipbuilding: one hundred years of change*, proceedings of the Third Shipbuilding History Conference at the National Maritime Museum, Greenwich, 13–15 April 1983. Marine Publ. Internat., London, 1983.

—— 'Redundancy and Solidarity: tripartite politics and the contraction of the West European shipbuilding industry', in *Cambridge Journal of Economics*, Vol. 10, No. 2, 1986.

Thommy Svensson, *Från ackord till månadslön*, Svenska Varv, Göteborg, 1983. English summary.

E.P. Thompson, *The Making of the English Working Class*, Vintage, New York, 1966.

Willie Thompson and Finlay Hart, *The UCS Work-in*, Lawrence and Wishart, London, 1972.

Rolf Torstendahl, 'Technology in the development of society, 1850–1980. Four phases of industrial capitalism in Western Europe', in *History and technology*, Vol. 1, 1984.

Paul Villox, *The capital crisis and labour. Perspectives on the dynamics of working-class consciousness in Canada*, diss., Uppsala, Sweden, 1980.

Heinrich Volkmann, 'Modernisierung des Arbeitskampfes? Zum Formwandel von Streik und Aussperrung in Deutschland 1864–1975', in H. Kaelbe *et al.* (eds), *Probleme der Modernisierung in Deutschland. Sozialhistorische Studien zum 19. und 20. Jahrhundert*, West Deutscher Verlag, Klett-Cotta Opladen, 1978.

—— 'Organisation und Konflikt', in W. Conze and U. Engelhardt (eds), *Arbeiter in Industrialisierungsprozess*, Stuttgart, 1979.

Max Weber, *Wirtschaft und Gesellschaft*, Tübingen, 1980.

Hans-Ulrich Wehler, 'Der Aufsteig des organisierten Kapitalismus in Deutschland', in Heinrich August Winkler (ed.), *Organisierter Kapitalismus. Voraussetzungen und Anfänge*, Vandenhoek Ruprecht, Göttingen, 1974.

Martin Weitzman, *The share economy*, Harvard University Press, Cambridge, Mass., 1984.

M. Welteke, *Theorie und Praxis der Sozialen Marktwirtschaft*, Frankfurt/M, 1976.

Frank Wilkinson, *Demarcation in shipbuilding*, Manuscript, University of Cambridge, 1973.

Heinrich A. Winkler (ed.), *Organisierter Kapitalismus. Voraussetzungen und Anfänge*, Vandenhoek Ruprecht, Göttingen, 1974.

Håkon With Andersen, Bo Stråth and Thommy Svensson (eds), *Olje, verft og redere. Et seminar om norsk og svensk skipsbyggningsindustrie og norske redere i Vårt Århundre*, University of Trondheim, Norway, 1979.

Charles Alexander Woolfson, *Working class culture. The work-in at Upper Clyde Shipbuilders*, diss., Glasgow, 1982.

Peter Wulf, 'Schwerindustrie und Seeschiffahrt nach dem 1. Weltkrieg: Hugo Stinnes und die HAPAG', in *Vierteljahrschrift für Sozial- und Wirtschaftsgeschichte*, No. 1, 1980.

Jonathan Zeitlin, 'Shop floor bargaining and the state: a contradictionary relationship', in Steven Tolliday and Jonathan Zeitlin (eds), *Shop floor bargaining and the state. Historical and comparative perspectives*, Cambridge University Press, 1985.

Bodo Zeuner, 'Solidarität mit der SPD oder Solidarität der Klasse? Zur SPD-Bindung der DGB-Gewerkschaften', in *Probleme des Klassenkampfes. Zeitschrift für politische Ökonomie und sozialistische Politik*, No. 1, 1977, Berlin, 1977.

Hans Ziegenfuss, Heiner Heseler and Hans Jürgen Kröger (eds), *Wer kämpft kann verlieren, wer nicht kämpft hat schon verloren*, VSA-Verlag, Hamburg, 1984.

Rainer Zoll *et al.*, *Krisenbetroffenheit und Krisenwahrnehmung. Eine empirische Untersuchung in der norddeutschen Küstenregion*, University of Bremen, 1980 (revised editions by Bund Verlag colonial in 1981 and 1984 — two volumes).

Index